BRENDAN BEHAN: MAN AND SHOWMAN

Brendan Behan at the Hotel Chelsea, New York, where he recorded
Confessions of an Irish Rebel on tape

BRENDAN BEHAN
MAN AND SHOWMAN

RAE JEFFS

HUTCHINSON OF LONDON

HUTCHINSON & CO (*Publishers*) LTD
178–202 Great Portland Street, London W1

London Melbourne Sydney
Auckland Bombay Toronto
Johannesburg New York

★

First published 1966

*This book has been set in Times, printed in Great Britain
on Antique Wove paper by Anchor Press, and
bound by Wm. Brendon, both of Tiptree, Essex*

To Diana, Val and Sheila

ACKNOWLEDGEMENTS

Many people have helped me write of my years with Brendan Behan and to them I owe a debt of gratitude. Particularly, I would like to thank Beatrice Behan for allowing me to publish personal letters both of her own and Brendan's, and likewise David Astor and Bernard Geis. I would like to record my thanks, too, to the editor of the *Irish Times* for permission to reproduce the review of *An Giall* and the record of the case in Bray, County Wicklow. To Colin Thubron I am indebted for his noble insistence on compiling the Index.

No formal acknowledgement could possibly convey my gratitude to Valentin and Sheila Iremonger, Iain Hamilton and Harold Harris, whose advice and encouragement gave me heart to persevere.

CONTENTS

ILLUSTRATIONS

A CHRONOLOGY OF THE MAIN EVENTS
IN BRENDAN BEHAN'S LIFE

1923	Feb	Born in Dublin.
1928		School of French Sisters of Charity, Dublin.
1931		Joins Fianna Eireann.
1934		Irish Christian Brothers' School, Dublin.
1937		Day Apprentice School, house-painting section.
1939	Feb	Arrest in Liverpool.
		Renounces Roman Catholicism.
		Three years' Borstal Detention.
1941	Nov	Deported to Dublin.
1942	Mar	Shooting incident at Glasnevin Cemetery.
		On the run. Order out to be shot on sight.
	June	Fourteen years' penal servitude.
		Sells first story to *Bell* (*I was a Borstal Boy*).
1946	Nov	Release by political amnesty.
1946–1951		House-painter, seaman and smuggler.
1947	Mar	Arrest in Manchester for breaking deportation order.
	July	Release from Strangeways Prison.
1951–1956		Free-lance journalist.
1952	Oct	Arrest at Newhaven for breaking deportation order.
	Nov	Release from Lewes Prison, Sussex.
1953	Oct	*The Scarperer* published as a newspaper serial.
1954	Apr	Begins weekly column in Irish Press.
	Dec	*The Quare Fellow* opens in Dublin.
1955	Feb	Marries Beatrice ffrench-Salkeld.
1956	May	*The Quare Fellow* opens at Stratford, London.

A CHRONOLOGY OF THE MAIN EVENTS

1957 Jan   Draft of *Borstal Boy* accepted by Hutchinson.
       Mar   Begins *An Giall* (*The Hostage*) in Irish.

1958 Jan   Goes to Ibiza. Begins *the catacombs.*
       Apr   Goes to Paris to discuss production of *The Quare Fellow.*
      June *An Giall* opens in Dublin.
       Aug   Goes to Sweden. Starts translation of *An Giall.*
       Oct   *The Hostage* opens at Stratford, London.
       Nov   *The Quare Fellow* opens in New York.

1959 Mar   Goes to Berlin for opening of *The Quare Fellow.*
       Apr   Goes to Paris. *The Hostage* selected to represent Great Britain at
           the *Théâtre des Nations* Festival.
      July *The Hostage* moves to London's West End.
           First serious breakdown.

1960 Jan   Tapes *Brendan Behan's Island* in Dublin.
       Mar   Begins *Richard's Cork Leg.*
           Goes to London. Second breakdown.
      Sept Goes to New York for opening of *The Hostage.*
       Dec   Returns to Dublin.

1961 Jan   Translates *Richard's Cork Leg* into Irish.
           Failure of *A Fine Day in the Graveyard.*
       Mar   Travels 11,000 miles across America and Canada.
           Two periods in hospital.
      July Returns to Dublin.
       Oct   Film première of *The Quare Fellow* in London.

1962 Feb   Returns to New York for opening of *The Hostage* in the Village.
       Mar   Returns to Dublin.
      July *The Hostage* elected in France as best play of the season.
      Sept Goes to London. Enters home for alcoholics.
       Oct   *Brendan Behan's Island* published.
       Nov   Goes to France to recuperate.
           Returns to Dublin after failure of cure.

1963 Feb   Final trip to America.
       Apr   Tapes *Confessions of an Irish Rebel* in New York.
      July Returns to Dublin and to hospital.
      Sept *Hold Your Hour and Have Another* published.
       Nov   *Brendan Behan's New York* taped in Dublin.
           Blanaid born.
       Dec   Enters hospital.

1964 Jan   In and out of hospital.
       Mar   Enters hospital finally.
           Dies.

I live, and yet methinks I do not breathe;
I thirst and drink, I drink and thirst again;
I sleep and yet do dream I am awake;
I hope for that I have; I have and want;
I sing and sigh; I love and hate at once.
O, tell me, restless soul, what uncouth jar
Doth cause in store such want, in peace such war?

Anonymous, 1609

PROLOGUE

On Friday, 20th March 1964, almost ten years after the first production of *The Quare Fellow*, Brendan Behan—house-painter, rebel, poet, playwright, journalist, autobiographer, and drinker —fought and lost his last battle. It was a sad end, as one had long and reluctantly foreseen, with Brendan lying unconscious in the Meath Hospital in Dublin, and his big heart succumbing at last to the fearful punishment he had for years inflicted on it. He had, I know, looked to his death with a fear and an awe no less profound than Dr. Johnson's; and during the week of his sinking my strongest emotion was one of hope that the moment, when it came, would not be as terrifying as he had feared. Let that anguished mind, I prayed, be spared that final terror. The end was peaceful; for days he had been unconscious; but I find it hard to believe that somewhere in the depths of his coma this man with his extraordinary powers of perception did not realise that at last he had pushed his luck too far. Like others who knew him well, I cannot believe that he wanted to die; if death came to him early it was not because he willed it but rather because he lacked the strength to change the pattern of life he had made for himself and which had only been strengthened by success.

But dead he is, and it is still hard to realise it.

For his friends there is no comfort in the legend that made him, while still alive, so much larger than life, for it is a legend that, for the moment at any rate, concentrates in the main more on his drinking attributes than on his limited output. As a result no truly convincing picture of him has yet emerged. There were many sides to Brendan Behan, despite his considerable preference for displaying one side only; and there is the added disadvantage that he was unable to share his completeness with any one person, possibly because he could not accept himself in his entirety. A great deal has already been written about him, but if all of us who knew him well give our separate interpretations, some more dispassionate biographer might in the years to come draw from our findings and present a true portrait of the whole man. And so our individual strokes on the canvas may yet have some importance.

Over the past two years I have tried to stand back and look as calmly as possible at the man as I had come to know him through years of close association. This has not been easy and indeed I have often been a prey to doubts as to my right to use a unique friendship and reveal certain details in his life that only became known to me as one of his intimates. In setting them aside, I have been prompted by two factors.

Firstly he asked me, only a few months before his death, to be his biographer. 'When I go for my tea,' he said, 'there'll be many people breaking into print about me. But you should do it, for you take my work seriously but not myself. On the whole, I would prefer to be remembered for my work.'

Secondly, Brendan was an extraordinary figure both as a writer and as a man, and in order to picture him fairly, if not definitively, it is necessary to merge the two aspects of him. In this respect I have an advantage, for my relationship with him during the last years of his life was equally extraordinary in that possibly I am the only person who came to know him well both professionally and privately throughout this time. I do not mean to imply that my findings are necessarily correct, but if they throw a new light on the complexities of Brendan's character, I believe the publication of this book is justified.

Few writers of our time can have experienced so much terror in their lives, so much crying need for the sanctuary of bars and hospitals, so many fruitless searches across land and sea for the

Never-Never-Land (Tir na n-Óg he called it) as Brendan Behan. And few writers have been able to put into words such immediate experiences or drill so closely to the very nerve centres without a vestige of bitterness or a trace of malice. Yet his writing is quite clearly autobiographical. It is all there, either as a whole or in pieces, and there can be no more than a tiny particle of himself that he has not left for posterity somewhere in his writing. And while it is certainly true to say that Brendan left a part of himself in every place he visited, his works have been collected and published while his personal impressions have not.

It is too soon for the compilation of these impressions, and the memory of him is too close for unprejudiced appraisal. A man would emerge possessing every virtue and fault alike, for Brendan inspired love or hatred but never indifference.

With his taste for publicity, he was capable of acting entirely out of character in his efforts to produce the reactions he wanted from those he was with. Ever the great showman, he enjoyed living up to what was expected of him, confounding his friends and his critics in equal measure, and for a while he was able to keep these various acts in surprisingly tidy compartments.

Slowly, however, his performances began to foster in him a consuming restlessness which only served to germinate the seed of self-destruction inherent in all doomed talents. He became caught in the trap of his own making. When could he stop acting and be himself? Timing was important. Was the auditorium really empty? There must be someone else out there in the dark. And so he acted the man well, hard and long, until somehow the true Brendan got lost in the character part and even he could no longer differentiate.

I do not believe that he was ever unconscious of the fact that he was deliberately playing the part of clown or bogman, or that his outrageous performances increased his notoriety and financial success. But the features of his own true being gradually grew into the grimaces of the clown's mask, and that was the terrible price that life exacted for his success.

Those of us who were destined to watch the change in him from the front row knew we were watching the last act of a great tragedy, but we were powerless to help him. He became the shell of himself—the unfulfilled, wasted talent.

It is true that alcoholism was a major factor in his life, but it was not everything, and with a little more perseverance he might have been able to overcome it. It is too easy to deal easily with a drinking artist and to compare him to every other drinking artist. Nothing annoyed Brendan more than his frequent comparison to Dylan Thomas, whose poetry he greatly admired.

'I may go out like him,' he said, 'as a sort of cumulative result of my excesses, but we had nothing in common other than the fact that we both got drunk in public and made spectacles of ourselves.'

The comparison goes further, however. They were both Celts, both weak men, and their weakness was drink, but Brendan never lost sight of the fact that his creative ability was the only force stronger than his addiction to alcohol and he made repeated and serious efforts to cure himself of his thirst. Unhappily, the Celt in him and the sudden experience of wealth enabled him to terminate his efforts at the least possible provocation and, unversed in the art of moderation, he would unleash the thoroughly recharged Mr. Hyde to destroy all the good achieved by poor Dr. Jekyll. He was an extremist all the way.

To a certain extent, this applied to his writing. In the early days, he would edit and re-edit, but later he began to settle for mediocrity in the knowledge that anything that bore his name was bound to be a financial success. I think it is significant, however, that the two works on which he worked the longest, *Borstal Boy* and *The Quare Fellow*, are the two with which he was most proud to be associated. I believe time will show them to be his best.

Of *The Hostage*, he told me that he felt it was too contrived in that it was based on the music-hall tradition of entertainment, although most of the incidents in the play were, in fact, taken from life. When he thought the audience was getting bored with the theme, he diverted them with a song or a dance. He agreed

with T. S. Eliot that the main problem of the dramatist today
was to keep the audience amused, but he did not feel this made
for great theatre.

He certainly never read the two books which were produced by
means of the tape-recorder, *Brendan Behan's Island* and
Brendan Behan's New York, nor would he even edit the raw
material. And he died before the tapes of *Confessions of an Irish
Rebel* had been fully transcribed. He was ashamed that he had
lost the will-power and the concentration to work and was forced
to resort to book-making in this manner.

At the same time, he also recognised that without his work he
could not survive. When an engine seizes up for want of lubrica-
tion, only a fool refuses the oil can and Brendan was no fool in
this respect. In 1960 when he first asked me to work with him, it
was not only because the heat was being put on him to fulfil his
contract for *Brendan Behan's Island,* but because he believed
that once having regulated his writing habits, he would be able to
continue to do so without any help. As such, he regarded the
tape-recorder seriously and used it only for serious purposes in
the sanctuary of his room. But he did not regard the finished
product as representative in any way of his talent. It was solely a
method of keeping things going until such times as he could write
again of his own accord. It was not, as so many people suppose,
a prostitution of art and a cheap way of supplying himself,
publishers and agents with easy money. It was his chance of survival and he was happy to accept it. Initially he found peace in
the act of writing and would become exalted with the sense of
realisation of what his genius could do with words. He was
always passionately interested in people and would remember
how they acted, talked, looked and smelt down to the very last
detail; and his memory was far more accurate than any camera.
But when the effort of concentration, complicated by increasing
ill-health, grew to be too much, he still found a limited peace
through the use of a tape-recorder. Indeed, in the end when all
else failed him, in this way he was able to work. *Brendan Behan's
New York* was completed shortly before his death, with his hands

too unsteady for the holding of a pen and his eyes too tired for reading.

'If I am anything at all, I am a man of letters,' he once said. 'I'm a writer; a word which does not exactly mean anything in either the English, Irish or American language. But I have never seen myself as anything else, not even from the age of four.'

Despite his constant protestations that he 'only wrote under the economic lash'—and clearly it did not lash him enough—I found little evidence of this. In fact he always claimed that the only articles he ever really enjoyed writing (and for which he received not one penny) were those for the *Irish Democrat* in 1936, when he was thirteen, about the Spanish Civil War. He was fervently anti-Franco and bitterly regretted that his age prevented him from doing more for the cause than indulging in a few street fights and collecting tinned milk and packets of cocoa and bags of flour for the Food Ship. And *The Quare Fellow* which was the least lucrative of all his major works—he sold the first production in Dublin for £30—was, by his own admission, one of his favourites.

Probably the explanation of his reluctance to talk about his work in his last years was the fact that while he was unable to write for sustained periods, Scott Fitzgerald and Dylan Thomas, to name but two with comparable problems, had managed to do so right up to the end.

The 64 million-dollar question as to what makes a man drink himself to death must always go unanswered, but while I am prepared to admit that Brendan had the soil in which an alcoholic thrives, I do not think he would have become one but for two events which took place at a stage in his life when he was the most vulnerable and impressionable. Even then, he might have saved himself had financial restrictions forced him to check his thirst.

He was born into a family of Republican idealists who had little other than a fierce patriotism to combat the tyranny of British rule in Ireland and, steeped as he was in Irish history, it was inevitable that Brendan should put on the cloak of their political beliefs with the uncompromising intolerance of youth. The bitterness generated by the Irish Civil War was to mark his entry into the world, for at the time of his birth in 1923, Stephen Behan, his father, was in prison rather than accept the fact that one blade of Irish grass should belong to the British Empire.

Along with his belief in his country, Brendan was bred and brought up to believe in God and the Catholic Church and he was a devoutly religious boy. On the day that he made his First Communion, he had prayed to God to take him, like Napoleon, straight to Heaven, and afterwards he had been a weekly communicant, and in spasms, particularly during Lent, a daily one. Later in adolescence he had had difficulties because the Church always seemed to be against the Republicans, but he had never given up the Faith and was glad of the solidarity it gave him to fall back upon.

In the early thirties, he joined Fianna Eireann, the Republican Boy Scouts who provided recruits for the more serious purpose of the Republican army. For the romantic and sensitive Brendan, the movement appealed to every fibre in his body and not only did he throw himself into all the activities of the Fianna with a burning sense of idealism, but he also contributed regularly both prose and poetry to the organisation's magazine. Soon he was on the fringe of I.R.A. activity, learning about the jobs that had to be done, until finally he became a full member and his big moment came: he was to go over to England and blow up new battleships that were being built in the dockyards at Liverpool.

In 1939, at the age of sixteen, and not twenty-four hours after he had landed, Brendan was arrested in Liverpool for being in possession of explosives and sent first to Walton prison and later to a Borstal institution. And it was in Walton that, rather than renounce the I.R.A., he was excommunicated from the Catholic Church and the first seed of self-destruction was sown.

'I sat down on the chair and leaned my head in my hands,' he writes of the moment in *Borstal Boy*. 'I felt like crying for the first time in years, for the first time since I was a kid of four or five. I had often prayed after Mass at home that God would not let me lose the Faith. I thought of Sister Monica, the old nun that prepared me for my first Confession and Communion and Confirmation, and Father Campbell, the old priest in Gardiner Street that I went to Confession to, and Christmas numbers of the little holy books we used to have at home. Never, never no more.'

The second seed was sown more slowly but with equally disastrous effects. In Borstal he learned to separate the English from that detested abstraction, England. Gradually everything he had stood for and believed in unquestionably had to be questioned. There were two sides to the problem after all and no longer could his sympathies go undivided. With his Faith and his belief in his country both immeasurably shaken, what could he put in their place? Not all at once but by degrees drink beat off his despair but for Brendan one drink was too many and a thousand not enough.

When I first met him he was still trying to hold onto the old ideals, but even had he wanted to, he did not have the money to squander on alcoholic binges. Nevertheless, *The Quare Fellow* had already been produced and success—and disaster—were knocking on the door.

I have written of my years with him as objectively as possible, without embellishments or exaggeration. I hope, in so doing, that I have done justice both to the good and the bad in him, measuring his talent fairly and without undue prejudice. There has to be, in working with someone, a relationship based on mutual respect, unfettered by chains of emotion; a dispassionate appraisal of each other which grows through experience of one another. It is an unique relationship; one of nearness and apartness alike. And I think it gives a far greater insight of the mind than is normally possible. As such, what I have to say may be of some importance, but failing this, I hope the book may have its own value as an account of a strange friendship between two very dissimilar people from two diametrically different worlds.

I

TEMPESTUOUS MEETING

'I'm tulip shape,' he said, as I entered Iain Hamilton's office somewhat apprehensively, and dispensing with the formalities of introductions, he proceeded to do a little dance around the room, whirling me with him, to the strains of 'Land of Hope and Glory', set to his own words of 'I Should Have Been Born a Tulip'.

I remember thinking at the time that this was rather an apt description, for underneath the billowing shape of his formidable figure, with his unruly hair cascading in ringlets over his forehead, were tiny, delicate feet, almost invisible under bell-bottomed trousers which somehow remained on him, in the best fashion they could, without the help of the wearer. His head leant to one side, like a tulip, in a kind of top-heavy way, and the jacket of his suit became the foliage up around his face. I had never met anyone like him in my life before, which was hardly surprising, for my sheltered, comfortable background and education at an establishment for prim young ladies would not have given me the opportunity of meeting the likes of Brendan Behan and the tough, rough, Dublin 'guttie' character he delighted in presenting on first acquaintance.

It was in the spring of 1957, and he had come to London for the broadcast of his play *The Big House*, commissioned by the B.B.C., and to deliver the almost completed manuscript of his autobiographical *Borstal Boy* to Hutchinson, his publishers. I

knew about the book's potentialities because earlier in the year
Iain Hamilton, the firm's editorial director, had gone to Dublin
on the advice of the poet Val Iremonger, of the Irish Embassy,
who had told him that Brendan was a roaring boy with a real
talent, and that an autobiographical fragment of his had been
circulating for a year or two. Iain was so impressed with the thirty-
odd pages of typed foolscap that he had signed Brendan up on
the spot for a £350 advance and returned to the office alternately
instilling his enthusiasm to the staff of Hutchinson and praying to
God that Brendan would finish the work. Already a photographic
copy had been sent to Bill Koshland of Alfred Knopf, the
American publishers, who was filled with equal enthusiasm and
had made a firm verbal agreement to publish it.

At the time I was employed by the firm as publicity manager,
and I knew little about Brendan personally except that he was
known to the English police, that he had written an extremely
good play, *The Quare Fellow*, and that he was the star of one of
the most talked about television interviews of 1956.

He had gone to the B.B.C. television studios in Lime Grove to
be interviewed by Malcolm Muggeridge on *Panorama*, following
the overnight success of Joan Littlewood's London production
of *The Quare Fellow*. By his own admission, he was already well
lit by the time he arrived at the studios, and was put in the entertainment room with a stiff glass of whisky to 'steady him up.'
His interview was to follow an important discussion, by two
generals, on civil defence. Hearing raucous and boisterous noises
coming from the room, interspersed with songs and obscenities,
the producer of the programme was naturally a little apprehensive about allowing the interview to take place, but Muggeridge
prevailed and Brendan faced the cameras. He was barely in-
telligible and no amount of subterfuge could disguise the fact
that he was drunk.

'Afterwards,' wrote Malcolm Muggeridge in the *New Statesman*, 'we returned to the entertainment room. I left him there
roaring out the "Internationale" at the top of his voice, with
the two War Office brass-hats giving every indication of being

about to join in. It was the pleasantest and most rewarding evening I ever spent in Lime Grove.'

Brendan received immediate recognition as well as notoriety.

It was hardly surprising that on my first meeting with him, I was chiefly concerned in discovering what manner of creature was able to behave so outrageously in front of the élite and unbending viewers of *Panorama* without incurring any serious wrath or indignation. I neither admired nor resented him for it, but was anxious to find out for myself.

The ease with which he came forward to greet me and his natural gaiety as we waltzed across the red plush carpet took me by surprise, and I must admit, not without a little alarm, but despite my inborn inhibitions I recall no embarrassment whatsoever. Within a very few moments our cavorting seemed perfectly normal behaviour, and at once I understood how twelve million viewers accepted him. Here was a character; a species of man distinctly rare. And they recognised it.

Beatrice, his brown-haired wife, sat quietly in the corner of the room watching us. Every now and again, Brendan would break away from me to shake her by the hand, and then return to continue the dance, or he would say something to her in Irish and she would simply nod her head in reply. I was struck by the obvious understanding between them.

The dance over, I tried to engage Beatrice in conversation but it was impossible. Brendan hosepiped all opposition into silence, drowning the trickles with torrential words of his own. His huge, red face expressed everything from the angelic to the diabolical as he told one uproarious anecdote after another.

With less unaffected literary figures this might have become tedious, but with Brendan, in those days, anyone would have gladly paid the price of a seat to listen to him.

For a brief moment Iain interrupted him to ask how much more work he had to do on *Borstal Boy,* and at once I detected the note of irritation in his reply as he dismissed the subject.

'It's all lies,' he said.

He had been touched on the one topic of conversation he was

not prepared to discuss, and for a gregarious man his reluctance
to talk about his work revealed itself quickly. In this instance
there was the added reason too, that he had written earlier to Iain
promising to 'kneel and explain why the lot is not finished when
I said it would be,' and now, face to face, he found it difficult
to offer spurious excuses. Without conceding the point, he
realised that I was a little bewildered by the sharpness of his re-
tort and he held out his hand.

'You know, daughter, I've got quite good manners sometimes.
There's an ould one in Dublin who would tell you the same. I
was hurrying along the street and I accidentally knocked her
down. Jaysus, Mary and Joseph, it was enough to put the heart
crossways in me to see the poor old lady down on her knees. I
helped her up, bent from the waist' (he imitated the gesture as he
spoke) 'and said, "Madam, I hope I have not incommoded you."

' "Listen to that," the woman said, "there's still courtliness
and gentleness to be found in Ireland."

' "Even from the lowest of the low, madam," I said, bowing
yet again. "Even from the lowest of the low." '

His laughter boomed out across the room to hit the walls and
resound back again and out of the door and along the passage,
taking my bewilderment with it. At ease again, I settled myself
further into the chair for an afternoon of entertainment. Brendan,
whose thirst took little account of licensing hours, called for a
drink. My thoughts immediately focused on Hilda, the stalwart
dispenser of tea and coffee from the urns on the trolley which I
could hear being pushed up the passage. I indicated as much to
Brendan.

'Do you call that a drink,' he roared, interpolating a stream
of unbridled Anglo-Saxon words which would not normally be
heard in a publisher's office. He made for the door saying he was
off to the Workers' Club in Fleet Street and would see us later
with the manuscript. At the very mention of the word, Iain
jumped to his feet, but with remarkable presence of mind he was
able to hide his unhappy fears of the consequence if Brendan
actually carried out his threat and merely suggested I go and get

a bottle of whisky. He managed to imply that there was a distillery round the corner in which thousands of bottles of the stuff were to hand for no more than the cost of asking.

Brendan sat down again and I left, shutting the door firmly behind me. God's help, they say, is never very far, for as I reached the street I met a local publican who was out for an afternoon stroll in the sun with his boxer dog. Within very short order, I was back in the office triumphantly clutching the bottle.

I suppose it would be true to say that our friendship began with this incident. I had left the office for so short a time that Brendan told me later that the inevitable barriers of class disappeared in his belief that he had found in me a fellow gargler, albeit a secret one, and supposed that throughout the day I was fortifying myself with the 'message.'

'If it's a thing I go in for in a human being, it's weakness,' he said. 'I'm a devil for it.'

For the rest of the afternoon he sang numerous folksongs and Dublin ballads, of which he had an unlimited repertoire. The entire office was agog to meet the cause of so much disturbance. They did not have to wait long, for Brendan, whisky bottle now empty, went into every room, hurling obscenities at the men and pinching the bottoms of any of the unfortunate girls who happened to be in the firing line.

Leaving chaos in his wake he made for the front door, Beatrice following. Before disappearing altogether he imparted casually that he had left the manuscript at the B.B.C. and would go and get it. Immediately Timothy O'Keeffe, Iain's editorial assistant and equally appreciative of the writer, the work and the importance of collecting it, was dispatched to accompany him, and the last I saw of them was bundling into a taxi which, at any rate, drove off in the right direction.

For those who never met Brendan it would be impossible to describe the scene following his departure. Complaints and admiration were meted out in equal measure, but certainly no more work was done that day.

Within a short while, Tim O'Keeffe returned. Brendan had been ugly and abusive and had forced him to get out of the taxi before they had reached the bottom of the street. Despair, gloom and utter exhaustion descended on us all until Iain suggested that perhaps I, as a woman, could handle Brendan in his elated state more deftly than a man. At least it was worth one final attempt.

I started out to look for him but I did not have to go very far. I heard his voice coming from The George, singing, somewhat more lustily than before, the same Dublin ballads. The pub was crowded and a galaxy surrounded Brendan at the bar, including Louis MacNeice. The others I took to be the producer and cast of *The Big House,* the one-act play he had written for the B.B.C. which was soon to be broadcast, and various casual acquaintances. Although barely five-foot-nine, Brendan stood out clearly amongst the crowd lined up at the bar, and I nervously inched my way across to him.

He hailed me enthusiastically all in one breath: 'Daughter, have a drink this is my publisher.' Everyone intoned the correct responses. A tall individual with sleek black hair disentangled himself from the others and came over to me, handing me a piece of paper as he did so.

'You might be interested in this,' he said.

It was an official hand-out and my companion was a press officer for the B.B.C. It was headed, BRENDAN BEHAN BURLESQUES THE IRISH AND ENGLISH (Home Service, June 7th, 1957). I read on:

'The producer, David Thomson, describes the work as "an Irish extravaganza, burlesquing stock English and Irish characters and pompous writing in plays and literature about the situation in Ireland in the 1920's." The English owners of a large house in the Free State decide they can no longer stand the Irish and their ways, so they return to live in Ealing, leaving their home in the care of an Irish agent. When they find they cannot tolerate their new English neighbours either, and return to their home, it is to discover that all their belongings have been stolen and even lead from the roof sold.'

I skipped over the bit about the cast and was just reading the autobiographical piece about Brendan, when the paper was snatched from me.

'For Jaysus' sake,' snarled Brendan, 'you are not in the office now, you know.' Again the irritation with it. I took the hand-out from him and quietly put it in my handbag, while the press officer, embarrassed now, moved away. I looked round the room for Beatrice and was surprised to see her sitting in the corner by the door in tears. I must have walked straight by her when I came in and I wanted to go over to her to apologise.

Brendan grabbed me by the arm, quickly let go and extended his right hand for me to shake. This was as far as he could bring himself to go by way of an apology but I recognised what it was costing him and he knew that I recognised it. The brashness returned.

'I'm singing two of the ballads in this f—ing programme,' he said to me, but it was really to the rest of the assembled company he was speaking.

Brendan began to sing one of the ballads in a light, lilting brogue which was altogether captivating, and as ballad followed ballad and folksong followed folksong, there were few in the pub who were not prepared to listen to him. Suddenly, without word of warning, somebody banged a fist on the counter and there were shouts of 'Up the Republic!' and 'Get up the cutting, you Kerry bastard from Limerick!' and other slogans which were completely incomprehensible to me.

A discordant note began to creep into the pleasure of the evening and uneasily I made a move towards Beatrice who was still sitting in the corner, but no longer crying. Once again, Brendan grabbed me by the arm but this time his action was not accompanied by any gesture of reconciliation, and a little frightened by his strength I wrenched my arm free. For a moment the expression on his face changed to that of a small schoolboy who had been rapped on the knuckles, and I was startled to discover that even in this high state of intoxication he was not unaware of simple protests. Insecurity and uncertainty were indeed not far from the surface of his bravado, and I realised that it would not be this day, nor the next, that his confidence could be won. I nodded my head in the direction of the 'ladies.' At the same time I held out my hand to him, and without seeing his face I knew by the pressure of his hand on mine that he would meet me halfway.

I remember wondering if that was the moment to ask him for *Borstal Boy* and immediately dismissing the thought. Of course the manuscript was important and I am bound to admit that its possession was uppermost in my mind. But there was something else as well; right from the beginning, I was not prepared for our relationship to be one of an entirely business nature. Brendan was well aware of the reason that had brought me to the pub in the first place, and had I used his moment of sensitivity to further my firm's wishes, all hope of friendship would have been destroyed.

The incident over, Brendan resumed his position at the bar and, once more the focal point, raised his voice to all opposition. I went over to Beatrice. She showed no visible signs of emotion at all, and I was annoyed with myself for not bringing her a drink. It was obvious that she neither asked for nor expected any attention, and she was genuinely surprised at my concern on finding her glass empty.

'If you go up there,' she said, looking over in the direction of the counter, 'you might have a job getting back again.'

I complimented her on her suit of white bawneen and this pleased her. Fortified by her response, I asked her why she had been crying.

'Brendan got it up for me because I did not like the way he was treating your man in the taxi,' she replied. 'If he does not want to part with the manuscript until he has finished it, why bring over any of it at all? Three hundred pages of foolscap are not light, you know.'

I was amused by the practicality of her remark, but at the same time I could see that unwittingly she had supplied Brendan with an excuse for his behaviour in the taxi. If I was to get the manuscript the approach would have to be direct and without help.

I asked her where she was staying and for the first time I heard her laugh. 'Now, Rae, I wouldn't be knowing that. It's early yet. We've left the stuff round at the B.B.C. where we can collect it any time before midnight.' She was obviously completely unconcerned by the possibility that they might not find anywhere to stay at all, and indeed, she did not even consider it a possibility.

Brendan was becoming more abusive and less entertaining, and already angry protests were beginning to circulate in the hot air of a May night. I opened the doors at the back of me to cool the atmosphere a little. People began to get up, scraping their chairs on the floor as they did so, and noisily walking out. I noticed the barman looking anxiously at Beatrice, who looked helplessly back in return. There was a clanking of glasses and murmurs of why don't they throw him out who is he anyway, the paddies are having a row I think I'll be off now.

My sheltered background had never prepared me for anything like this and my first reaction was to run away as quickly and as far as possible, for I had horrible visions of my daughter Diana learning of her mother's involvement in a public-house brawl from the front pages of a newspaper in the headmistress's study at her boarding-school. Suddenly my fear was replaced by overwhelming anger. Why had I been given this type of assignment at all, and why couldn't someone else have given up their evening to standing in a pub? The hunger I hadn't had time to feel until this moment, although I had not eaten for many hours, hit me like a hammer, but before I could give vent to my feelings, I saw Brendan dancing a jig round the room, weaving his huge frame in and out of all obstacles as nimbly as a needle through the threads of a loom. The dance over, he proceeded to sing, in a voice which it would be complimentary to describe as falsetto, 'The Boy That I Marry.' Unfortunately most of the words escape me, but I can remember the last four lines quite clearly:

Stead of sittin', he keeps knittin'
For a sailor he met in Thames Ditton.
I must find another, for he loves my brother,
Not me!

It was impossible to remain angry for long, and an enormous
cheer went up as he swam slowly and gracefully towards the end
of his song. For a while I joined in the general mêlée surround-
ing Brendan, answering 'yes' and 'no', which was all that was
required of me, and then, while my patience was still with me,
I slipped it in.

'Could I have the manuscript, please, Brendan?' The words
paraded in front of me, heavy as lead.

I remember once at school wanting to perform the usual func-
tions of nature during a lesson, sitting in anguish and despair
until I finally put up my hand and asked, rather too loudly, to be
excused, and found on having actually accomplished so daring
a feat that I no longer wanted to leave the room at all. I
experienced the same reaction now.

Perhaps Brendan sensed this, for he immediately turned and
shouted to Beatrice to go and get it for me. I was to learn in later
years that indifference was always the best approach to Brendan,
though at the time I was certainly not resorting to cunning. When
the full implication of his response became known to me, however, indifference soon changed to elation.

People collecting their cheques from the football pools have
not felt more excitement than I as I walked the few steps up the
street to the B.B.C. with Beatrice. I was glad too for the breeze
and the stars that shone in the sky and the neon lights and the
people who passed us, giving an air of reality to the unreal events
of the evening. There was sanity on the hard pavement under my
feet and I trod heavily for fear I might lose it.

The Behan luggage consisted of one small hold-all and
Beatrice must have sensed my surprise at this, for without my
actually mentioning it, she explained that she always travelled
light for she never knew when she might be carrying Brendan as
well. Suddenly I realised the significance of her previous remark

about the weight of the foolscap pages. She unzipped the bag, took out the manuscript and handed it to me. As I glanced superficially through it, I was struck by one thought: if the man himself was undisciplined, certainly his work was not. It was clean and well typed, and what corrections there were—and there were few—were written neatly and precisely in his own hand.

It is more than a pity that by his own wish all but a few pages of this manuscript have been destroyed, for it would have supplied one further piece of evidence of his contradictory nature.

I read the first paragraph and was hit by the torrential force that poured off the paper. No wonder Iain had been so anxious to get hold of it, and even I, tired as I was, became determined to read it for myself before handing it over to him in the morning. I would have left at once, but Beatrice stopped me because she felt Brendan would like to say good night to me personally, and again his friendship took precedence over duty. Nevertheless, I made up my mind that I would simply put my head round the door, pay the necessary courtesies and bid a hasty retreat. Looking back on it, my innocence appalls me.

What confronted us was a drinking-school of immense proportions which drew us into its midst more firmly than any magnet almost before we had set foot in the place. I made several attempts to extricate myself, but gave up.

What cannot be cured must be endured, and endure it I did until across the alcoholic haze I heard a voice shouting that they had telephoned for the police. Using physical force—for my own part I do not know where I found it—we had Brendan out on the pavement and into a taxi before the noise of the police bells warned us of their approach. As the Behan cab turned the corner into Regent Street, I realised that, after all, I had not said good night to either of them.

I have no recollection of getting to Great Portland Street tube station, but after such an evening my brain probably prefers not to record mundane trivialities. I only know that I did get there, that I sat in an Inner Circle train, and that I got out at South Kensington station, unfortunately without the manuscript. As the

door of the train slid to a close with a sickening thud of finality,
I caught sight of the cause of all the disturbance sitting peacefully on a seat entirely by itself.

I was up the stairs and into a taxi like an arrow, covering the
distance to St. James's Park station before there was time to
contemplate the gravity of the situation. Nor did I concern myself with the taximan's reactions as I fled down the stone steps
on to the platform to find the train indicator blinking merrily,
No. 1. INNER CIRCLE. Marshalling panic into a semblance of
order, I remembered exactly where I had been sitting so that,
when the train came in, I was in it and out again as quickly, but
this time clutching the manuscript with a force that would have
frightened even the Prodigal Son. And to those who raise their
eyebrows in disbelief, I can only say that this really happened. I
assume that luck must have been on my side and there was a
hold-up somewhere along the line.

Some time later, I told Brendan the story. 'It's a good job for
me that you found it, kiddo,' he commented. 'I did not have a
duplicate manuscript.'

Late that night and far into the dawn I read the uncompleted
Borstal Boy and I knew that the escapades of Brendan Behan
that day, or any other day, were of no lasting importance to anyone but himself. What was important was that he was an artist
and a superb writer and that by a stroke of good fortune I had
come to meet him and to know him, if only superficially. Happy
in this knowledge, I fell asleep.

II

BRENDAN AT WORK

Brendan was back in the office early next morning. I was with Iain at the time and explaining to him a few of the difficulties I had experienced in capturing the manuscript when he was announced. Hastily Iain pushed it into the middle drawer of his table which he then proceeded to lock up.

Brendan was aggressive, his health no more improved than mine as a result of the night before. He came straight to the point without waiting for the conventional exchanges. He wanted his typescript so that he could get finished with it; there were certain revisions and one or two libellous passages that had to be taken out, and he would have said more but Iain firmly interrupted him.

'*A chara.* Wouldn't it be a better idea for us to get on with editing the 300 pages while you are finishing the work? Added to which I am receiving one letter per day from a gentleman in New York who is waiting to launch your book upon the many scores of millions in that republic. I would like to send him what we have and then when it is completed we can show it to the lawyers *intacto* while you complete your revisions.'

Brendan's reply thundered across his words almost before he had finished speaking them. An author knew best when his work was ready for submission to his publishers, he boomed, and in the name of the Blessed Virgin Mary would we ever let him have it back? As he spoke his eyes searched every object on the table, and his hand was poised in readiness to grab the cause of his concern. Before I could stop myself I told Brendan that if he thought I had spent the evening lugging his manuscript around just to have it handed back to him in the morning, he was greatly mistaken.

'It's not light,' I added, remembering the effect Beatrice's words had had on me, but the outburst over, my conventional upbringing reasserted itself and drawing little comfort from the startled expressions on the faces of both Iain and Brendan, I could only think of all those brave men who, in the course of their duties, carried time-bombs in their hands. There was only a pin separating them from total extinction too. I slunk to the door.

'You'll not be leaving us,' said Brendan, and to Iain, 'That girl's got pluck. I wouldn't have handed the manuscript over to anyone else.'

Out came his hand to mine, an easy smile on his face and a wink of such proportion that, not only did it obliterate his right eye, but the flesh on one side of his face winced and crumbled under the pressure of it. The awkwardness passed and Iain used the opportunity of Brendan's change of mood to talk about Borstal Boy, and in particular his doubts about the aptness of the title. It would not do for the States because it would mean little or nothing there, he said, and he was not sure it was really an adequate label in England for a book of such quality. What was needed, Iain felt, was a title with the harsh salty taste of poetry about it; a phrase out of a Gaelic song or a Dublin ballad or anything else less merely label-like, and would Brendan turn his thoughts to it when he had a moment of leisure?

There was something about Brendan's complete agreement that told me his mind was not on his work, and indeed within a matter of minutes it was obvious his thoughts were turned more in the direction of the Mason's Arms across the street. With no further reference to the manuscript, he suggested I accompany him.

Over in the pub, he was friendly and courteous and asked me

to tell him more about myself. On hearing that I came from Sussex, he recalled his experiences in Lewes Prison, of which he had pleasant memories, if memories of this nature can ever be so described. And then he told me a little bit about himself and his own background.

'As I explained to Kenneth Allsop in a recent interview,' he said, 'ten years ago in Strangeways Prison I stopped trying to find political solutions and began seriously to write. I don't argue the political issues involved between England and Ireland any more. In my work, I try to mirror what happens to the people involved and leave it to the literary intelligentsia to expound their own theories afterwards.'

Here he broke off to give an imitation of a normal literary interview, phrasing the imaginary questions with devastating accuracy, his answers unfortunately unprintable. He was back again as quickly, picking up the threads of the original conversation.

'I have written a play for Gael Linn,' he said, 'on the taking of a National Serviceman as a hostage by the I.R.A. It is basically about the ordinariness of people—which is an extraordinary thing at such times. The only solution I suggest in it is for people not to allow themselves to be fooled by the Establishment of any side. Some people say they've got friends on both sides. I'm proud to have enemies on both sides. I won't bore you with talk about Partition and all the killing that's going on up on the border now, but I cannot be indifferent to the fact that young Irishmen on both sides are being killed. All that I am trying to show in my play is that one man's death can be more significant than the issues involved.'

We were alone, without audience, and there was no irritation in his voice as he went on to speak about his hopes and fears for *Borstal Boy*. He knew it would be banned in Ireland, but that did not worry him. 'The number of people who buy books in Ireland would not keep me in drink for the duration of Sunday opening time,' he explained. 'I don't want the Irish to read my book—I don't want to corrupt them by giving them too high an opinion of themselves,' and without waiting for my laughter, his own was sufficient for the pair of us.

'I must admit,' he continued, 'fair field and no favour, I still prefer to live in Ireland, though I have a great admiration for the British people. No one but they would have used Churchill during the war and then thrown him out at the right time afterwards.'

The pub was beginning to get crowded now and I noticed that Brendan was looking for a larger audience. This annoyed me because I wanted to ask him more about the book before the mood changed and the clown in him took over. To my question as to what he felt about a change of title, he snapped that only nuns and civil servants wanted to put tags on everything, and if they couldn't put a label on your soul as well, then your body would be held in a ferment of pain below on this earth.

The favourable reaction that his remark drew from the crowd delighted him and expansively he ordered drinks all round. I began to feel out of my depth and edged slowly towards the door, but Brendan, perhaps conscious of the fact that he had been hurtful, called me back.

'I've had enough f—ing work for the one day,' he whispered. 'For Jaysus' sake, relax. I'm not going to break up the bar or anything and after a little sustenance, I am going back home to finish the book.' And in case he had not made his gesture of friendship clear, he added, 'It's not everyone I talk about my work to, you know.'

I was pleased that he had confided in me but as he was now quite drunk I deemed it wiser to leave while there was still a modicum of contact between us rather than chance my arm and become involved in a situation beyond my control.

I did not see him again until August for, true to his word, he returned to Dublin to finish his book, but almost immediately I sent him a set of publicity information sheets, the questions printed in dark blue on light blue paper, with suitable gaps left for the answers. For me, this was normal office procedure as soon as a book was accepted for publication.

Within forty-eight hours, Brendan had returned the completed forms with the accompanying letter:

Thursday, the 6th June, 1957

Dear Rae, Me lovely Sussex chickadee—I was going to write poule—and show off me French but that has a double meaning. Beatrice tied me hand and foot to this bastarding machine till I filled in this form.

Love to Eileen[1] and Margaret,[2] Paudrig O Caoimh[3] and Bob Lusty[4] and the Highland Chief himself, Iain the Slasher,[5] in haste to ketch the post, Brendan.

These forms I still have and the parts reproduced here are not, I think without interest.

Writing Career: My own writing habit is that I write when absolutely sober. I started writing for Irish Republican and Irish Left Wing papers and was published first in a magazine called *Fianna*, the organ of Fiann Eireann, the Republican Scout Organisation founded by Countess Markievicz, and of which I was a member from the age of seven to the age of fourteen, when I was transferred to the I.R.A. as a courier or messenger boy. I was published first at the age of twelve but the first article I was ever paid for appeared in the June, 1942 issue of the *Bell*. I have written for love (political writing) and for money, radio, newspaper work, in English and Irish, and poetry.

Special interest or pursuits other than professional: I swim a great deal in the summer (in water I mean) and am very fond of race meetings—particularly a point-to-point. I spend most of my spare time with non-literary fellows that I have known from youth—mostly fellows that are mixed up in the greyhound business. I myself like the company and am of course always very well informed as to the form of dogs at any track in England or Ireland, but don't like racing myself, because the track racing is too dull, and the coursing is too cruel. I go coursing sometimes because the screams of the hares give me an excuse to stop in the tent drinking whiskey. I like city people, in Dublin or from the East End.

[1] Eileen Horrocks, Iain Hamilton's secretary;
[2] Margaret Taylor, assistant in publicity department;
[3] Timothy O'Keeffe;
[4] Robert Lusty, chairman of Publishing Group;
[5] Iain Hamilton.

In a general summary on *Borstal Boy*, Brendan wrote the following:

It's the story of an Irish boy of sixteen arrested and sentenced in England for I.R.A. activities, of his fears, hopes and relationships with the other boys in an English reformatory. (The only thing about which I am not garrulous is my own work.) I have tried not to be heroic or any more abject than people sometimes are. I have attempted also to reproduce the conversations of adolescent prisoners about sex and religion and sometimes about politics and sometimes about crime and sport. It is a book of 'innocence and experience.' Some people may say that my book shouldn't be read, then I say that adolescence should not be lived. I was excommunicated from the Catholic Church when I was arrested and refused to disavow the Irish Republican Army in prison, and I think the book tells of my loneliness in exile from the only church I had ever known, or taken seriously, the church of my people, of my ancestors hunted in the mountains, and of my bitterness about this. But I must admit that I find more Marlowe than Mauriac in the book and when the sun shone and we worked together in the fields or ran down the beach naked for an illegal swim, the Church or poor old Ireland were well forgotten.

And finally, under the heading *Review Copies*, Brendan supplied the names of one or two people whom he felt were entitled to free copies of his book.

Thomas Barbour, *Hudson Review*? America (He praised me once.)
    William Maas, some University, America. If you don't know him then he's not much good to either of us.
    Jean Shepperd, a radio commentator. (I was invited to have dinner with him but didn't but he's my only contact with U.S. radio.)

The forms were completed by the following statement: 'I wrote for many expatriate magazines in Paris—*Points, Paris Review* and *Merlin*—but do not wish to remind anyone of the fact—hunger makes pornographers of us all.'
The whole operation had been carried out neatly and pre-

cisely and the professional attitude he adopted to the compilation of the publicity forms was obvious. Iain however was not
meeting with quite the same professionalism with regard to the
submission of the finished manuscript, and he was getting
anxious. At the end of June he received a post-card from Brendan
from the west coast of Ireland.

> Tá mé, Leaping from roasted rock and spangling the shimmer-
> ing quivering air with showering Rainbow fragments gaily jang-
> ling between the Atlantic and the sun's mad glowering. Also graft-
> ing like a bastard and will send instalment of 100 f/cap pages for
> you to have on Sat 29th morning. Love to Rae, Eileen, Mr. Lusty
> and Margaret, Breandán.

But several days later still no material had arrived and Iain
telephoned him to be promised that it would be in the post by
return. Indeed on July 8th, Brendan wrote the following letter:

> Iain, a chara, Here's the finished copy to date, and I am truly
> sorry that I have not sent you more. I got the readies o.k., and
> thanks a lot and have not very much to do—at least no more than
> I can do in a fortnight from this date. As I told you, you will have
> the whole thing finished, as far as I am concerned, on the 1st
> August. I am drinking tea at this moment and feeling ghastly.
> There's some Anglo-Indian old one just now on the B.B.C. and
> she's been taking elocution lessons from the Duke of Edinburgh.
> Get a load of this . . . 'London in April was just what I'd expected
> it to be . . . I remember asking Granny why she was such a funny
> colour and wondered why she changed the subject.' Jesus and me
> trying to stop off the gargle. The Archbishop of Dublin says I am
> a communist—Harold Hobson of the *Sunday Times* said I was
> an R.C. bigot—but like yourself I most certainly am a Gael. I often
> thought we should have taken up something else, did you? I some-
> times think I am a crypto Englishman, the kind that wears a
> bowler hat and goes round the streets with a water-cock . . . some
> of my grandfathers looked like that . . . and refers to a glass of
> beer as a half, although I am bound to say my grandfathers knew
> what a half-one was.
>   Gradh mo chroidhe to you, and your ladies and Mr Lusty and
> everyone. One consolation for both of us; the next book is a
> smasher—if we're not outlawed over it and have to go back into

our ancestral bogs. In the meantime I shall get on with this book. It has cheered me up even writing to you, and you are certainly the first publisher to get a message like that. Love from Beatrice to Rae and Eileen and yourself and Margaret and Mr Lusty, Brendan.

July came and went and still there was no sign of the missing forty pages. Iain again wrote a gentle reminder and Brendan's reply to it was prompt.

Monday the 12th of August, 1957

Iain, a chara mo chroidhe, I really am very sorry that I have not sent you the last of the book ms before this, but matters sometimes get very complicated. What is the good of telling you now, but I have some very fucked up snafoos in my affairs and am only now getting out of them. They were all financial, but I did not like to call on you again, so soon. However, in one fortnight from now, as God is my judge, you shall have the last word of *Borstal Boy*. I was getting a lot of dough off a French company for the film rights of *The Quare Fellow*, and ironically, by C.B.S. of America wanting to televise it. They all start wrangling about a thousand or so, when a couple of score would have saved my life last week. Things are easier now, I hasten to add, in case you'd think I was putting the arm on you, and I am just going to address myself to some Dubonnet, new peas, steak, Graves de Vayres, Irish tomatoes, brack (a sort of cake brom 'breac', spotted, you know 'barm brack') and I'll send you the last word in a fortnight. Slan agat anois, a Iain o, Breandán.

At the end of August, he paid a fleeting visit in person to the office, but as Iain was away on holiday, Brendan conceived the idea that I was the next most likely person to tap for more money. At the same time he made it perfectly clear that he had no right to be asking me for it as he gave me a detailed summary of what had taken place beforehand. The sum involved was only £10, so I gave it to him on his assurance that the final part of the manuscript was almost on the point of being sent off.

Encouraged by his success and the co-operation of his publishers, Brendan had not been back in Dublin for long before he was asking once more for 'a few bar,' but this time Iain was adamant: no typescript, no money. Almost immediately the final pages were despatched with the accompanying letter:

20th September, 1957

Iain, a chara, This is the first letter I ever wrote you in long hand (which I am not too good at). I think you were perfectly right in your letter. I sat at the old typewriter till 8 p.m. without eating or drinking till I finished the job—I cannot drink if I'm writing because it's all rubbish and I cannot eat because I haven't been drinking. If you had not written the letter—and if you *had* sent the chicken's neque we would still have been fucking around with the mss. next week. As it is, when I was finished I just got to the pawn with the old typewriter and pawned it for four quid. I then went and drank a glass of whiskey, a ball of malt—three English ups, isn't it?—some soda and a half one with a bloke I met. Here it is anyway and I hope we all get a few nicker out of it. I am tired now but will ring you up early in the week. Love to the girls and indeed to Bob Lusty. Mo z Rae dhuit feín (agus ó Beatrice) do cara, Breandán.

At last *Borstal Boy* had been delivered in its entirety and Hutchinson, at least, learnt the lesson never again to advance Brendan money. If only others had done the same, the ending could have been different.

The hard and closely detailed work on the manuscript began in earnest and, with Brendan's complete co-operation, all the difficult libel problems were ironed out with the lawyers. He was now determined to confine his attentions to serious writing, even if it meant a financial loss, for previously he had been employed as a free-lance journalist with little heart and enjoyment in his work.

30th September, 1957

Iain, a chara, I miss my poor old book [he wrote shortly after its submission] though long and lovingly I cussed it. However there's more where that came from as the mother of twenty said. I refused yesterday the job of Dublin corr. for the *People* newspaper, which meant a Sunday column in the Irish edition and some newsgathering. I have just bought a cottage in C. Wicklow and am putting it into repair, so I don't just booze it all. Pay me— for half the time, will you Iain, and I can keep on writing my own stuff, and yours I hope? I am not doing anything with an eye to you now, because I'm writing a play in Irish,[1] but in a couple of weeks I'm starting a book called *the catacombs* (the lower case is intentional) which I will submit to you and Bob Lusty. I do not expect you to commission it—my neck is not that hard—but if I do journalism I cannot write it and if I took the job off the *People* I would finish up in the D.T.'s anyway. With a tenner a month I'm like Goldsmith's Vicar, passing fair, mo ghradh thú, Breandán.

There was still one further problem, however, before the printing wheels could turn uninterrupted. The doubt that had existed originally concerning the title of *Borstal Boy* remained and although Brendan had come up with an alternative of '*What Matter*' from '*O what matter when for Erin dear we fall!*', Iain felt the allusion was obscure and did not sufficiently convey the nature and flavour of the book. He offered instead, '*Me son, me son, what have ye done?*' Brendan answered:

13th November, 1957

Maybe you're right about *Borstal Boy*, but you're dead wrong about that Me son miaow thing. You told me to go and search the scriptures in the form of the old songs and I've come up with this, 'This Young Neck.' How is that? Will you settle for *This Young Neck* for the English edition? I don't care a fiddler's fuck about the American edition except for the readies, but whether you or I like it or not, London is the capital of the English language. I don't mind standing in the dock and being charged with high treason, for there can be no treason where there is no allegiance, but the language is as much yours and mine as it is the Duke of Edinburgh's (for example) and to be truthful with you I'd sooner lose money even, than be disgraced in London with that title, Me son me son etc. I have *This Young Neck* for the English edition and you call it anything you like for any other editions? Is this all right? *This Young Neck* comes from a song called *The Prisoner of Clonmel,* translated from the Irish by J. J. Callanan. It's in *1000 Years of Irish Poetry*. do chara, Brendan.

After a great deal of toing and froing on the matter, Brendan's

---

[1] *The Hostage.*

patience snapped and in a brief little note in his own hand (the brevity of which he excused as due to being in bed with the 'flu) he recorded finally that 'the title of my own book is "Borstal Boy" in the English edition.' Having made his point, he left, with Beatrice, for Ibiza, not only to get away from it all, but to write his novel, *the catacombs*, in peace, a feat he accomplished at least to the extent of thirty pages of typescript by the time he had returned to Ireland at the end of March.

While he was still in the Balearic Isles, however, Brendan had the idea that it would be a good thing if *Borstal Boy* carried a photograph of himself in his 'teens, as this would match the book better than an up-to-date portrait. But he did not possess one of himself during the period concerned, and could scarcely ask the Home Secretary for an official photograph, so he persuaded a Spaniard, who resembled him closely at the same age, to stand in for him wearing a large I.R.A. placard around his neck with the words, BRENDAN BEHAN, 47383501, written in block capitals underneath it. The prints he dispatched to Iain:

8th March, 1958

Herewith pictures—front-face for front jacket and profile for back. It will cost you or me, £10.10.0. and Knopf $30 and I think will be most satisfactory.

The years that followed did nothing to obliterate his regret that the faked photographs were never used, nor could he appreciate that it would have been absolute madness to do so.

I was beginning to understand the difficulties I was going to encounter in promoting Brendan solely for his literary ability. Already in his absence in Ibiza, there had been a good deal of talk about *Borstal Boy* and every move he made appeared to be attracting the attentions of many of the more popular newspapers. To stop it would have been no more difficult than stopping the ebb and flow of the tide, and it was not long before the name of Brendan Behan was again in the headlines. After his return, he had gone quietly to Paris with Beatrice to discuss the French production of *The Quare Fellow*. On the flight back, while the airliner was over London Airport, the pilot announced that he was turning back because the plane's radio had broken down. Beatrice felt it was her duty to wake the sleeping Brendan to tell him what was happening.

Awake he was indeed on hearing the news and up at the door of the pilot's cabin, only to meet restraint in the form of two stalwart over-anxious passengers and a near-hysterical steward, who physically forced him back to his seat. This alarming treatment could not do otherwise but further increase the fear in an already terrified man. A scene followed and Brendan tore up his plane tickets under solemn oath that never again would he fly Air France.

Back safely in France, but before he had time to make his official complaint, the thought of which had apparently kept him alive high up over the English Channel, Brendan was himself arrested and taken to a police station, where he spent the night in a cell in the company of two Algerians. On his release the next morning, while waiting for the boat train from Paris to Dieppe, he was besieged by the press.

'Listen,' he was reported as saying in one newspaper, 'I may not be an expert radio engineer, but you can take it from me I'm an expert passenger and I have no intention of dying for Air France. That plane was broke.'

Asked if it was true that he had spent the night in the police station, he nodded. 'Sure. But don't ask me why. All I know is that they put me in a cage with two Algerians. Mark you, I didn't mind the Algerians. But I must say I can't take too kindly to the French police.'

But whatever harm the adverse publicity may have done to him personally, this was soon counteracted by the excellence of the reviews which followed the opening of his new play, *An Giall*, in Dublin a few weeks later.

> June 22nd, 1958 (Feast of St. Joseph Stalin)
> Iain, a chara mo chroidhe, I enclose a piece from the *Irish Times* about my new play, partly as exculpation of my dotty dilatoriness in the matter of 'B.B.' I am attacked by some citizens who

maintain that my poor old play is Pro-British! Jesus, I've heard it
all now. However it is a tremendous success, and is being retained.
Being Scots or Irish is a great thing in the days of our youth, when
we look good in a kilt, and associate it with giving us a good excuse for tramping the mountains, but sometimes I wish I was born
something else. Not French (Algeria) nor English (Cyprus and
Kenya) nor Russian—my affection for them is in their role of
spectres haunting Maynooth College—but Swedish or Mexican
. . . Gneu, gou, gu. *The catacombs* goes like a bomb. I have thirty
pages of it done, and will send them to you whenever you like.
do chara, Breandán.

The review he enclosed is worth quoting at length because it
does show that *The Hostage* did not owe everything to Joan
Littlewood's able direction as has so often been claimed.

Irish Times, June 17th 1958.

One expects the unusual from Mr. Brendan Behan and one is
seldom disappointed. He is one of the few writers in Ireland who
writes in both French and English, and last night at the Damer
Hall, St. Stephen's Green, Dublin, he proved to an overflowing
audience that he was equally at home writing Irish. Mr. Behan's
Gaelic might not be approved of by the purists, but it certainly
suits the working-class Dublin of which he writes.

His new play *An Giall* (*The Hostage*) is set in a lower-class
Dublin brothel owned by a fanatical Gael, the son of an Anglican
bishop, who was educated at Oxford, and managed by a one-
legged old I.R.A. man willing to use it for his own ends. A young
English soldier, stationed in Armagh, is kidnapped by the I.R.A.,
brought to Dublin and imprisoned in the brothel. It is only by
accident that he discovers that he is a hostage and will be executed
by the Republican soldiers if a young man, under sentence of
death in the Crumlin Road Jail, Belfast, is hanged. He falls in love
with the maid in the house and she with him, and they find that
both have more or less the same background—that neither cares
a straw for any war or battle which Ireland and Britain might
have had in the past or would have in the future. The manager of
the place also understands the futility of carrying on the 'Old
fight', but he is powerless to intervene.

An Giall is a very cleverly written play. Indeed, in the first act
the writing was possibly too clever and the dialogue was over-
loaded with witty lines that were of little use to the play as a

whole. However, this was a small fault and did not detract from the over-all picture of excellence.

Mr. Frank Dermody's production was of a high quality which, coupled with Mr. Behan's pen, presented a most entertaining show. It is hoped that Mr. Behan translates his play into a language which more people can understand and more theatregoers enjoy.

Ironically, it was not Brendan who caused the first controversial headlines to be written about *Borstal Boy*. It was myself. There was some doubt in Hutchinson as to whether the book should be published in its entirety, or whether some of the four-letter words, which cropped up in every other line, should be expurgated. No decision had been reached on the matter and it was deemed unnecessary, at this stage, to warn Brendan of the dilemma. I was getting frequent telephone calls from the press enquiring when the book would be published and now they were beginning to get curious about the cause of the delay. Finally, in desperation, and assuming it to be 'off the record,' I gave one reporter the background story so that he might have a clearer understanding of the difficulties involved.

A few days later, I had a very clear understanding of the difficulties I was facing as I tried to explain how the story had appeared in print at all. And there was little encouragement, from the wording of the article, that Brendan might take a different point of view.

I read:

Brendan Behan, that wild man of Ireland who astounded London theatregoers two years ago with his play, *The Quare Fellow*, and everyone else with his drinking capacity—remember that tipsy TV interview—will be in a four-letter mood today. For I can tell him that his Publishers are having second thoughts about his book, *Borstal Boy*.

The clock was not made to pass the hours waiting for Brendan's reply to my letter, but never have the Customs House and River Liffey, Dublin, Ireland, looked so sweet on a postcard as on that day. Simply addressed to 'Rae (of Sunshine)', Brendan had written:

24.6.1958

Dear Rae, I have not seen the paper which does not circulate here these days. I should be obliged if you would send me a copy for the laughs. I got a wire from them, signed blank, asking me to ring them, which I did not because said blank is an ex-Fascist and a scab journalist. Don't bother about it, for [and here the four-letter word had been scored out heavily in green ink by the censor] sake. All publicity is good except an obituary notice. Send me a copy of it though, love as ever to you, Eileen and all—Brendan.

Immediately, I sent the newspaper cutting to him, and again by return of post came another card, this time of the Four Courts, The Quays and River Liffey.

1st July, 1958

Rae (of Sunshine), I loved it—thanks. But not the picture— Beatrice loved it all and we both love you—not Jeffs but [here a drawing of the sun illustrated the point.] Brendan.

It was a charitable ending to an unfortunate error on my part, but for those who knew Brendan well, his attitude to the incident came as no surprise.

At the beginning of August, he went to Sweden with Beatrice at the invitation of Dr. Olof Lagerlöf and his wife, Dagny, whom they had met in the preceding year while in Dunquin, Co. Kerry. There, in a summer-house at Ljusterö, not far from Stockholm, Brendan put the finishing touches to *Borstal Boy* and began the English translation of *An Giall*, which as *The Hostage* was to be produced later in the year by Theatre Workshop under the direction of Joan Littlewood. For three weeks he worked hard, drinking little, and his few visits to the capital did nothing to alter his concentration. Very soon he had sent Iain back the corrected proofs of *Borstal Boy* with the accompanying letter:

15th August, 1958. Sweden.

Iain, a chara mo chroidhe, I enclose the corrected book proofs and will bring the long sheets with me when I come back on

Saturday, 23rd. The parcel may take some days so I am sending
this page by post. No wonder Charles Dickens used to drink two
glasses of port and an egg before he'd start work in the morning;
navvying couldn't be much worse than writing in longhand.

Regards to Eileen and Rae (tell her we're looking forward to
the party on pre-publication day) and Bob. Regards to Margaret
too, and the married one—ask her how it feels these times.
beannacht dhuit féin uaim-se agus ó do chara, Brendan.

Years later I was to meet Olof and Dagny Lagerlöf and spend
a day with them at their home. I cannot imagine a more fairy-
tale setting in which to work. Small wonder that Brendan was
reluctant to leave it.

In the meantime, interest in *Borstal Boy* was gathering momentum. The early copies had been sent out for advance comments,
a normal procedure which rarely bore fruit. This time, however,
the response was immediate.

'A vital and moving book,' wrote Canon Collins, 'which ought
not to affront anyone who is genuinely in search of the truth
about life. To anyone concerned about the British penal system
—and this, surely must apply to everyone who professes to
Christian and liberal values—this book is a "Must"!' Emanuel
Shinwell felt that 'if you dislike the truth, don't read this book,'
adding as an afterthought that if he had to review the book, he
would 'advocate that it should be publicly burned, but only after
it had been read.' Frank Swinnerton was more direct in his praise:
'I call this book a smasher. It is as precise as a document and as
personal and dramatic as a novel by Victor Hugo. It should be a
great success.'

Brendan and Beatrice returned from Sweden to a London
poised expectantly for adulation or notoriety or both and, surprisingly, Brendan showed little pleasure at the attention he was
attracting. He was aware of the hazards of success to a man of his
weakness and unconsciously tried in bouts of unpredictable
irritation to turn away from it before it was too late.

'I would prefer not to be treated as a national figure like Chi-
Chi the panda or Billy Hill,' he said pathetically after a particu-

larly bad day of constant interruptions by exuberant well-wishers. 'Why don't they leave me alone?'

But it was not to be, and as his bolt of resistance was tackled by every conceivable type of spanner, his capacity for living, coupled with a real fear of loneliness, would not allow him to resist for long the constant invitations to the feast. His ability to shut himself away to write now began to diminish as success grew and the unfinished translation of *The Hostage* did not appeal as much as the pub or the binges that brought the newspaper headlines. Money was no obstacle for there was plenty to be had for the asking and more to come. *The Quare Fellow* was to open in New York at the 'Circle in the Square' in November, under the direction of José Quintero who had staged Eugene O'Neill's *Long Day's Journey Into Night*, while Boris Vidan's French translation of *The Quare Fellow* was due for production in December at the Œuvre, in Paris. *Borstal Boy*, although still not published, was assured of financial success and various translation rights had already been sold.

Brendan had known too much poverty not to be dazzled by the gold dangling in front of his eyes and now he began to boast of the money he was spending each day on drink. Finally, and in desperation, using the plot of the play as his guide, Gerry Raffles, the manager of Theatre Workshop, forced Brendan, at the point of a gun, to complete the translation of *The Hostage*.

On the 24th September 1958 there appeared this brief announcement in the press:

> After several months of uncertainty, following the withdrawal of most of their grants, Theatre Workshop announced last night that the Theatre Royal, Stratford, would reopen on Oct. 14th. The production will be the first of a new play *The Hostage*, by Brendan Behan, author of *The Quare Fellow*.

It was the last major work that he was ever to write.

III

FIRST NIGHT

If it is true to say that the task of promoting *Borstal Boy* had certain difficulties, it would be equally true to say that this was not entirely the fault of Brendan. Although he enjoyed the full glare of the spotlight, he was not meeting any rebuffs to check his enthusiasm, for the newspapers recorded his every move so efficiently that only the deaf, dumb and blind could have remained oblivious to his existence. With no financial necessity to work and plenty of encouragement to do otherwise, Brendan spread his wings and flew round London, and if there were some who wondered where it would all end, they wondered from afar and were not actually in the nest with him.

Even his visit to Whitstable for the opening of the oyster season drew nothing more in the way of criticism than a cryptic comment from Beatrice: 'Oysters mean stout. You know what it is, Rae,' she said as I met them on their return, battered but still in one piece.

At the end of September, Brendan went back to Dublin to give himself a breather, and Beatrice as well, in readiness for the opening night of *The Hostage* in London and the publication, a few days later, of *Borstal Boy*. In the confusion that was beginning to dog his departure from anywhere, Brendan missed the train from Paddington and had to travel from Euston to Liverpool, so making his existing ticket null and void.

As he disappeared down the platform at Euston, ignoring

Beatrice's valiant efforts to get him on to the train before it
actually started to move, I called out to him that he could get his
ticket refunded, only to receive a wave from the back of his hand
in acknowledgement, or what I presumed to be an acknowledgement. The last I saw of him he was being pushed through the carriage door, like a reluctant greyhound into a trap, as the train
eased its way out of the station.

Back in the office, I tried to readjust myself to a certain degree
of normality but the prospect of publishing a book of *Borstal
Boy*'s literary merit was hardly an everyday occurrence, and as
the day of publication came nearer a feeling of excitement swept
through the office. There were so many requests for personal
interviews with Brendan both from the press and television companies that it became impossible to deal with them with the Irish
Sea separating us. I was detailed to go across to Dublin to
straighten out a few of the entanglements that must surely follow
without Brendan's full co-operation. I was to stay in the house of
a senior counsel at the Irish bar, a man who knew Brendan from
his earlier days and whose wife was also an acquaintance. They
would be prepared for emergencies. As the aircraft touched down
at Dublin airport on the first of my many visits to Ireland, I could
not help wondering whether the return flight would find me in a
comparable state of health.

With my hostess, I went to see Brendan and we carefully
selected the hour between 2.30 and 3.30 to do so as the pubs
would be closed during that time. (The Holy Hour, Brendan
called it, adding that the politician who introduced it in the Dail
was shot dead an hour afterwards.) I was several minutes knocking on the door of their ground floor flat in Herbert Street before
Beatrice half opened it. Her assertion and regret that Brendan
was out, followed by Brendan's booming affirmation from the adjoining room that he was in, were somewhat bewildering. As we
hovered on the doorstep, there was no time to decide on our next
move for a hand pulled Beatrice to one side swinging the door
wide open, and Brendan stood in front of us, barefooted, the
bottom of him just covered from the point of indecency by

pyjamas, while the top half sported a white shirt, the collar of
which was stretched tightly around his neck as he manfully
struggled to do up the button.

The extent of his welcome for me was totally in opposition to
the look of distaste he gave to my companion and I was confused
and embarrassed, both on her account and my own. Beatrice,
who had still not recovered from being made to look a barefaced
liar in front of comparative strangers, was unable to help. He
ushered me in, and the sight of the room which we entered did
little to alter my confusion for it looked as if it had been ran-
sacked by a burglar. Brendan beckoned me to sit down while
seating himself in the only other available chair and, while I trod
gingerly across the floor, Beatrice apologised for the mess and
explained that the builders were trying to combat the dry rot with
which the house was plagued. All at once I felt stupid and rude
for not having warned her of our visit. Of course she would object to our seeing her home for the first time in this condition.

Slowly Brendan began putting socks on his feet, but with a
lack of concentration revealing that his mind was not on his
work. Deliberately and with a dignity completely out of character, he turned towards my hostess.

'Would you ever tell me what you had to do to get those briefs
for your husband?'

The unfortunate woman receded under the blow but came forward again with a smile on her face to indicate she had taken his
remark as nothing but a joke. She was soon to learn her mistake,
for Brendan now began to give his own views on her personal and
matrimonial affairs until the very sinews of her soul lay exposed
and bleeding. She stood helplessly, with the tears hurrying down
her cheeks, and her eyes implored me to do something. Although
a thousand actions sprang into my mind I could only sit in the
chair loathing my lack of courage for not being able to do any
one of them. Instead I wished that I was a million miles away
before the asp-like barbs of Brendan's tongue became directed
at me and I excused my appalling indecision in the belief that the
fierce cruelty I had witnessed would not have been unleashed

without some provocation of which I had no knowledge. The noise of my chair grating on the floorboards broke the silence and in the hollow of my mind I heard Brendan apologise to me for the lack of drink in the house, and politely suggest that as soon as the pubs opened, we go out for a 'jar.' The tension eased a little, though none of us spoke a word as he shuffled off into the next room, returning a few minutes afterwards with the index and second finger of his left hand supporting his shoes while his right hand clasped his trousers to prevent them from falling round his ankles. He put the shoes down on the floor beside my chair, craned up his trousers by the braces and took a sheet of typed paper off the mantelpiece.

'Now you be looking for their letter,' he said to Beatrice, who immediately began rummaging through a pile on the table. It was not long before she found it and handed it to Brendan.

'You'll be the mother of a bishop,' he thanked her jovially before passing the letter to me. It was from British Railways, in the person of an official who had signed himself, 'for N. H. Briant.' I read:

> Before giving consideration to your claim for a refund I should be glad if you would be good enough to let me know the circumstances which prevented you from using the ticket.

Scarcely had I time to digest it, before Brendan thrust his reply into my hand, snarling oaths on the head of every John Bull bollox of petty officialdom, dead or alive, as he did so. On the paper he had typed:

> Dear for N. H. Briant, I don't know that it matters, but we missed the train from Paddington and had to travel from Euston to Liverpool. If you do want to give me back my twelve quid, do so. If you need it, keep it. I am not depending on it . . . God help any poor traveller that was. I have more to do than be answering your silly letters. Send the money or don't. My time is valuable.
> I am usually paid more than twelve nicker for writing as much as this. for Brendan Behan, Brendan Behan.

I laughed and handed the letter to my hostess to read, but before it had reached her hand from mine, it was in Brendan's. 'That's business,' he snarled.

Suddenly I was very, very angry and this time I said so, continuing my wrath up the windy street, across the bridge and into Mooney's bar on the corner of Bagot Street. Brendan interrupted me to ask what I'd be having but when this did nothing to stem my flow of words he did not press the point. Instead he ordered four glassheens.

'There you are,' he said, as he handed me a glass of draught Guinness. 'That'll soften your cough.' And he grinned at me. I collected my degrees of rage into one lump and told Brendan that I had not realised he was capable of so much viciousness; that I was disturbed by his lack of remorse and could see no connection between the man who had written *Borstal Boy* and the man whose behaviour I had just witnessed. Despite the rough manner in which he retaliated, 'In the name of Jaysus, will you ever stop giving out the pay?' he was obviously sorry and I left it at that.

For the rest of the afternoon, we adjourned from one bar to another, Brendan scattering his greetings like a king. He sang, he danced, he told innumerable stories and put his hand in his pocket on more than one occasion, but as his rowdiness increased along with the trembling of the glass partitions in the bar, his gaiety appeared more contrived and less spontaneous, and it was not difficult to detect that somewhere, not far from the surface, he had a large conscience.

I had not intended to discuss business with him in this explosive atmosphere, but he took me aside and seemed anxious to know some of the arrangements. He had been booked for television interviews with Dan Farson on *This Week* and Kenneth Allsop on *The Bookman* while *Tonight* had also expressed an interest in him. Robert Pitman I knew wanted to fly to Dublin to write a full-page article on him for the *Sunday Express* and there was the matter of invitations for the pre-publication party of *Borstal Boy* which Hutchinson were giving.

Brendan listened attentively, nodding his head from time to

time but without interrupting. He was quite happy to leave the plans to me, he said, and would make himself available any time he was needed. He would rather not come to London before the first night of *The Hostage*, but would of course if it became necessary.

Briskly and to the point I explained that his book was being published on October 20, six days after the opening of *The Hostage* at the Theatre Royal, but as far as I was concerned he would not be needed before October 16, the date of the Hutchinson party. I ignored his attempts to break through my business-like approach and his remarks, 'You're a great girl,' 'May your shadow never grow less,' 'Your blood's worth bottling,' had little effect. Finally and irresistibly, he broke through my reserve.

'You know, for a gentle person, you can be very stubborn,' he said. 'I don't go a great smack on that woman you're staying with. I'm sorry but there's an end on it and I've got two tickets for you for the first night of my play.' He pushed them into my hand as he spoke. 'If you don't want them, you can sell them for a few bar. It's all the one to me.' He was back up at the counter downing a pint before I could answer.

I looked at the tickets and on the back of one was written, 'To Rae with love, Brendan.' I put them into my handbag and joined Beatrice and my hostess who seemed to be hitting it off well, though I detected a certain restlessness in the latter to be away. I mentioned this quietly to Beatrice and suggested I telephone for a cab and that while I was doing so, my hostess could slip out unnoticed, for although Brendan had ignored her for most of the afternoon, I was afraid he might consider one last salvo in her direction to be of no harm. Beatrice agreed and they both went out into the street. I ordered the taxi and went back up to the bar, but something told me that my departure would not be quite so easy. Unlike the pubs in London, the few people around Brendan were paying little attention to him as his shouting increased and his behaviour became more garrulous.

'I must go,' I began rather abruptly, to have the rest of the sentence cut short in the air.

'Hold your hour, daughter. I'll be with you in a moment when I've finished settling up a matter here.'

'But I'm not asking you to come with me,' I replied. 'My hostess is in a taxi outside and she is waiting for me.'

His reaction was instantaneous. 'For the love of God, it's not a train you're catching, is it?' and then immediately, 'You're my publisher, aren't you?' He turned his back on me and faced the bar again.

I considered his attitude both presumptuous and impertinent and saw no reason why I should put up with it. I got straight into the cab. As the wheels rumbled over the cobbled streets and rolled on to the outskirts of Dublin, I became increasingly more puzzled as to why I could not dismiss the incident as one of the hazards of being a publicity manager and I tried to define my relationship with Brendan in a clinical fashion. I was not fully aware that he had already forced upon me a personal concern in excess of my duties, and was bewildered by my own regret at leaving him in this way. He seemed to demand the whole of my attention, and while one part of me enjoyed it, another rose up in revolt. I could neither reject nor accept the situation.

The Hostage opened in London the following week, and although I waited all day for a telephone call from either Brendan or Beatrice, it was not until I reached the theatre with Brian Inglis, to whom I had given the second ticket, that I knew they had arrived. They had seats in the dress circle, a little further back from our own. Brendan looked clean and well groomed and I recall no surprise that he was wearing a dinner-jacket. I smiled at them both and waved my hand, but although I received a response from Beatrice, Brendan ignored my gesture and nodded to Brian. I walked back to speak to him and for a moment I thought he was going to disregard me again, but as he looked straight ahead, a faint flicker of a smile moved his lips and I knew he would not keep up the act of offence for long.

I returned to my seat and glanced through the programme.

Brendan Behan needs no introduction to regular patrons of

this theatre [I read]. This playwright of the Irish and British peoples made an unforgettable impression with *The Quare Fellow* in May 1956. He has hatred for the political forces who divide and subject Ireland: but for the people—even if those people are the instruments of antagonistic political forces—he has only love and understanding. If a stranger attacks Britain, no one will support this country more strongly than Brendan Behan, but when he talks of Ireland—of a country where, outside the cities, there are almost no young and active men left, where the villages are now but rows of empty houses, where Irish butter and meat are dearer than they are in England, and where partition gives such a sense of continuing betrayal and defeat that the brilliant and useful ones leave for abroad to escape the internecine quibbling and denigration—he grows angry with the anger of a man who loves his native place as passionately as Shakespeare loved his.

By the end of the first act, I was astounded that the play could have been judged anti-British. If anything, it gave me the impression that it was pro-British, except for the fact that it was pro everything that was good, fine and fair in man, regardless of class, creed or country. And for one such as myself, ill-versed in Anglo-Irish history, despite the surface wildness and the constant interruption of song and dance, the plot was easy to follow. I do recall wondering how it was that Brendan, who had so much cause for bitterness, had managed to write the play without a trace of it; instead a compassion that showed the futility of patriotic fervour when it led to hatred and violence.

In the interval Brian and I walked across the street to the pub opposite, but as I reached the saloon-bar door, I felt a touch on my arm. 'I was asking after you,' Brendan said. 'Beatrice said you'd just gone out. Did you know I'd written most of the songs in that?' and he nodded his head in the direction of the theatre, 'while one or two of the others were written by my uncle, Peadar Kearney, the same who wrote the Irish National Anthem. Aren't they great gas?' He was as pleased as Punch with himself.

I would have liked to have told him that I thought his play wasn't so bad either, but he slipped back into the theatre so quickly that I doubt if more than a few of the crowd in the street realised he'd been there at all.

When the curtain rose on the final act, I remembered the reviews I had read of *An Giall* and could see little basic difference in the plot, which had now been turned, by the addition of song and dance, into a musical tragi-comic extravaganza. I noticed too that not all the cast had been changed for the Theatre Workshop production, for the part of Teresa, the maid, was still played by Brendan's sister-in-law, Celia Salkeld, for whom it was specially written.

At the end, as the entire cast came forward to take their bow, a thunder of applause echoed round a packed auditorium. Perhaps not great theatre, if *The Hostage* had nothing else it had life in abundance, welling out from every corner of the stage, enveloping the audience with its zest and enthusiasm. It was a wonderfully exciting evening and one that left even Brendan a trifle bewildered. At any rate, there was no sign of the showman as he came forward to make his curtain speech.

With dignity he thanked the audience for their reception and said he was proud to have his play produced by the best producer (Joan Littlewood) and the best company (Theatre Workshop) in the world, and went on to describe the proceedings as 'my comment on Anglo-Irish relations. As to what it is about, you will find out from the critics.' Indeed the following morning, the critics were so enthusiastic about the play that, for once, Brendan's literary achievements took precedence over his other less creditable attributes.

He was staying at the time with Joan Littlewood and Gerry Raffles at Blackheath and early next morning he walked the short distance to the station with Beatrice and bought all the papers.

On the train somewhere between Blackheath and the centre of London could hardly be described as the best place to discover one is world-famous; but this is exactly what happened to Brendan as he read one glowing review of his play after another. His flow of vivid language increased along with his warmth and gaiety. His fellow passengers facing the prospect of a hard day's work, hid themselves behind their newspapers, or stood stiffly to attention with expressions of disgust, like soldiers on parade when one of them has fainted. But it would have taken a different character from Brendan to be affected by tea-and-toast decorum, unless it was to encourage him to raise his voice still louder, and he sang from the heart all the songs from *The Hostage*, the sweat on his forehead glistening as much from his efforts as from the proximity of the passengers. It must have been, as Milton Shulman described the play itself, 'a rare and invigorating experience.'

It was from the George in Great Portland Street that he telephoned me a few hours later and asked me to come down and meet him. He was in wonderful humour and equally fine voice and the weather seemed brighter for all of us standing at the counter listening to him. His delight was in the pleasure he was giving, and not from the contents of a bottle.

I was not prepared for the sudden seriousness in his voice as he whispered to me: 'All this will help my book, won't it?' It was a question asked in earnest but quietly so that no one else could hear.

'Can do no other,' I replied truthfully. I had not realised, until this moment, how real was his lack of confidence in himself as a writer, or how much it mattered to him what people thought of his work. All the praise he was getting for *The Hostage* could not quite obliterate his apprehension over the publication of *Borstal Boy*. The ordeal of watching the English translation of his play performed in public for the first time was over. Now he was beginning to get anxious about the reception of his book and wishing the hours away.

Although Brendan had the capacity to make everyone with whom he came in contact believe there was an immediate intimacy between them, and special only to them (though on the occasion of their next meeting they might not be even recognised), he bestowed on few the privilege of hearing him discuss his work. For him, this was the bridge between a temporary relationship and a lasting one. Now he had taken me aside from the others as if my opinion on the matter was of some consequence, and I knew I must not attempt to allay his fears by joking references for his need to polish up his glass belly.

Because of this, I did not mention the *Borstal Boy* party or the fact that I would have to leave almost at once to make the final arrangements for it. The pub was buzzing with editors, broadcasters, journalists and 'ardents' as Dylan Thomas called them, and Brendan's worries, at any rate on the surface, soon appeared to be smothered under the weight of their congratulations. As I reached the door, I called back to him over my shoulder: 'See you Thursday night, Brendan,' and louder, 'around five-thirty.' He gave no positive sign that he had heard me, but I knew that he had.

IV

THE NIGHT OF THE PARTY

Brendan and Beatrice arrived punctually. I had made up my mind, as we sat around waiting for the party to begin, that our conversation would be of an entirely superficial nature. This was not simply on Brendan's account but because I knew that the members of the press who were coming—and there were many —had probably formed in their mind before the event the stories they'd be writing afterwards. I was not going to be the match to light the gunpowder for their big bang.

Brendan was in the best of form, eagerly devouring the sandwiches that had been cut for him, but it was not long before I realised he was in no mood for frivolous banter. All in the one breath he told me that I ought to know more about his novel, *the catacombs*—abortions in Dublin and so on—that the two companies concerned were still quibbling over the film rights of *The Quare Fellow*, and that he had just heard the televised version of his play was shortly to be seen on Associated Rediffusion.

'To tell the honest truth,' he added, 'I'm not out of my mind about the latter bit of news, because I am sure there's not a deal of similarity between my play and theirs.' And he looked up into my face for the reaction that he expected from an alert and publicity-conscious individual. But I was neither of these things; I was irritated that he should have chosen this time to tell me matters of such importance and expect me to grasp the whole picture from the sketchy outline he had given me. He misunderstood my silence.

'I'm not saying these things by way of any boast,' he said, tetchily, 'but rather marking your card in case you are asked any questions tonight.'

'I could hardly answer any questions, Brendan,' I replied, 'from the little you have given me, and as Iain is in America, I can hardly call upon him for help.' He gave me a look of despair and shrugged his shoulders to indicate my stupidity. All I had to do, he explained with bored patience, was to say that his novel was set in Dublin in the forties; that Sam Spiegel, in America, and Blondefilm, in France, were both interested in the film rights, and that *The Quare Fellow* was shortly to be seen on television.

Actually my nerves were so knotted inside me at the thought, in Iain's absence, of having to take the responsibility for the impending party (for I knew Bob Lusty, the firm's chairman, was leaving early for a conference) that it was a miracle I was still able to listen to anything at all. I do not know if Brendan understood, but as soon as he had finished speaking, he held out his hand to mine and shook it firmly but kindly.

'And if you get bewildered by me sometimes,' he added, chuckling, 'so does Beatrice. For I have a mind that would burst rather than sustain a mood or a subject for long.'

Never will I forget the party for *Borstal Boy*: the imposing panelled room in which it was held; the waiters impeccably dressed in white jackets and pin-striped trousers; the brave occupation-for-gentlemen faces of the staff as they nervously made conversation; the suspended what-is-going-to-happen shape of the eyebrows on some of the guests. And always Brendan, coat wide open to reveal scarlet braces; Brendan factual and formidable, entirely diminishing his own portrait from the dust-wrapper of his book which had been multiplied many times and took up the length and breadth of one wall. There was Hugh Delargy, the Socialist M.P., who had met Brendan many years previously when he was on the run in Manchester and knew that he would never forget him, not only on account of his strange story but because of the goodness and tenderness that were so much part of him. And Emanuel Shinwell, too, who talked of his own prison experiences for his part in the famous 'forty-hour' strike in 1919, but said he thought the prison scenes in *Borstal Boy* were exaggerated. 'The warders never used language like that to *me*,' he insisted.

Then with Bob Lusty's departure, a reasonably controlled but free-for-all attitude pervaded the room and the general hubbub increased. Patrick Campbell announced his intention of giving his rendering of 'The Old Musheroon' to which Brendan responded, loudly and clearly:

'Oh, the praties they were small over there,
Oh, the praties they were small over here,
Oh, the praties they were small, but we ate them skin and all,
They were better than f—— all, over here.'

and everyone laughed and accepted it without surprise. There were songs and more songs, only silenced by a solo from Val's wife, Sheila Iremonger, which she sang quite beautifully in the Irish language. No matter that few of us understood the words; we did not need to.

Brendan, on the grounds that one good solo deserves another, began his with tremendous volume, only to discover that he had a partner in Hugh Delargy, who was standing at the opposite end of the room, as together they sang the chorus of 'Glory O, Glory O, to the Bold Fenian Men.' In the middle of the concert, two young boys arrived whose presence in the doorway was of such pleasure to Brendan that he left his unfortunate duettist in mid air to come over and greet them, before serving them personally with two very strong drinks which they took without the slightest tremor of indecision.

I do not remember how the next incident started but I imagine Brendan must have been expansive about his prowess in selling the film rights of *The Quare Fellow* to two different companies, and Jacqueline Sundstrom of Blondefilm, who was at the party, must have overheard his indiscretion.

My recollection begins with a sharp exchange of words between Jacqueline and Brendan, followed by a rush of reporters who swooped upon them, anxious not to miss anything that might be going in the way of a barney. Forced into positive action, I was not long after the heels of them, airily dismissing whatever Brendan had said as 'complete and utter nonsense,' and adding, 'You know what Brendan is' with as much charm as I was able.

For the most part, they believed me. At any rate, they dispersed and became once more part of the general hilarity. All but one of them, that is. He, more persistent than his colleagues, stayed on to ask Brendan one or two extremely pertinent questions which Brendan answered arrogantly and abusively to the increasing hostility of the man who now became very, very angry. All at once, I was in there, between them, one hand pushing Brendan away, the other similarly employed on the reporter. The result was incredible. Brendan, only too happy to be out of an ugly situation, suddenly recognised an old friend at the other end of the room, while the reporter, willing to face the likes of Brendan in the line of duty, was certainly not willing to face the wrath of a near-hysterical woman. He went straight out of the room, picked up his fawn mackintosh from Reception and left. No more than a handful of people had been aware of the incident.

Brendan obviously thought it wiser to leave me alone for a while, but later he came over to tell me that he had been unable to find the man in question to apologise to him. Judging by the unrepentant look on his face, he had more in mind than an apology.

All the same, he was remarkably sober, whether from fright or 'with intent' did not matter, and I was grateful for the fact because I needed his help to remove one or two of the more inebriated guests. It must have been the only time in his life that he was called upon to use the art of gentle persuasion on others less well than himself.

There were not many at the dinner afterwards. I had taken the precaution of reserving an upstairs room at the back of Bertorelli's, an Italian restaurant not far from the office. To begin with I sat back and listened to a friendly and hilariously funny sparring match between Brendan and Paddy Campbell which, for sheer entertainment value, was second to none. But Paddy was a member of the Irish aristocracy, the heir to the title of the Glenavy estate and a protestant, and soon the inevitable gulf between the autochthonous Irishry and the West Britons made itself felt. Brendan began snarling at Paddy for having policemen in his pedigree, whirling the meat round on his plate with his fingers in the gravy and shovelling up the peas with a knife as he did so. Paddy retaliated and slowly their friendliness turned to anger and our laughter stopped.

A pretty Italian waitress came in and asked politely for a little less noise, but left abruptly as the lash of Brendan's tongue stung across her face. I doubt if he even saw her, far less understood what she was saying, but he had been hurt and all of us sitting there were part of his hurt and none of us proof against his revenge. Displaying the worst version of himself, he paced up and down the floor drinking rapidly to fortify his anger and obliterate all reason. It occurs to me now that I should have stood up and told him we were for him and not against him; that his row with Paddy was something that only concerned the two of them in which the rest of us had no part. But by the end of the evening, it was not only us he had to contend with; he was shadow-boxing with his past and the bell for him would only come in oblivion.

We were asked to leave as I knew we would be, and Brendan stumbled out into the night to look for further solace for his troubled mind. It was a sad finish.

For the press however, who had not been at the dinner, it was a tame affair although they did their best with the poor copy available. 'Mr. Behan's Rebel Songs Make His Publishers Wince,' headlined one newspaper, bracketing the statement with the words, 'He's not drinking tea at the moment.' But apart from one small reference to the film rights of *The Quare Fellow*, for which we were thankful, and an equally small one to *Borstal*

Boy, his work was not mentioned. I cannot pretend that I was aware at the time that this kind of attention could only destroy him, but I do remember feeling uneasy that Brendan might, in future, behave more outrageously in order to be sure of getting the recognition he craved.

The next morning in the office, he looked surprisingly well and was clean and neatly dressed in a rough tweed suit. He made no reference to the newspapers and sat quietly at a table in the corner of the room signing copies of his book. After a while I noticed he was having to stop at regular intervals to brush the sweat off his brow with his right hand, and assuming that he was feeling the effects of the previous evening's bout, I suggested a chaser. To my amazement he refused, becoming harassed and distracted as he asked me to tell him about the plans for a television interview. I explained that I would collect him from Blackheath the following afternoon to go to Birmingham, the headquarters of A.B.C. Television, and that Kenneth Allsop, the interviewer whom Brendan had met previously, was to travel on the train as well. He met my remarks in morbid silence, becoming increasingly more hang-dog in manner and appearance. Suddenly, but not unexpectedly for it was quite in character, his attitude changed, but the reason for it startled me. He made it emphatically clear that he loathed and detested the 'goggle-box.' It was my first experience of the anguish he suffered each time he appeared on television, and later I was to learn that, for a man who loved to be in the public eye, the mental and physical strain it imposed on him was extraordinary.

The next afternoon I collected Beatrice and himself as arranged, and having met Ken on Euston station, we settled ourselves in the dining car of the train and ordered our meal. The journey up was uneventful. Brendan ate well, entertaining both himself and us with talk which ranged from Kingsley Martin, editor of the *New Statesman*, to the day he locked up a policeman in a cell on the Aran Islands, and his limitless fund of stories did not end before we arrived in Birmingham. In the taxi, his humour began to deteriorate and as soon as we reached the hotel, he pushed past the television team who had turned out in force to meet him, and made straight for the bar. He downed several drinks in quick succession when, fortified but sober, he joined the rest of us in the lounge. For a while he took up other people's conversational leads, improving and enlarging on them, until inevitably and unconsciously, he appeared to have gathered around him everyone in the hotel. But beneath his gay appearance, each of us who knew him detected a strong explosive element which he was nobly trying to hide, and we were thankful when he finally went to bed before the warning rumblings became too apparent.

Brendan and Beatrice were already having their breakfast by the time I was up. Brendan looked wretched and depressed and obviously did not want to be engaged in conversation. He asked for a second cup of tea, complaining of an incurable thirst, and after Beatrice had refilled his cup, I automatically handed him the sugar bowl.

'Brendan's not allowed sugar,' Beatrice intervened quickly, and then more gently, 'he's a sort of diabetic.' Not until that moment had I the slightest inclination that he was not constitutionally a fit man, and I raised my eyes in horror at the thought of the added punishment his body must endure. He finished his breakfast with alarming alacrity, the expression in his eyes defying us to mention the subject further, and disappeared through the door as if his life depended on his going.

'He doesn't seem to want anyone to know about it,' explained Beatrice. 'But I would not want you to think that his incurable thirst was entirely due to villainy. He needs the liquid and when he is behaving himself, he is perfectly happy to be drinking tea.'

I was not anxious to lose sight of him, so I excused myself from Beatrice and went out to look for him. My anxiety on finding him neither in the hall nor in his bedroom increased to blood-chilling alarm when I realised he was not in the hotel at all. For two hours I waited and no Turkish bath ever accomplished weight reduction so effectively, until by the time Brendan returned, I was only a shred of my former self. He had been round the city, he said, and like every other f—ing joint on a Sunday, the mortuary would give more comfort to a dying man.

We were due at the studio almost at once so we grabbed a taxi and instructed the driver to take us to the A.B.C. Television Theatre at Aston on the outskirts of the city. As soon as the rehearsals began, Brendan began to show the strain he was feeling. Red-faced and tousle-headed, he muttered to himself, argued with the producer, abused Ken Allsop and dismissed the list of questions Ken had prepared as utter rubbish, and each coherent sentence he spoke contained at least one obscene word. When we sat down to lunch he demanded a drink and refused to eat, but on a promise that he would accept a slice of cold meat, he was given a beer which he swallowed, coughing back some of it on to the table before shouting for another. The programme was being transmitted 'live' and a repeat performance of the Malcolm Muggeridge interview seemed an odds-on certainty. Nor were Brendan's opening remarks on the air likely to give encouragement that it could be otherwise.

'I'll start talking,' he thundered, 'when I know which camera I'm supposed to be looking at.'

It was Ken's unruffled but assertive reply, 'Forget the cameras; just look at me,' that produced a remarkable change in Brendan, and sitting straight up in his chair, he proceeded to give ten minutes of first-class entertainment to confound and relieve the studio audience. He appeared to be completely sober, and after making one or two unfavourable comments about the British— 'You suckers. That's what you English are. You give me nearly all my drinking money'—he settled down to talk seriously and sensibly about *Borstal Boy* and Borstal institutions. He concluded the interview with a selection of songs from *The Hostage* to be faded out singing, 'Don't muck abaht with the moon.' Indeed his performance was so professional and assured, it was difficult to imagine that his earlier mood had not been manufactured for the pleasure of watching the chaos he was causing, and that Ken's indifference to his antics had brought him to his senses.

The ovation that greeted him as he walked into the reception room was tremendous, but the strain he'd been under began to reveal itself in the sweat which ran copiously down his face. With the arrival of the press and each successive tilt of the glass in his hand, the clown in him returned to cover up the jangling of his nerves.

The hundred questions he was asked, he answered belligerently. 'What do I think of Birmingham? It's like Louis Armstrong said when they asked him what he thought of Dublin: "What's Dublin?" he says. "Can you play it?"' 'Sure I drink all the time I'm writing.' 'You can say I was drunk again.' And a host of similarly degrading statements which were bound to give a false impression of himself to people who were likely to get no other.

It was at this point that a feeling of guilt enveloped me for I was partly responsible for the afternoon's exhibition, and I knew positively that my affection for Brendan exceeded my desire to promote him and shine at my job. I did not kid myself that without my help the promotion of so easy a subject would not be the same, but at least I could be sure that I had not contributed to his need, under these circumstances, for obsessive drinking. Above all, I knew that I wanted to step down off the band-wagon, to understand him as a writer and to try to protect him, if possible, from himself.

The drive back to Birmingham station brought no change, and Brendan sat dishevelled in the corner of the taxi shouting rebel songs interspersed with abuse until the veins on his face stood out in angry protest. And there was worse to come. On the platform he skated ahead, picking up the suitcase of a middle-aged woman on his way, and all eyes turned as she chased after him screaming, 'That's mine, that's mine,' alternating her cries with, 'Help me, help me.'

Beatrice fled up the platform after them and catching up with Brendan, she snatched the case from his shoulder where it was precariously perched and returned it with apologies to the unfortunate woman who was now in a state of near collapse.

Brendan sat down on a bench, but he did not hear our remon-
strances for he had fallen into an exhausted sleep. Beatrice looked
distraught, and the calm and control I had come to associate
with her was missing as she explained that whoever woke Brendan
in this condition would be treated to a series of thumps on whatever part of the body happened to be in the line of his fists.

'It dates from his days on the run,' she said, 'and he imagines
it is a policeman come to take him away.'

Hardly were the words out of her mouth when I saw, from the
corner of my eye, the unmistakable blue of the arm of the law
beckoning from behind a nearby pillar. I walked slowly over to
it, my eyes taking in the face which owned it so that I might have
a better idea of what I was up against. He was gruff and to the
point. There had been complaints, he said, and if there was any
further trouble, he would have to take the man to the police
station.

'That's Brendan Behan,' I replied, as if the identification was
all that was required for the matter to be dropped.

The policeman remained unmoved. 'I know who it is, and I'm
telling you . . .' He repeated his first statement with added
emphasis.

I rejoined Beatrice who was now approaching Brendan from
behind, giving him short, sharp jabs, but well out of reach of his
fists. 'You do the same,' she pleaded, and the pair of us syn-
chronised our attacks. The double-backed assault had its effect
for Brendan woke up, using his hands, legs and tongue all at
once. The policeman took several steps towards us, thought better of it and retreated to his pillar.

It was Ken Allsop who actually got Brendan to his feet. He
had been nonchalantly browsing through the papers on the stall
unaware of the impending crisis or of the dangers of disturbing
Brendan. As the train inched into the station he approached innocently to give him a helping hand. Hurling abuse and using
both arms Brendan lurched himself forward for better contact,
but as he did so Beatrice gave him the mother and father of a
push from behind and he went sprawling past Ken in the direc-

tion of a carriage door from which people were alighting.

'Push him, push him,' screamed Beatrice and between us we more or less lifted him bodily into the train where a seat was immediately vacated by a passenger with remarkable anticipation. As the train hissed and steamed out of the station, I leant out of the window and called my thanks to the policeman who waved back and smiled, not I thought without relief.

Brendan again fell into a heavy sleep, and we removed ourselves to a compartment along the corridor where we could sit and talk in comparative peace. Periodically, we took it in turns to have a look at him, but throughout the journey he remained comatose. Finally, ten minutes before we were due at Euston, we decided to wake him up, only to discover that he was no longer in his compartment. A knock on the door of the most likely place produced the reply, 'F—— off,' and patiently we waited for him to come out.

Ten minutes later my patience was wearing thin. *Borstal Boy* was due to be published the next day, and that morning I had ordered the Sunday papers to be sent up to my hotel bedroom. Although I had glanced superficially at the reviews of the book, I had not had time to digest them, and I wanted to do so quietly at home. The train began to empty and we were still standing waiting for Brendan. In exasperation, I shouted from the platform to the lavatory window above my reason for wanting to go. This time there was no answer and alarmed by the possibility that, if we did nothing, Brendan would be involved in a shuttle service to Birmingham, we searched out the station master to ask him to break down the door. As we came back up the platform, Brendan was standing on the train steps, his trousers down by his ankles, his shirt unbuttoned to reveal a bare chest, and looking both mentally and physically ravaged. Impassively he stood on the train steps while Beatrice dressed him before he appeared to brace himself for the rigours of catching a taxi as if he was utterly alone with no prospect of assistance. I tried to make contact, but I had not appreciated the extent of his loneliness and neither the reviews nor the success of his television appearance

made any difference to the insecurity inside him. Aimless and
without anchor, conventional standards meant nothing to him.

His footsteps stumbled up the platform and out to the fore-
court; alternately he accepted and rejected a guiding hand with
a softness and a brutality that defied comprehension. Suddenly
I recalled Cyril Connolly's review of *Borstal Boy* in the *Sunday
Times* in which he had complained that the book was uneven because Brendan had not realised the dangers of anticlimax in passing too quickly from sternness and savagery to sweetness and
light. This was Brendan himself, ever at war, his seesaw
emotions pitching him up and down on a base of uncertainty
that he could never shift. Alcohol might bring about a temporary
truce, but the after effects only served to intensify the battle and
weaken his ability to combat it.

The reception given to *Borstal Boy* did not exceed expectations, but rather lived up to them. Despite Cyril Connolly's
criticism in the *Sunday Times,* he recognised that Brendan was
a 'natural writer, his rare descriptions of scenery are poetic, his
accounts of Christmas relaxation among the warders and
prisoners almost Dickensian,' while Maurice Richardson in the
Observer enjoyed it without reservation. 'An excellent book,' he
wrote, 'vivid, solid, very warm and full of human observation.
There are sharp sketches of fellow Borstalians, in brilliantly
characterised dialogue.' The *Times Literary Supplement* recorded that 'his book is a brilliantly evocative account . . . and
his stupendous gift of language, exuberant, ungoverned and
indeed ungovernable, creates the very image of the rackety, reek-
ing life of his wide boys, ponces and screws. But beneath the surface of this lewd and riotous book lies an essential charity which
is altogether moving and memorable.' But Christopher Logue in
New Statesman and Nation went further in his praise: 'The most
important book of its kind to be published this century,' he
wrote.

Within a very few days, fifty-two newspapers in England and
Ireland had reviewed the book and few contradicted the general
acclaim that it was a masterpiece. Brendan himself read them

with consuming interest and without conceit and never once asked how the book was selling in the shops. In fact the Hutchinson sales department was kept very busy replenishing the orders and the first 15,000 print number quickly became exhausted. The banning of it in Ireland merely formalised a decision expected months previously, but when Australia refused to accept the book and New Zealand followed suit, only Brendan remained unmoved by the news.

> My name is Brendan Behan,
> I'm the best-banned in the land,

he sang to the tune of 'McNamara's Band.' He refused to meet members of the Australian press in London to give his views on the banning and his only comment, 'Oh! God, Oh! Canberra. Where's Australia?' was considered best left unrecorded.

After much consideration, Hutchinson decided to print a special edition for the Australian market omitting a few lines of doggerel and replacing some of the compulsive swearing by dashes. H. G. Kippax wrote in the *Sydney Morning Herald:*

> One despairs that such a decision should ever have been made necessary. Enjoyment, as Judge Woolsey said of *Ulysses,* is 'a matter of taste.' Mr. Menzies is quite entitled to feel that this book is 'almost a collection of what the Italians call graffiti— things written on the walls of certain places by adolescents'— incomprehensible though that judgement may be to literate people. But to apply his own taste and standards to the justification of a grotesque censorship decision is nothing less than a gross abuse of power calculated to make us and him the scorn and laughing stock of the civilised world.

As Brendan's humour had restored itself completely by the morning after the Birmingham trip and he was congenially at ease with himself and everyone else, I suggested cancelling his proposed television interview with Dan Farson, but he would not hear of any alterations to the existing arrangements. We were due to meet Dan at the Wig and Pen Club in Fleet Street for lunch and Brendan had agreed that on his way he would call in at the London offices of the *Manchester Guardian* for David Low to draw him. On the appointed day, we hailed a taxi but as we approached our destination, the way was blocked by a net of preparations which precluded all traffic that was not part of the State procession for Germany's Dr. Heuss. Paying off the taxi, we walked the rest of the distance through a milling crowd of spectators who lined the streets anxious to catch a glimpse of the representative from a former enemy country.

Brendan's bawdy language shot through their midst. 'I always thought you English were mad,' he roared, 'now I f—ing know it.' Hastily I pushed him through the doorway of the *Manchester Guardian* office, but throughout his two-second sitting for David Low, his lunch with Dan Farson and the tele-recording afterwards, he could not dismiss the incident from his mind and kept harping back to it. It was a blessing in disguise, for his concern over the oddities of the British people far exceeded his dislike of the television cameras and the interview did not trouble him.

Since he was expected to say shocking things, he rarely failed to do so but on this occasion, with one exception, he answered Dan's questions seriously without losing the uninhibited gaiety he had shown throughout the day.

'What is your ambition, Brendan?' Dan enquired.

'To be a rich red,' replied Brendan, breaking into a full and natural laughter.

Rich he may well have wanted to be, but for him money would not make life more tolerable, nor could he be contained within the limited framework of any organisation.

The interview took place at the bar of the Theatre Royal, Stratford, to add to his congeniality, but he had little to drink and as soon as the cameras were removed he hurried off to join the cast of *The Hostage* who were arriving for the evening's performance. When I left I heard him tell, once again, the saga of the State visit of a German minister.

Brendan and Beatrice returned to Dublin before the television production of *The Quare Fellow* had been seen by the public.

It was shown on Guy Fawkes night—perhaps by accident—and while it translated reasonably well to the small screen, the gusty theatrical exuberance of the stage had been turned into an almost serious documentary for television presentation, and the running commentary on the walk to the scaffold didn't quite come off the way it had done in the theatre.

I doubt if Brendan ever saw it. He certainly never mentioned it and in a letter to Iain he revealed his mind was on another line of business.

2nd November, 1958

Dear Iain, As you may know, I am a housepainter by trade—though not by inclination and though it is many a long year since I have held a stockbrush or a scraper, I still have an interest in a firm here which paints (sporadically) but on the whole profitably.

At the moment if you could advance me £——, it would do us a great deal of good, because we are getting the painting of the Big Stand in Croke Park—one of the largest objects in the country.

I do not know how we stand, but I have a play opening in New York in a fortnight, and if you wished we could consider the matter in the light of a loan, and I would pay you from my New York royalties, till the royalties on *Borstal Boy* came in.

Give Bob Lusty my word that it is for business purposes and for no other that I need these readies. Good luck, Brendan.

The money he required was sent to him, but I do not know what happened about the project. The play in question was *The Quare Fellow*, and whilst Brendan had been asked to the opening night at 'Circle in the Square', an off-Broadway theatre, he had declined on the grounds that the travelling would interfere with his intention to finish *the catacombs*. Simultaneously with his refusal he heard unofficially that he would not be allowed into America anyway as the United States immigration authorities were not prepared to grant him a visa because of his prison record. This knowledge hurt him, but he tried to disguise the fact in loud words to the press.

'I never had any intention of going there,' he said. 'I never even applied for a passport. I don't give a fiddler's damn about America or Americans. It is only Americans who think America is important; no one else does.'

The play was not a success. The *New York Times* called it 'a loose, sprawling, loquacious play,' but said it was 'redeemed by the grimness of its subject, by the intimacy of the author's knowledge of the strange, dark manners of prison life and by the rude exuberance of the dialogue,' adding finally that Brendan as a craftsman 'is no great shakes—he has an uncertain command of the theater medium.'

The *New York Herald Tribune* wrote that 'by its triteness, it fails to make a major indictment. The occasional outburst, the cynical remark, these somehow gather no momentum.'

My next direct communication with Brendan was to learn that, after much searching, he had bought a house in Anglesea Road at Ballsbridge ('rather a snob area,' he explained by telephone, 'and opposite the Royal Dublin Society building') and that he and Beatrice were busy moving. He was finding time, however, to celebrate the absence of his book in Dublin, and would I post him as many copies as possible to his father-in-law's house, heavily disguised in different wrappers.

Meanwhile, Boots, who had lending libraries all over England, announced the absence of *Borstal Boy* from their shelves too.

'We don't think its popularity will last,' they said. 'In a month's time the demand will have fallen off. We don't think it is worth our while.'

Boots' libraries have now closed and *Borstal Boy* is still selling in all editions.

V

INTERNATIONAL CELEBRITY

Brendan telephoned me from his new house to tell me the news, but not directly. He was incapable of handing out information in a straight manner, but preferred to slip it in from a tangent.

I listened patiently while he explained that his home was being decorated by an old I.R.A. friend, the very same who had been charged with him many years before for the attempted murder of a policeman at Glasnevin Cemetery, and how much more recently, he had done his spot of decorating as master of ceremonies and operator at the official turning on of hundreds of fairylights on the large Christmas tree in Lower Parnell Street.

The mention of the street sent his mind racing off on a different train of thought. Did I know Lower Parnell Street? He would have to show it to me when I was next in Dublin for it had a definite place in the history of Anglo-Irish relations. Despite the fact that, by now, I was impatient to know the real purpose of his telephoning, I was fascinated to learn that Michael Collins, the Sinn Féin leader, had once hidden his guns and I.R.A. documents in a bar in Lower Parnell Street after narrowly escaping capture by a military patrol at Ballsbridge. His car was searched but, unrecognised, he had sat smoking a cigarette with the officer-in-charge of the patrol and all the while his I.R.A. papers and his gun were hidden beneath his coat. He was allowed to go on but not wishing to chance his arm further, he deposited his documents in a secret room at the back of the bar (now renamed Mick's) and hardly had he done so before the place was raided by the Black and Tans and he escaped again through a side entrance.

'I must show you the photograph up in the bar commemorating the occasion,' Brendan said in a way that somehow implied that I doubted the authenticity of his story. 'I know I'm capable of kidding you English in all kinds of nonsensical ways,' he continued, his laughter crackling down the wire, 'but I'll tell you one thing and that's not two, *The Hostage* has been chosen by the French director of the International Theatre Festival to represent Great Britain and will be performed in Paris in April. Now there's a thing. It seems you limey suckers can't resist a spot of culture, for first you put me in jail and then you make me famous. You take the bombs as well as the plays from out me pocket; fair field and no favour,' and his self-congratulatory applause was deafening.

It had taken Brendan half an hour to come to the point of his telephone call and I assumed, wrongly, that he wanted me to release the information to the press. But he was hurt by my business attitude and explained, touchily, that in God's name wasn't he trying to write his novel, not to mention the film script of *The Quare Fellow* before going to Paris for the festival? Would I protect him from, and not involve him in, needless distractions? As I put down the phone, I wondered if I would ever really understand him.

Borstal Boy was published by Alfred A. Knopf in America on 23 February 1959 and was well reviewed: 'Mr. Behan can write prose that sings or snarls or chuckles,' wrote Orville Prescott in the *New York Times,* while *Time* recorded that 'he had Gabriel's own gift of the gab, a cold eye for himself, a warm heart for others, and the narrative speed of a tinker.' John K. Hutchens in the *New York Herald Tribune* felt that 'he is, first and foremost, at artist,' while W. S. Merwin in *The Nation* found that 'one of the most impressive things about the book is the feeling it gives ... of Behan's growing up, becoming wiser ...'

Now foreign countries clamoured for the book and rights were quickly sold in Germany, France, Italy, Spain, Sweden,

Norway, Denmark and Holland. Brendan as a writer had arrived. But as a man, he was beginning to take the first steps along a path which could only destroy him, and success dazzling his vision he was blind to the danger.

A month before he was due to go to Paris, every English newspaper carried the story of his arrest for drunken and disorderly behaviour at Bray, County Wicklow, and some of them even considered it important enough for feature treatment. Because it was the first of many such incidents in which Brendan discovered that his impossible behaviour paid dividends, I feel it is not without point to reproduce, without exaggeration or embellishment, the record of the case which appeared in the *Irish Times*.

Mr. Brendan Behan, playwright and author, aged 36, Anglesea Road, Dublin, was yesterday fined 40s. at Bray District Court by District Justice Manus Nunan, for being drunk and disorderly at 1 a.m. at Greystones, Co. Wicklow, on the morning of March 4th last.

Mr. Behan insisted that the case should be heard in Irish. He admitted that he was drunk and apologised for his language. Witnesses said that he called policemen murderers, scruffhounds and dirt birds.

When the case was called, Mr. Behan said (in Irish): I want this case to be heard in Irish, please. According to the Constitution of this country, I have a right to be heard in Irish.

District Justice (in Irish): Sit down.

Inspector James Kelly (in Irish): Be quiet.

Mr. Behan (in Irish): I have a right that only the Irish language is used in this case.

Guard J. A. Molloy, who began his evidence in Irish, said that on the morning of March 4th, he got a call from a civilian named Terence O'Reilly that a man was lying in Church Road, Greystones. At 12.45 a.m. he went to Church Road where he saw the defendant, Behan.

Mr. Behan (in Irish): Justice, can I speak to you for a moment?

District Justice (in English): No.

Mr. Behan (in Irish): According to the Constitution of this State, I can speak in Irish, and have the right to be heard in the language of the State.

District Justice (in Irish): Sit down.

Guard Molloy then began his evidence in English. He said that he went to Church Road. 'I saw the defendant . . .'

Mr. Behan (in Irish): That man is not talking in Irish. I want the case to be heard in the first official language of the country.

Guard Molloy, continuing his evidence in English, said that he asked the defendant what he was looking for. He was lying down. A local doctor, who was also on the scene, told him that Mr. Behan was not ill and that it appeared to be a case for the police. He said that he was 'looking for his wife,' the witness said, and added that 'she was in one of the local houses.' He was dishevelled and appeared to have been in a struggle. He said, 'Here are the —— bloodhounds,' and 'You are —— murderers.'

Mr. Behan: Correct.

Witness: He then left the scene, and went towards another hotel, where he hammered on the door to gain admittance. I remonstrated with him, and he used vile language. Then I telephoned for a patrol car, and two *gardai* came along in it.

Mr. Behan (in Irish): Well, at least you know one word in Irish—*gardai*.

Guard Molloy: He said that we were '—— bloodhounds.' He resisted violently when we tried to arrest him, and used foul language. You could hear him all over the place.

Defendant (in Irish): No doubt it was not in the Irish language.

Guard Molloy said that the defendant had to be forced into the patrol car, and had to be forced out of it again at the police station. He was forcibly searched, and then forcibly put into a cell. He added: He kicked at the cell door from 1.30 a.m. to 4.30 a.m. He said that the police were '—— murderers,' and said: 'You are no —— good.' He was discharged at 8 a.m. when he was still in the same tone of voice.

Defendant: As I always am.

Guard Molloy said that when he attempted to take the defen-

Brendan and the snake at Phoenix Park Zoo (see page 121)

Beatrice, Brendan and Rae. An interlude on the *Queen Elizabeth* before sailing home from New York

Brendan and Beatrice enjoying a break in Sweden where he translated *The Hostage* into English (it was originally written in Irish)

Photograph by kind permission of Dr. Olof Lagerlöf

dant into custody he had no idea who he was.

Mr. Behan, cross-examining the guard in Irish: When I asked you for a drop of water during the night, did you give it to me?

Witness: Yes.

Mr. Behan: You gave it to me five minutes before I left in the morning. Now you know I have no great love for you, don't you? You are a perjurer.

Addressing the district justice, still in Irish, he said: He said to some of the others: 'We have the quare fellow now.'

Inspector Kelly: I must ask you, Justice, to treat this behaviour as gross contempt of court. He has abused this guard, and has called him a perjurer. This should not be allowed.

The next witness, Guard Denis O'Leary, said that he was called to Church Road in a patrol car on the morning of March 4th. When he attempted to arrest the defendant he called him a bloodhound and said that he would get him in the morning. He had to be forced into the patrol car and out of it at the station.

Defendant: You recognised me as Brendan Behan?

Witness: Yes, I had seen your photograph in the *People*.

Defendant: Not in *Fogra Tora*?[1]

Guard L. C. McEntaggart said that he was in the patrol car which came to arrest the defendant. When we tried to get him into the car, he called me a '—— guttersnipe,' said witness.

District Justice: It would be hard to translate that one.

Mr. Behan (in Irish): I'll do it for you.

Witness added: His language was vile, and he could be heard all over Greystones.

Mr. Behan: Did you recognise me?

Witness: I did not know him, and I do not know him. I have never heard of him and never read him.

Mr. Behan (in Irish): Can he read at all?

Asked to make his defence, Mr. Behan, speaking in Irish, said: I went to the Grand Hotel, Greystones, on the evening of March 3rd because I wanted to do some writing for a film. I was in the bar, and was having a few drinks. I had booked into the

[1] *Hue and Cry*, the Irish equivalent of the *Police Gazette*.

hotel for a couple of days. While I was in the bar, a man, who said his name was Charlie Reynolds, came up to me. He wanted to drink with me. He told me that he was an old policeman. I told him that I would not give a drink to any policeman, old or new. Then I went out into the open and the police came. They put me in the car. They would not even give me a drink of water in the cell. I have been in jail in Belfast and in Britain and have never been refused a drink. I am on my oath now, so I must admit that I was drunk on this occasion.

District Justice Nunan called Mrs. Beatrice Behan to give evidence. She said that when her husband left Dublin for Greystones he was sober, and that he had gone there to finish some work so that he would not be interrupted.

District Justice: Isn't it obvious that he went there on a skite?

Mrs. Behan: I did not think so. He just wanted to be somewhere quiet.

District Justice: I am trying to keep him out of jail. I don't seem able to do that. You don't seem able to control him.

Mrs. Behan: I would have if I had been there.

Inspector Kelly said that if the case had been carried on in the proper manner, he would not press it. It was a shame that an otherwise very talented man should behave like a blackguard. He was drunk and he was violent, and he had behaved very badly.

District Justice: Will you make an apology for your behaviour?

Defendant (in English): How can I make a sincere apology? I regard you as representative of the Irish people. But I will apologise for my language.

District Justice: Is that an apology?

Defendant: Which would be the greater insult—to apologise if I was not sincere or not to apologise?

District Justice: That is a matter for your own conscience.

Defendant: All right, I will apologise.

District Justice: Fined forty shillings.

After the case was over, Brendan immediately repaired to the nearest bar where, according to one newspaper, he celebrated his meagre fine with a series of boastful remarks. 'I hate policemen—whether they are Irish, British or Russian.' 'Proust says that to work all you need is chastity and water—neither would suit me well.' 'I gave them their forty shillings' worth. It was well worth the trouble.' These are a few he is reported to have said. He treated the bar and sang songs in Irish before returning to Dublin satisfied that only the Lord God Almighty would have had a better reception. This knowledge would hardly encourage him to settle down to the less flamboyant business of writing, but what better excuse for having that extra drink to help him with his act of performing clown?

With the memory of Bray still fresh in his mind, Brendan left with Beatrice for Germany for the opening night of *The Quare Fellow* at the Schiller Theatre in Berlin. But the legend of Brendan Behan had not yet fully penetrated the ears of the German people, and they were not amused by his uncouth, tattered appearance on the stage or the incoherent curtain-speech that followed. 'A scandal,' reported the German newspapers as they panned both him and his play.

Brendan could not end his performance on this note. If he shouted long enough and loud enough, surely he could convince himself that it is better to be abused than ignored? 'I was drunk. I am usually half-shot and why not? I'm an enemy of the State—every damn State. Maybe the critics don't like me, but the people do. I understand my play is well booked up,' he retaliated.

But his bravado was short-lived for he had been knocked where it most hurt him. If he did not object to the false reputation that he was building up around himself, he did mind when this reputation coloured people's opinion of his work. As he left with Beatrice for the four-day *Théâtre des Nations* festival in Paris where *The Hostage* was being presented by Theatre Workshop, he was determined not to make the same mistake again.

Unlike his many previous trips to France, Brendan had every reason to celebrate. The success of *The Hostage* in London had averted the closure of Theatre Workshop, financially embarrassed owing to the withdrawal of the Arts Council subsidy, and the play had now been chosen for presentation at the finest international drama festival in the world. This was no small accolade, for the *Théâtre des Nations*, in bringing the actors, dramatists and producers of twenty-three countries together, is the stage's equivalent to the Olympic games. Indeed, the original Olympics included contests among poets and players which were as important as the sports events.

Reporters and television companies besieged him for personal interviews, editors of magazines badgered him for articles with pressurised dead-lines, but despite the strain these requests must have imposed on him, he conducted himself with dignity and rarely drank more than soda-water. He ignored the idle gossip which was circulating around his friendship with Shelagh Delaney, who was also in Paris for the festival. Although he was naturally pleased to have the attention of a young and attractive girl, at this stage his marriage and his love for Beatrice were all that he required.

On the morning of the première, Brendan was at Le Bourget Airport to meet the DC3 aircraft that was bringing Joan Littlewood, Gerry Raffles and the Theatre Workshop cast from London. Travelling with them was Frank Norman whose *Fings Ain't Wot They Used T'Be* was the play of the moment at Theatre Royal. If the visitors were flustered and excited, Brendan was not as, throughout the journey from the airport to Paris by coach, he listened attentively to Joan Littlewood's direction and advice and Gerry Raffles's insistence that not a drop be touched before the final curtain had dropped. Spontaneously and naturally, he sang one or two of the songs from *The Hostage* and appeared unaffected by the magnitude of the occasion. On the outskirts of Paris, as the coach eased at the traffic-lights, someone noticed that the posters advertising the play as being 'under the patronage of the British Ambassador,' had been overprinted by the statement that the Ambassador, Sir Gladwyn Jebb, would be unable to attend the opening.

'Sure,' Brendan replied amiably, 'but haven't we plenty of ould ambassadors coming anyway?'

At the Sarah Bernhardt Theatre, he led the way into the office of M. Julien, the festival's director, on whose walls hundreds of telegrams from well-wishers were pinned. Nor did he draw attention to the fact that the telegram from the British Embassy was conspicuous by its absence.

That night, as he stood in the foyer of the Sarah Bernhardt Theatre drinking iced water, he watched the arrival of the American, Polish and Irish Ambassadors along with the glittering gowned and bejewelled host of celebrities as they fought their way through the crush. Naturally he was recognised, but he accepted the handshakes in a way that suggested that whilst he was proud of the attention he was receiving, he was humble too.

Any fears he may have had that a cosmopolitan audience of such sophistication might be more critical of his play he soon discovered to be unfounded. And contrary to expectations, the British Ambassador did arrive, although he was an hour late. 'I couldn't get away earlier. I had a dinner party going on,' he explained.

The evening ended in ten curtain calls, a brief speech in French from Brendan and a three-minute ovation from the crowd of 1,250 people. The lesson he had learnt in Germany was not in vain.

Afterwards, at the celebratory dinner at La Mediterranée, everyone beseiged him, but as interview followed interview, he began to be irritated by the slick questioning of the long-haired young men from the broadcasting companies and the equally long-haired women from the glossy magazines. Their interest in him appeared to be more in his penal background than in his work. Since his youth had been directed towards the fight for Ireland's freedom, and since most of his impressionable years had been spent in prison as a result, inevitably his work would be drawn from his experiences of both. But nothing annoyed him more than the insinuation that he would not have been a writer had his background been different. He was neither proud nor ashamed of his prison record, nor of the reason that took him there.

'Anyone who makes capital out of acts of violence and hatred, is a fool,' he said. 'The whole damn world is *ipso facto*. Now you'd almost be needing to go to jail before you'd be accepted as a bloody writer.'

The wind, for a while, began to blow more gustily, but it was only the froth off his beer and he ended the night with his resolution intact to 'stay away from the hard stuff.'

The Hostage was hailed as 'a triumph,' and Martini, one of the world's richest liquor firms, gave a cocktail party in Brendan's honour at their headquarters in the Champs Elysées. It was at this gathering that he revealed a new conception of himself. Hitherto, he had always avoided making it known that there was any struggle between himself and alcohol; that perhaps he could not hold his drink as well as the next man. And on the occasions when he felt his complete abstention was a matter for derision, I have seen him snatch at the whisky bottle and forget the consequences. But on this day he remained impervious to the jibes from the press and disregarded their efforts to get him to have a drink. Instead, he encouraged them to take photographs to prove that he had no glass in his hand and allowed himself to be quoted as saying that his temperance was due 'to a promise I have made on account of all them interviews.'

But the international respect he received, both as a playwright and as a man, during the four days of the festival was a new experience for him, and on the last evening he crumbled under the weight of it. Resisting discipline—his own and everyone else's—he began to celebrate in earnest and was unable to appreciate his role as guest of honour at a party given by Jean-Louis Barrault.

Once having started his own kind of celebration Brendan could not stop, and although the festival was over he remained on in Paris to hide the anticlimax in his inimitable way. Unable to get his usual brand of stout he used the excuse to sample every other type of liquor, until he finally settled for cognac, a drink hardly likely to improve the health of a diabetic. The more he drank the less he ate, and no amount of cajoling from Beatrice could make him do otherwise. After getting into a few fights—some innocently provoked and some deliberately engineered—he came to

London, dishevelled, dejected and utterly exhausted, and I felt more sharply than ever the difficulties of communicating with him as he hid, alternately spiky and moronically morose, under a shell.

I tried to interest him in news of *Borstal Boy*, but he neither cared that it was selling well both in England and abroad nor that the Minister for Customs in New Zealand had removed the ban on the book. I had been asked by the B.B.C. television programme *Tonight* if I would persuade Brendan to face the cameras to talk about his days in Paris, but not wishing to add further to his distress I had been evasive. In one of Brendan's less irritable moods, I mentioned the matter to him and he was furious.

'It's me they want, not you, isn't it?' he snapped. 'I'll say what I want to do and I'll do as I f—ing like.'

'In that case, Brendan,' I replied, 'you had better arrange all the interviews for yourself. I have a job to do, but it's no skin off my nose to be relieved of some of it.'

As I turned to walk out of the room, he clutched my arm. 'No, you do it,' he said, but then paused to utter more gently, 'Will you do that for me, daughter?' The old Brendan was still around. He had his own way of apologising.

The television appearance was not a success. Brendan savagely told Derek Hart, who was interviewing him, how much he loathed appearing on television and denied emphatically that his success had been of any benefit to him. 'I go to better beds, if you like,' he shouted angrily, 'but I sleep less well.'

The interview over, Brendan demanded a drink and was taken into the reception room and handed a bottle of whisky. 'Jaysus,' he shouted, 'what are you trying to do? Kill me? You know I'm not supposed to drink that stuff.' He did not stay long in the room, nor did he touch the whisky. He was restive and anxious to be out of the place. Bidding hasty goodbyes—and, on my side, apologies—to Derek Hart, we climbed up the steps outside to Lime Grove and into a passing taxi.

Once settled in the cab, Brendan's tension burst out of him in volleys of abuse at Beatrice. He was over-wrought, desperately unhappy and mentally and physically sick, and had to release his pent-up emotions in this way or be devoured by them. Beatrice sat impassively without saying one word. She understood completely. The lull would come when the storm was over. But I was confounded and dismayed by his unhappiness and, pleading a headache, I asked to be excused from travelling further with them.

Brendan was in the office early next morning, and while I was getting used to his mercurial changes of mood, I was once more astounded to find him in good humour, calm and completely at ease. He had signed a contract with Hutchinson to write a comprehensive book on Ireland, he said, and had agreed to return to Ireland because Paul Hogarth, who was illustrating it, would shortly be coming over to work on the project with him.

We had a farewell drink at the Mason's Arms, and when I waved him off from Great Portland Street I did not expect to see him again for a while. A few days later, however, Beatrice telephoned me from Dublin to say that while Paul Hogarth had arrived as arranged, Brendan's contribution was to take off immediately for London. 'He's on his way to you at this very minute,' she said. 'I thought I had better prepare you for the event.'

Indeed, within a few hours Brendan was in the office and asking for money. He gave no reason for the purpose of his return, nor did he mention that Paul Hogarth was in Dublin. He merely indicated that he would be staying with Joe and Kathleen McGill, friends of his from earlier days. As I knew that both Joe and Kathleen would be largely tied to their flat by domestic duties, I became aware that Brendan had not called on me simply to collect money. He was expecting me in some way to be responsible for him and to be part of his erratic and abnormal behaviour so that he could gallop around London on a free rein and be sure of a friend to pick him up when he fell. For a moment I wavered. I resolved to get rid of him and spare myself the appalling state of anxiety which accompanying him necessitated. But then I reflected that the demands he made on me, consciously or unconsciously, were part of a real need for self-protection and were well worth the indignities which I might have to endure. It became plain that he had come back to London to drink, and I was not prepared to watch him drain his talent into the sewers of the Thames without some effort to stop him.

In the next few weeks I was turned out of more pubs with Brendan than I care to remember. People who had previously sought his company now avoided him, and I was left standing on the corner of the street, one arm propping up Brendan while the other waved in anguish at the taxi-drivers who passed without caring to notice us.

His health deteriorated rapidly. The strain of the continental tour, coupled with his junketing around London, had left him in considerable need of medical help. But to get him into hospital willingly was an impossible task for he was without a vestige of common sense in his loathing for the place, and looked upon his admittance as a form of drastic punishment. I waited for the inevitable collapse but while he still had the determination to stand on his feet, he announced he wanted to go home and asked me to make the necessary arrangements. His gratitude was both touching and pathetic.

'If the Lord God Almighty were to tell me that your friendship was not genuine,' he said, 'I would not believe him. You're a gentle and understanding person, and I would rather cut off my right arm than hurt you. When I've had a few, I may say a lot of nonsensical things, but I don't mean them. You know that.'

'Brendan,' I answered. 'I wish I could help you more. I believe so much in your work and I hate to watch you throw away your talent.'

A shy smile broke across his lips and his tired eyes reflected momentarily the humour as he replied. 'Ah, that's the rub. Success is damn near killing me. If I had my way, I should prescribe that success should go to every man for a month; then he should be given a pension and forgotten.'

He did not laugh, but sat gloomily looking at the floor in front of him; I wondered now if there ever could be a cure for Brendan Behan.

VI

PERSONAL APPEARANCE

'I've lost three stone in a month and I'm not feeling so good,' Brendan told waiting reporters as he came down the gangplank of the Liverpool packet at Dublin. 'It's all that foreign stuff. I can't stand the muck.' In future, he said, he would only drink his 'own brand of stout.'

After recuperating at home for a few days, and on his doctor's advice, he and Beatrice left for the little white cottage they rented every summer from Patrick Griffin in Carraroe, on the west coast of Ireland. With them, hopefully, went Paul Hogarth and his wife, Pat. It was to be a weight-restoring holiday with Brendan bravely asserting that if he couldn't be putting it on with Guinness, he'd be drinking milk as well.

The postcard I received from Beatrice was not encouraging:

June 11th, 1959

Arrive at our Atlantic refuge at last. Yesterday we sailed to Aran with the Hogarths. There was a *cérh* aboard, and the islanders sang and danced the whole way over. There was a battery of cameramen and reporters when we got off the boat at Galway. I think they'd nearly have swum across to get a story. However, Brendan was too tired so we just went home. Many thanks for all your help. Love, Beatrice.

It was a pity that Brendan could not be left alone to recuperate in peace. He was badly in need of rest and the cottage, standing on a little bay with the Atlantic rollers breaking right beside it, as much part of the sea as a stalwart defence against it, was the ideal place in which to find mental and physical relaxation. Previously, Brendan had always managed to work in these surroundings and, for an essentially city-loving man, he found a strange contentment in the untamed elements which raged around the cottage. But now, on two accounts, peace eluded him. His so-called romance with Shelagh Delaney had attracted a great deal of attention and Beatrice, who was being hounded by the press for her comments on the rumours, wrote in an unguarded moment an article for *Woman's Mirror*. But she did not appreciate that the words she would use when speaking to a friend would not convey the same impression when embodied in print, and the effect of her writing was to exaggerate and falsify the extent of her concern over the matter. Far from quietening the rumbles, she increased them, and Shelagh Delaney was forced to issue a flat denial of all the accusations. The whole affair was a stupid storm in a tea cup and I only mention it because it did cause ripples in Brendan's pool of discontent at a time when he was trying to reform. The second factor was much more serious.

On July 11, 1959, *The Hostage* opened at Wyndham's Theatre, in the heart of London's West End, with most of the original cast, but Avis Bunnage and Murray Melvin who were playing in Shelagh Delaney's *A Taste of Honey* had been replaced by Eileen Kennally and Alfred Lynch as Meg Dillon and the British soldier, Leslie. I was at the first night and was not surprised when, at the end of the performance, the shouts of 'Author' from the audience brought forward an actor who read a postcard message from Brendan: 'Tell the audience I was asking for them,' he had written. 'You see,' commented the actor, 'he's with us all in spirit.' At the time, I did not know the truth of these words.

The next morning, the critics were even more enthusiastic in their praise for *The Hostage* than they had been previously, although with Séan Kenny's settings and Joan Littlewood's direction, both productions were virtually identical.

'Mr. Behan's irreverence for the established rules of society strikes us as going deeper than Mr. John Osborne's,' wrote *The*

Times. 'His flouts and jeers, however outrageous, are essentially warm-hearted. The wounds inflicted are never poisoned. He can arrange for one of his characters to sing a bitter anti-English ballad and turn away offence by putting into her mouth the comment: "Why doesn't the author come up here to do his own dirty work?" '

Indeed, in the programme of the play, I had noticed a quote from a recent interview with Brendan which explained his code for living. 'I respect kindness to human beings first of all, and kindness to animals. I don't respect the law; I have a total irreverence for anything connected with society except that which makes the roads safer, the beer stronger, the food cheaper, and old men and old women warmer in the winter and happier in the summer.'

But he was showing little respect for himself as I read of his escapades on the news pages of the same papers who were cheering his play. If he could not be at the first night of *The Hostage* in the West End, he was not going to be left entirely out of the shouting. Downing whiskey and stout chasers, he drank his way, in one pub after another, from Connemara to Galway, singing songs, telling stories of I.R.A. battles during the times of The Troubles, holding animated conversations in Irish and generally making as much noise as possible, with never a thought to be giving up drink, nor the harm it was doing him. Between the drinking and the singing and the rumbustiousness, he told one reporter: 'You are right. I am not well. I sometimes feel terrible. But I don't know what the trouble is. So have another drink . . .'

Worried, I wrote to Beatrice and she answered at once.

I'm worried to death, but no one can control a man like Brendan. It is too much for anyone. He drinks too much and won't eat at all. He has been told to stop drinking completely. But what can I do with him? I do my best and every morning before he leaves the house, I give him a raw egg in milk, but it has too much to compete with. He is ruining his health. I wish he would stop for a little while.

Brendan did not stop. Soon he was beyond the stage of being

persuaded to take his diabetic pills, his moments of drowsiness drifted into periods of deep unconsciousness and he had his first alcoholic seizure to bring him back to Dublin and straight into hospital. Someone should have shown Brendan a film of himself during these appalling attacks, for the sight might have convinced him that he should never touch another drop, and even sent him running to join the ranks of a Temperance Society. I say this in no sense as a joke, for drunks or drunkenness are never subjects for mirth, but in the belief that it might have averted his walk into the endless tunnel of alcoholism. It would certainly have helped him to make the effort of will that is necessary to overcome the addiction.

For a short while, Brendan remained in hospital and despite the intervention of misguided friends who smuggled him in the occasional Baby Power whiskey he appeared contented. Under medical care his health rapidly improved but, far from being grateful for the attention he was getting, Brendan's temper deteriorated and by his grumbles and complaints it was obvious that, given the slightest pretext, he would walk out of the place in protest. Tactfully, the nursing staff avoided troubling him more than was necessary, and the stubble on his chin was allowed to grow undisturbed. But Brendan was not to be thwarted. He was only waiting until he felt strong enough to make the journey to England to see *The Hostage* in the West End for himself. And when that day came, he grabbed his clothes—at this stage no one thought to hide them—dressed, discharged himself, hailed a taxi to take him to his cousin, Seamus de Burca, from whom he borrowed a dinner-jacket before driving out to Dublin Airport to fly on to London.

I have not the slightest doubt that there was villainy in his heart as he fortified himself with liquid courage throughout the flight. By the time he reached London Airport he was not in the best of health, but his shouting and singing startled the airport officials no more than the growth of beard on his face or his tousled hair hanging down over his eyes. Immediately, he went to Paddington to see his sister-in-law, Celia Salkeld, but on finding she was out, he lay down on a couch and fell into an exhausted sleep. With alarm-clock precision he was awake again in time to go to the theatre and more to spare for a few adjournments on the way. The rest had caused no change of heart but only served to renew his energy. As he stood at the bar of the Salisbury, next door to Wyndham's, bolstering himself up for the grand entry, all thoughts of dressing for the occasion had been forgotten. Through the haze, he heard a voice raised in opposition to his own, singing in the street outside, and he left to investigate. There, on the pavement, stood an old man in a bowler hat, doing no more harm than trying to entertain the gallery queue for *The Hostage*.

'For the love of Jaysus,' shouted Brendan at him, 'why don't you sing them an Irish song?' The man in his innocence began a bar or two of 'When Irish Eyes Are Smiling.'

The queue, patiently waiting in the cool air of a summer's night to take their seats in the theatre, must have been totally un-prepared for the language that thundered across the poor man's solo almost before he had started it.

'Do you call that an Irish song?' bawled Brendan from a height as he snatched the bowler hat out of the man's hand and began singing himself an Irish ballad. The song over, he walked the length of the queue badgering them for contributions before handing the hat and the takings over to the flabbergasted old busker. Satisfied with his cleverness, Brendan went into the theatre, pounded his fist on the box-office desk, demanded a tic-ket and took his seat in the stalls.

The events that followed are utterly inexcusable and unfor-givable. When Brendan set out to attract publicity, the methods by which he did so were always regrettable. But that he should have shown such a lack of consideration both for the audience, who were paying their respects to him as a playwright, and for the cast who, night after night, worked hard to perfect their pre-sentation of his play, I find out of character and incomprehen-sible.

He sang, he shouted. He continually interrupted the actors and called the audience idiots until he finally clambered up on to the stage and unsteadily attempted to dance a jig. The curtain dropped on him but his shoutings could still be heard after the theatre was cleared. The next morning there was not a newspaper that did not carry the story and, through half-drunken eyes, Brendan read them one by one with unashamed delight. What matter if the photographs which illustrated the text did reveal for posterity the image of a drunken, rumpled, crumpled, tieless Brendan Behan as long as there was admiration, rather than reproof, in the accounts of the Behan shindig?

Brendan was staying with his old sculptor friend, Desmond Macnamara, at his house in Hampstead, and when Beatrice telephoned to plead with her husband to come home and stop risking his life in the manner so faithfully reported by the press, Brendan became abusive, arrogant and finally disinterested. Throughout the day he made a tour of the pubs in Fleet Street and although Desmond tried every means to keep him out of further trouble, his efforts convinced Brendan that he was only a death's head at the banquet, and encouraged by the reporters who were awaiting the next instalment, Brendan charged off to the theatre to repeat his performance of the previous evening. He could get no further than the door. Sir Bronson Albery, the owner of Wyndham's Theatre and father of the show's impresario, Donald Albery, had left specific instructions that Brendan was not to be let in to see his play without having written permission.

'Nobody's giving orders to Brendan Behan,' he shouted into the face of the anxious doorman and although he was fighting his way to become the life of any newspaper story, his physical strength waned and gave out under a bout of sudden sickness. Still accompanied by the press, he allowed himself to be taken home by Desmond, where immediately upon arrival, he collapsed groaning on his bed.

Beatrice telephoned me at the office. Brendan had slipped out of the house in Hampstead very early in the morning and had gone to the Mayfair home of Garach and Tara Browne, sons of the former Lady Oranmore and Browne of the Guinness family and old friends of Brendan with whom he spent every Christmas at Lugala in Ireland. Only Tara, the younger son, was at home, she explained, and he was quite unable to deal with the seriousness of the situation. Brendan, she believed, was in a diabetic coma and had not passed out, as was suspected, from the drink.

'Would you ever call a doctor,' she pleaded, 'and go down and collect him and get him into hospital where he can be treated properly?'

Up until this moment, I had made up my mind that as long as Brendan behaved in the manner of the last few days, I would not be counted among his retinue. I believed in him as a writer and would have done anything to help him in this direction, but I was not prepared to witness the spectacle of a man who was capable of writing *The Quare Fellow*, *The Hostage* and *Borstal Boy*, imitating the antics of a partially-trained grizzly bear. Now I realised that if I was to remain a friend, it was impossible to divorce the explosive elements in his nature from the force of his words when he poured them out on paper, for if he controlled one, the other must necessarily suffer. And as long as I acknowledged that his writing possessed a quality far beyond the ordinary, I should be willing to move into his orbit and try to temper his violence and channel his energies in the direction of the written word. Added to which, Beatrice was worried out of her mind and frustrated beyond endurance as to know what to do from Dublin.

I telephoned my doctor and arranged to meet him at the address off Curzon Street. When I arrived I was taken up by Tara Browne to the drawing-room where Brendan was stretched out on the floor with a cushion under his head. His appearance shocked me and he was breathing extremely irregularly. I spoke his name but he was obviously far away and his eyes, when I lifted the lids, were without a vestige of colour. Quickly, Tara filled in the background.

Brendan had arrived early and, ignoring all attempts to get

Brendan and friend on the isle of Ibiza where he began work on *the catacombs*, a novel which he never finished

Brendan and Beatrice with their daughter Blanaid, aged five days. This was one of the last photographs of Brendan

Brendan and the author in the snow in Dublin while working on
Brendan Behan's Island

him to eat, he had demanded a drink. Although dazed, for a while he had mumbled incoherently and appeared to be struggling to make himself talk, but eventually he had drifted off into a restless sleep which soon became heavy and somewhat unreal. Tara was frightened and had telephoned Beatrice. It was now several hours later, and still he had not moved.

Dr. Eppel's arrival relieved our anxiety but only for as long as it took him to step into the hall, for at that moment Brendan came tottering down the stairs, perspiration breaking out on his face which was flushed, menacing and contorted with aggression. Slowly, I walked towards him and held out my hand to help him negotiate the remaining tread, for his eyes were so firmly fixed on the doctor that I was sure he would fall.

'This is Dr. Eppel, Brendan. He's come here to put you right.'

'Nobody f—ing asked him to,' was Brendan's only reply as, ignoring my hand, he advanced on the object of his gaze in a most unfriendly fashion.

'Indeed they did,' I shouted, trying to hide the quivering in my throat. 'Beatrice asked me to get the doctor. If you won't go home for treatment, you'll have to have it here. Only make up your mind one way or the other for the doctor has plenty of other patients without wasting his time on you.'

The flow of obscenities which followed my words left Dr. Eppel in no doubt as to what Brendan had decided to do, and he disappeared out of the front door before the barrage had quite ended. Like a wounded animal, Brendan charged round the house until his eyes focused on a whiskey bottle standing on an oak chest in the hall.

'Oh! go ahead,' I heard myself expostulate, my patience rapidly declining. 'Drink yourself to death, only give me one as well.'

Brendan was not to be fooled by so simple a piece of cunning. The more I had to drink, the less there would be for him. It would be over his dead body, he bellowed, before he allowed any f—ing limey to taste a drop of Irish whiskey and, as he spoke, he picked up the bottle by the neck and waving it in front of him, he lurched over towards me. For a second I experienced cold, clammy fear and imaginary nine-inch nails rooted my feet to the floorboards, but when he came within inches of me, I knew instinctively that he would never physically attack me. I took the bottle from him, gave a look of disgust and put it back on the hall chest. 'For a man who professes publicly to respect kindness to human beings above everything else,' I remarked, 'I'm seeing very little of it at present.'

He looked at me quizzically as if his ears were deceiving him, but when the full realisation of what he had done penetrated through the fog to his brain he became overwhelmed with misery and stumbled off to an adjoining room. 'Everyone's against me!' he cried with utter despair in his voice. He was sick and dejected, groping through the dark curtains of his mind to find some justification for his behaviour which he knew was despicable.

'Certainly I'm against you when you come at me with a bottle,' I answered him. 'And you have a wife who is not only running round Dublin doing your work with Paul Hogarth, but is being hounded by the press on your account and worried out of her wits as well.'

I knew that I should not leave him in his present mood, but I was overwrought and did not have Brendan's ability to forgive, nor was I sure that either the man or his talent made up for my recent experience with him. Despite his protests, I returned to the office. As I entered the room my phone rang.

The newspaper reporter was brief and to the point. Brendan had been arrested and was in Savile Row police station. He had a black eye and could I give him any idea how this had happened? He had seen me leave the house in Mayfair not half an hour previously and he felt sure I could throw some light on the matter. As I put down the telephone receiver, I was completely mystified. When I had left Brendan, his face bore no traces of physical violence and yet when he reached the police station twenty minutes later he was sporting a large bruise under his left eye. Nor has the passing of time solved the mystery. Brendan himself had little recollection of the incident except he 'didn't get it from the cops. They were very civil and decent,' he is reported as saying.

Desmond Macnamara and Duncan Melvin, the publicity agent for *The Hostage*, went at once to bail him out, determined to force him on to a plane for Dublin as soon as he had appeared at Bow Street. Having deposited the ten shillings bail, they all left the police station in a police van in an effort to shake off the press, and picked up a taxi in Regent Street. From there, they drove to Belgravia with the intention of taking the Underground from Victoria to Hampstead, where Desmond lived. But at Victoria, as the taximan was collecting his fare, Brendan escaped.

Diligently, but in a state of near-panic, Desmond and Duncan, like a sheriff and his deputy, combed Soho and St. Martin's Lane on pale ale and tomato juice with total lack of success. Finally, as the press hazards thickened, they separated homewards with gloomy prognostications, and Desmond found Brendan waiting on his doorstep, oblivious of the chaos he had left in his wake.

The next morning Brendan was taken to Bow Street where already a queue had formed half an hour before the court opened. He was charged with being drunk, pleaded guilty and was fined five shillings and ordered to pay fifteen shillings to the doctor who had attended him at the police station. His three-minute appearance over, the Queen would hardly have had a more royal send-off as hundreds of spectators cheered him into a waiting car on his way to London Airport. Nor would the convoy of cars that followed him act as a deterrent for future escapades. Encouraged by the ballyhoo, Brendan insisted upon stopping at the Osterley Arms, where, in the company of the press, he began drinking heavily, sending out his words in the certain knowledge that they would find their way into print.

'I have been very patriotic since my stay in Her Majesty's prison,' he is reported as saying. 'I will only speak Irish.'

From pub to pub, from the Osterley Arms to London Airport, he proceeded to entertain the hangers-on to stories and songs in Irish, each one increasing in volume the more he had to drink.

Nor did the intervention of Desmond and other genuine friends produce anything further from Brendan than 'The publicity? I don't care. It will do the old play a powerful lot of good.'

After stampeding round the lounge at London Airport lustily singing The Red Flag—in English—Brendan eventually boarded the plane and his three-day binge was over.

The harm it had done to him physically was no greater than the harm it had done to him mentally. If he chose to ignore the disgust of his true friends, there would always be spurious ones to take their place and boost his ego along with a pile of newspaper cuttings.

Yet somewhere in his subconsciousness, for he was too drunk for it to be otherwise, Brendan must have been aware, as his aircraft headed for the east and Dublin, that his past few days in London had neither improved his health, brought him happiness, nor helped him to live more at peace with himself. If *The Hostage* was playing to packed houses as a result of the publicity he had attracted, this was poor compensation. Across the Irish Sea, he took off his shirt, parted his hair and decided to treat himself with a little more respect.

Many wild theories have been put forward as to why Brendan went on his terrible batter in London, but I believe the truth is simpler than any of them. After the excitement of his continental tour, life in Dublin was tedious; he wanted to collect some money which was held, on his instructions, both by Hutchinson and Theatre Workshop for protection against himself, and perhaps most important of all, he had a play running in the West End. This fact signified to Brendan, that as a playwright he had arrived, and had nothing whatsoever to do with finance. Many years earlier, the Abbey Theatre Company in Dublin had turned down *The Quare Fellow*—or *The Twisting of Another Rope*, as it was then called—and afterwards, despite the great success of the Theatre Workshop production at Stratford, he did not feel he could call himself a playwright until the play had been performed at the Abbey.

'I was offered a two weeks' run in the Gaiety,' (also a Dublin theatre) he said, 'but I turned it down for one week at the Abbey for thirty pounds.'

When he arrived in London he was already a sick man, and the only way he could justify his stupidity in discharging himself from hospital before he was fit, was to have a drink and forget all about it. But once having started the snowball, Brendan, in his total inability to do anything in moderation, could not stop it; nor was he encouraged to do so by the bunting and the flag-waving which lined whatever route he chose to take.

But it was a very different Brendan who walked down the steps of the aircraft at Dublin Airport, across the tarmac, ignoring the reporters who were waiting for him to supply the colourful *finale*. Grabbing a taxi, he drove straight to his home and to bed.

Like a frightened child who is trying desperately to put right some naughty damage he has done, Brendan made a real effort to repair the harm he had done to his health, but unable to eat without spells of vomiting which wracked his body he was forced to go back into hospital. Determined to 'beat it yet,' he took his typewriter with him.

Four days later, he wrote an article for the *People* newspaper and because it took the form of a confession and was the only time he stood back in public and wrote the truth about himself as he really believed it to be, I feel some of the contents are worth quoting:

For a start let me tell you that I'm neither dead, drunk nor dotty. I'm just damn sick, but getting better all the time. My liver, I'm told, is like a sole of a hobnailed boot; my inside feels as if it's been scoured out with sulphuric acid and my head occasionally thumps like a pneumatic drill. But sure I could be worse and indeed I often was.

It is true, however, that I am an alcoholic and that excessive gargle is responsible for my present condition. But I am not without hope. I have been in hospital now since last Wednesday night and I've been gradually getting off the drink all the time. As a matter of fact I had nothing to drink yesterday and I will be back to work and dry as a sponge next Wednesday.

Why do I drink so much? That's easy answered. First because I

like the stuff. Secondly, because I like company and thirdly because a pint of orange or lemon juice is twice the price of a pint
of stout. Furthermore, it would be very hard for me to miss the
beer bug seeing as I was at the stuff with me grandmother since
I was six. By the time I was ten I knew the taste of it better than
tea.

Anyway I'm a lonely so-and-so and I must have people around
me to talk with. Bars are usually the best places because most of
them are full of poor people, hard-chaws, ex-convicts, chancers
and tramps who'd lift the froth off your pint if you didn't keep
your nose well in over the edge of the glass.

So long as I am working I am O.K. I'd never ask to stop writing. It's only when I've nothing to do that I hit the bottle. Lately,
it has been with more serious impact than in former years, but
that's simply because of my different financial position. My pockets kept a strict rein on my drinking then, but nowadays I can
afford a little more.

I know I can cure myself from drink and that's what I am doing
here in hospital. Remember that during that skite last week, my
average consumption was between two and three bottles of
whiskey a day, washed down with, maybe, a dozen or two of
stout or beer. Since I came into hospital on Wednesday, I cut
that down to a dribble and I took nothing yesterday or today.
And I will take nothing until I come out a new man this week.

I'll go back to work then and take an occasional drink just like
I used to before all this rumpus started a few months ago. I'll go
for walks with Beatrice then and we'll go to the sea and we'll talk
just like we used to.

That seems to me to sum up Brendan's views on himself in
July 1959. Sensibly, he recognised that his work was the only
interest more powerful than his love of drink; that it was his
safety-valve to enable him to release his inexorably squabbling
emotions profitably on paper instead of disastrously on the air;
and that if he could muster the will-power to keep writing, it
was his salvation.

As soon as Brendan was discharged from hospital, Beatrice
telephoned me, and although she was not foolish enough to believe that from henceforth all would be sunshine and flowers, she
was delighted to report that Brendan was still behaving himself
and working hard on *the catacombs*. He had, apparently, given

her a blow-by-blow account of his jauntings in London, except that he had omitted to mention our little skirmish or indeed that he had even seen me.

The winds from Ireland blew lightly for a while. Tommy Steele had been in Dublin to captain a team of film and television stars in a charity football match, but Brendan, who had been chosen to captain the Irish opposition, failed to turn up. He did turn up, however, at the International Theatre Festival, but apart from offering four words of advice about the theatre, 'Stay away from it,' had said little else.

When I first met Brendan, he was always very prompt in answering letters, but lately I noticed a change and he was now using the telephone instead, possibly because he found it a less troublesome, if more expensive, way of communicating. I had not been in touch with him since the bottle incident, and was therefore surprised one morning when I answered my telephone to hear, not the customary opening, 'Hello', but Brendan's unmistakable voice already in the middle of an explanation about the revisions he had done to his novel. Without waiting to hear to whom he was speaking, he began reading what turned out to be the opening paragraphs of *the catacombs*.

There was a party to celebrate Deirdre's return from her abortion in Bristol. Ciaran, her brother, welcomed me, literally with open arms, when I entered the Catalonian Cabinet Room where the guests were assembled. Even her mother, the screwy old bitch, came over with a glass of whiskey in her hand and said, 'You're welcome, Brendan Behan.' Bloodywell, I knew why I was welcome. It was I squared the matter for Deirdre to go over to England and have her baby out under the National Health Service, so to speak.

Suddenly he stopped. 'It is yourself I'm speaking to?' he enquired apprehensively. I answered that it was, but as these were the first words I had uttered throughout the length of the call, it could well have been a stranger. His uninhibited laughter clapped like thunder and rumbled into the distance. 'You've got some-

thing there,' he condeded. 'But wait till I tell you.' He began
reading again :

> The mother was supposed to be a very good Catholic, and I
> was a bit shocked to see the matter of fact way she accepted the
> situation, and even put up the money for the trip, and the readies
> to pay the quack. She never let on to know, of course, that there
> was anything amiss (no pun) and pretended to believe that
> Deirdre was 'going on a bit of a holiday to the other side.'

He paused for my reaction and I remarked jokingly that yet
another Behan book would be banned throughout the world.
'Oh f—— the censor,' came his reply. 'I have set up my own
bloody censorship board, and I hereby censor all censors,' and in
the next second he had slipped it in. 'Have you censored me?'

'I'm not worried, Brendan,' I answered truthfully. 'But as a
matter of interest, why didn't you tell Beatrice that you had seen
me in London?'

His reply was instantaneous. 'It has never been a habit of mine
to say anything bad against myself.'

A few days later Brendan paid a fleeting visit to London
bringing Beatrice with him. 'I had five minutes' notice and we
were off,' she commented philosophically. He looked fitter and
happier than he had done for a long time and was both eating
and drinking in moderation. Working was a tonic to him and he
was genuinely excited over the amount of progress he had made
on *the catacombs*. I was surprised to discover, however, that in
all the interviews he gave to the press he spoke of his next play,
the theme of which appeared to be identical with that of his novel.
I do not know whether the idea came to him on the spur of the
moment or whether in actual fact he had begun to execute the
change at home, and when I asked him, he merely winked. Tactfully, I did not press the point.

He went twice to see *The Hostage*, the ban now lifted, and
during the first visit he sat through the show without a word to be
led on to the stage at the end of the performance. But his second
was not quite so successful and he was smuggled out of a side

door before his interruptions became too noticeable. Wisely, he returned to Dublin before the temptations proved too much for him.

Shortly after his departure, word reached the press that Dominic Behan, his brother, had written a play which was to be performed in the West End. Like *The Hostage*, it was set in Dublin with the I.R.A. as its theme. I was apprehensive as to how Brendan would take this news, for the two brothers did not appear to get on very well.

I need not have worried for Brendan's attention was diverted by an explosion of a different nature. He had been tele-recorded for Ed Murrow's show, *Small World*, on the Columbia Broadcasting System, and the half-hour programme on 'The Art of Conversation' consisted of the film and sound track of a telephone exchange of words between Ed Murrow in London, Brendan in Dublin, and Jackie Gleason and John Mason Brown, the literary critic, in New York.

Despite the fact that it was tele-recorded, when it actually went out on the air, Brendan was eliminated halfway through the programme. Sitting in a friend's house, watching, he was naturally furious.

'They had no right to cut me off,' he fumed to the reporters. 'They never told me there was any defect in their recording apparatus. If there was any fault, it wasn't mine.' The *New York Times*, however, didn't entirely agree and described Brendan as a 'spirited and incoherent panelist' before his part in the discussion was 'abruptly and sensibly terminated.'

'There did not seem to be complete communication between the three guests,' were the reported words from the co-producer of the programme, 'and so it was decided to continue with only two.'

'Well, Mr. Behan was coming through a hundred per cent proof,' was Jackie Gleason's only comment.

It was a strange affair, for although Brendan was always the first to admit when he had been unruly, he insisted that whilst he had had 'a jar or two and was perhaps too outspoken,' he was

certainly not drunk. 'I don't suppose Mason Brown liked my
calling him a liar, any more than the Americans would like to
hear that the art of conversation went out when the atom bomb
came in, because it had been murdered by lunatics, mostly from
the United States.'

Inevitably, he began to drink heavily and Princess Margaret's
visit to *The Hostage*, which coincided with the incident, gave him
a further excuse for excessive drinking. If he was not accepted
by some, at least he was under royal patronage.

Unbeknown to myself, a decision was being taken at this time
which was to alter the entire tenor of my life. Paul Hogarth, who
had long since returned to England with his drawings for *Brendan
Behan's Island*, was getting a little concerned that there would
ever be any text to go with them. He appealed to his agent and
she conceived the idea that perhaps if Brendan would not write
the words, he might be persuaded to talk them into a tape-
recorder. She mentioned the matter to Iain Hamilton, who at
once telephoned Brendan to get his reactions. Brendan was delighted but assumed that I would be the natural choice for the
assignment.

Neither my parents nor my daughter, Diana, were happy about
my tackling the project, but I managed to convince them that the
Brendan Behan who appeared in the newspapers was a very
different person from the man himself. Three weeks later, after
Diana had returned to boarding-school, I was relieved temporarily of my duties as Hutchinson's publicity manager and
crossed the Irish Sea with a tape-recorder as an essential part of
my luggage. I did not know how long I would be away or what
I would have to face before I eventually set foot again on English
soil. I only knew that throughout the journey I had a gnawing
pain in the pit of my stomach, and I tried to comfort myself with
the words I had used previously, and with success, on my family.
I certainly did not know that one simple telephone conversation
would lead to my becoming Brendan Behan's collaborator.

VII

THE COLLABORATION BEGINS

Despite Beatrice's kind offer of hospitality, I had decided to avail myself of the loan of a flat on the top floor of an office building near O'Connell Street. The building would be empty at night, except for an elderly widow and her daughter who occupied the flat directly beneath mine, and I felt the peace and quiet might be necessary if my job was to be successful.

On arrival, I took a taxi to Ballsbridge, a smart continuation of Dublin and about a mile from the centre of the city. Anglesea Road is broad and tree-lined, flanked from the Dublin end on one side by a low grey stone wall, from which one can see the river below and a vast flour-mill beyond, and on the other by the public library and high palings which hide the Royal Dublin Society in whose grounds the famous Dublin Horse Show takes place. There are no private houses up to this point, but now the grey wall ends in a row of Victorian semi-detached houses with a view of the Royal Dublin Society; further along they change to detached houses, hidden in the main in their own grounds. The Behan home was—and is, for Beatrice still lives there, although she has had it converted into two flats—the third house in the row from the end of the grey stone wall. A wooden board on the iron gate in the front displays the word, 'Cúiz,' and as the taxi-man assured me that this was Irish for five, I gently pushed it open to hear it groan on its hinges. I walked up the tiny garden to the door, and on finding there was neither a bell, nor a door knocker, I rattled the letter-box cautiously. A tortoise-shell cat appeared out of nowhere, rubbing itself around my legs, the ominous quiet broken by its purring. I peered through the letter-box but could see nothing but darkness and I rattled it again, this time with more force.

Within a few minutes, I heard sounds of movement, indistinct at first before echoing the patter of someone running down the stairs, and Beatrice opened the door. Of course she was expecting me, she gasped, the effort of having to wake up suddenly and scramble into clothes making her temporarily breathless, but she and Brendan had been to a party the previous evening and were still sleeping off the effects when I rattled. She took the tape-recorder from me, hurrying with it into a room to the left of the hall, and the cat raced past me down a long passage ahead through a door at the end of it. I looked around. The chest in the hall was littered with letters, unopened, and the floor was furnished with a number of empty beer bottles, some standing, some leaning in drunken fashion, while a few were on their side and the dregs had left the inevitable stain.

Beatrice ushered me into the dining-room to wait while she cooked the breakfast, and a pang of uncertainty and homesickness shot through me as I stared out of the window and into the larger garden beyond. Noises from the room above interrupted my loneliness. Brendan was awake and coming down the stairs, calling my name as he did so. My first sight of him entirely altered my mood. If he had been tired when he went to bed, the few hours of sleep had apparently refreshed him, for he appeared in the doorway alive, animated and quite determined to look after his guest and to ensure that she had a good time. This new conception of Brendan startled me, and somewhat overcome by apprehension and weariness, for I had had a night-long passage of rough weather across the Irish Sea, I had little to say. But I was amused by the reversal of our normal roles. Metaphorically, it was I who had the hangover and it was he who was trying to cure it. Throughout breakfast, he made polite conversation about people, places and things in Ireland, and as soon as the meal was

over, he insisted that we go out for the day, instructing Beatrice
to order the taxi without delay. He gave no intimation as to
where we might be going, but once in the cab, we collected his
mother, Aunt Maggie—not really his aunt, but given this dis-
tinction through years of family friendship—and Carlos Kenny,
a friend, and drove out into the country.

It was to be a whirlwind tour of some of Brendan Behan's
Ireland, I discovered, but quite different from the normal guide-
book version as he pointed out the places where he and Beatrice
used to walk, and drew attention to a prison-like building where
a man, said to be mad, had once been imprisoned.

'The I.R.A. decided he wasn't mad, so they rescued him,'
Brendan explained. 'But when they put a tommy-gun in his hand,
they found out just how mad he was,' and his laughter at the
thought swallowed up our quieter chuckles.

The foothills began at Rathfarnham. Invited to get out, I
looked down on the roofs of Dublin city and the beautiful curve
of the bay. Higher up we drove across the Featherbed Pass and
through miles of wild, rugged, primitive country, bare of life except for an occasional cottage nestling between the hills, with its
chimney billowing smoke from peat gathered nearby.

From Glencree, we moved on to Glendalough where a saint
had once lived, since immortalised in a famous song which
Brendan sang quite delightfully. Enjoying his function as The
Host, he described every inch of the neighbourhood, until finally
our taxi came to a halt outside a large stone building which
turned out to be a hotel.

Sitting in the lounge Brendan ordered pints all round, and
although we were the only customers, our talking and singing
produced a volume of noise not far removed from a crowded pub
at closing-time. Revived by the buoyant atmosphere, I began to
speak to Brendan's mother, Kathleen, of whom, beforehand, I
had been rather frightened, but for no reason that I could name.
A small woman, with glasses, she had a personality and a manner of speaking similiar to Brendan and was as much devoted to
him as obviously he was to her. Brendan was the eldest of her

second family, she said, for she was only two years married to
Jack Furlong, a '16 man, before she was widowed. She had had
eight children in all, two sons by her first husband and five sons
and a daughter by her second, but the last son had died. She was
of course proud of them all but never had hopes of any of them
being writers, although she was happy that Brendan had his trade
as a house-painter to fall back on should anything happen. He
was like his father in appearance, but she'd say he took more
after her brother, Peadar Kearney, the same who wrote the
National Anthem of Ireland.

'Did you ever meet the Da?' she asked, continuing at once as
I shook my head. 'He's always jolly, and never bad-tempered or
moody. I never had a cross word from him in the thirty-eight
years I am married to him, excepting I raised it myself.'

Beatrice interrupted our conversation to suggest, sensibly, that
we have something to eat, and we trundled into the dining-
room to have an excellent lunch which Brendan devoured
eagerly.

Later, we returned to the lounge but I had barely sat down
again before I heard Kathleen Behan call across, 'You killed
Kevin Barry.' On looking around the rest of the company I was
forced, by the direction of her stare, to acknowledge that she was
speaking to me. I hadn't the slightest idea to whom she was referring, but guessed that the remark was provocative because
Brendan angrily told his mother 'to leave the girl alone. She
knows nothing about these things.' I felt the storm clouds gather
above my head, but in the next breath, Kathleen Behan blew them
away by singing the lovely song about Kevin Barry which I now
know so well.

> In Mountjoy Jail, one Monday morning,
> High upon the gallows tree,
> Kevin Barry gave his young life
> For the cause of liberty.
> Only a lad of eighteen summers
> Yet no one can deny
> As he walked to death that morning,
> He proudly held his head on high . . .

We clapped our applause and asked her to sing more, but Brendan shouted down our appreciation in order to tell the story of Judge Lynch of Galway who hanged his son because nobody else would do it. 'There are plenty of Irish bastards too,' he emphasised. Beatrice, Aunt Maggie and Carlos intoned their agreement.

For the rest of the afternoon, we remained at the hotel paying little regard to 'the Holy hour,' so that by the time we piled back into the taxi, the previous shadow of stress was entirely removed by our shining faces of contented well-being. We sang in turn Irish ballads, popular ditties, rock-'n'-roll, and 'Land of Hope and Glory', which Brendan soloed magnificently, and it was with genuine regret that I bade farewell to his mother, Aunt Maggie and Carlos, as we delivered them back to their homes. For myself, I was ready to call the day over, but Brendan, more awake than ever, suggested a light supper before returning in search of more gaiety. We went to Crowe's, the localest of his local pubs, and pushing through the crowd in the front room, we threaded our way through the more closely assembled pack of people in the back to a row of chairs which lined the far wall. Brendan ordered the drinks, but a young man at the counter, partially intoxicated, demanded attention which Brendan was not prepared to give to him, and downing his pint with remarkable speed he expected Beatrice and myself to do likewise so that we could leave the place quickly and go somewhere else to drink in peace. All at once, in a way that I came to know was characteristic, he was showing utter distaste of the man's tipsy exhibition; I can only presume that he saw in such behaviour a reflection of himself. But too tired to stand on my feet, I said I would like to go home and Beatrice telephoned for a taxi. Brendan had already done more than enough in the way of taking care of me, but graciously he insisted he accompany me in the cab, and I did not say good night to them until I was safely on my doorstep.

When I arrived at Anglesea Road early the next morning, Brendan was up, though in his dressing-gown. The sunny smile with which he greeted me radiated warmth in contrast to the bitter cold outside where the snow was falling in large, persistent flakes. Beatrice was waiting breakfast for me and as soon as she had cooked it, she joined us to talk and linger over innumerable cups of scalding hot tea. In the euphoria that surrounded me, I became unconscious of the reason which had brought me over to Ireland, and asked casually what the new day might bring. Brendan leant across the table and said, apologetically, that if it was all the one to me, he would like 'to knock out a few words into the tape-recorder before getting dressed.' Hastily, bolt upright in my chair, I donned an attitude of efficiency and concurred. We moved into the room next door where Beatrice had put the tape-recorder and which overlooked the road. I set up the machine at once, while Brendan settled himself comfortably in a high-backed ebony chair which was to be his choice for every future session.

'If the Mycenaean Greek poets could do it, then so can I,' he chuckled happily. 'I do not set myself up as an authority on these matters, but if Homer is to be believed, the Greeks wrote their books by improvising them in talk. Now I'm getting in on their act.'

I put the tape-recorder on a chair next to him and sat myself on the other side of the machine. But when I handed him the speaker he was so horrified that I placed it on the arm of his chair where he could still talk into it without being constantly reminded of the mechanics of the operation. People who believe that all that was required to capture the golden words as they poured out of Brendan's lips was to set the tapes rolling are badly mistaken. He gave as much thought to working in this manner as he would have done had he been physically writing the words on paper.

I had a set of questions with me, prepared by Iain Hamilton, and a list of Paul Hogarth's illustrations so that by question and answer in this way, the drawings would complement the text. Before we started recording, I gave Brendan the list of questions and he studied them carefully before giving them back to me. Then he stared in silence at the fire, noisily cleared his throat, spat into the grate and nodded to indicate that he was ready to begin.

I had scarcely spoken a few words of introduction before Brendan stopped me. 'Better play that back. Just to make sure we're not wasting any words on the air.' I did as I was asked and heard the echo of my voice with relief.

We began again, Brendan's pauses acting as a signal for me to turn off the recorder while he rephrased a sentence or considered more carefully the pertinence of his answers. Occasionally he would voice his thoughts aloud to get my reaction before they could be captured, or he would tell me some anecdote in connection with his discourse which, for reason of libel or obscenity, was best left unrecorded.

As the morning progressed, the operation became less of a radio interview, until the single mention of a place-name drew from Brendan a wealth of fascinating and sober information. Throughout he remained seated in his chair. Nor would he tolerate any interruptions, and the groaning of the front gate which heralded the arrival of frequent visitors diverted his mind no more than a quick glance out of the window. No one was allowed in the room and I knew better than to go out of it. By lunch-time we had recorded 4,000 words and we both felt we had accomplished enough for one day.

I started to close up the machine, but Brendan insisted that the success of our joint venture be celebrated on tape with a song. Standing in the middle of the room, the froth on his pint swilling over the side of the glass in his hand, he pushed out his chest and sang lustily:

> Don't quarrel, hearts too precious to break,
> So drink up and have a pint for Jaysus' sake.

Work over, Brendan was out of the door and up the stairs and down again as quickly, dressed and anxious that I should accompany him up the road for a jar. I was hungry more than thirsty but in this gee-whiz atmosphere, I did not like to mention it, and anyway he was already out of the front door before I could answer him. I flung on my coat, picked up my handbag and raced after him, and we covered the distance from where the houses end, along by the side of the grey stone wall to the top of the road, with remarkable speed.

Panting and out of breath I sat on a stool in Crowe's, while Brendan ordered a pint for himself and a glass for me. I was curious to know the reason for his great haste, but sensed it was not entirely a desire for drink. Soon he was telling me how much he loathed and detested the walk from his house, with no possibility of waving his hand at the friendly faces as they popped up over their garden hedges, or even the comfort of less friendly faces peeping from behind their net curtains hanging in the windows.

'You'd be needing a drink to give you the courage to face such loneliness,' and although he laughed as he spoke these words, I knew he meant them seriously.

After lunch Brendan became The Host once more as he guided me into the heart of the city. 'Tomorrow we shall be talking about Dublin for the book,' he said, 'so you had better see it for yourself today.'

Our first stop was Mick's Bar in Lower Parnell Street, but before I had time to really look at the photograph of Michael Collins, a stranger tapped Brendan on the shoulder and congratulated him on a recent television appearance. The gesture embarrassed rather than annoyed Brendan, and as several other customers moved closer in to speak to him, he backed to the door exchanging polite farewells as he did so. I followed him, surprised that his public image should confuse him and bring out a shyness that I had not noticed before. Out in the lamp-lit streets, the snow which had stopped earlier was renewing its efforts half-heartedly but quickly turned to slush as soon as it brushed the pavement. We moved on to another pub and into a dimly lit room where Brendan told the barman I was just over from England, to which the barman responded convivially that if I came from Manchester, I'd be used to the weather outside. With a fresh pint in his hand, Brendan began to bring himself up to date with the Manchester he remembered—Strangeways Prison and Platt Lane police station—but before he'd finished his recollections, his words fizzled out in a mouthful of beer as he drained the bottom of his glass. Again he was at the door, this time muttering that he 'was fed up with going over the same bloody prison ground.'

He was beginning to become irritated that he no longer had the privilege of indulging in life's simple pleasures; of showing a friend round Dublin without being stared at or stopped to have his hand shaken or, worse, treated like Santa Claus in a big store at Christmas with nothing better to do than speak civilly to strangers. He'd put up with it in London for the English lined his pockets, he grumbled, but there was nothing for him in Ireland. Most of the people wouldn't know a book when they saw one, unless it was the Bible and that out of fear, while the nine or ten who could read decided his work was unfit for their cultured minds.

In O'Connell Street, the sight of Nelson's Pillar restored his humour a little, but only because he had once managed to climb to the top of it and not because it was there. 'That one-armed, one-eyed Admiral of the British bollock-shop institution, the Royal Navy,' he snarled, 'has no business on his perch at all. He has no f—ing place in Ireland's history but a wrong one.'

Our next stop was the General Post Office and as it was shutting up for the day the inhabitants were too busy completing their postal arrangements to notice Brendan when he walked in. It had been the headquarters of the Easter Rising of 1916 from whose steps Padraic Pearse proclaimed the birth of the Irish Republic as a sovereign independent state and as such, historically, is one of Ireland's most important buildings. I read the Proclamation of Independence, POBLACHT NA h-EIREANN, The Provisional Government of the Irish Republic to the People of Ireland and so on, until I came to the end where I noticed seven signatures. 'They're all dead,' Brendan said, pointing his finger at their names. 'They were executed, the Lord have mercy on them, not at once, in the heat of the moment, but in the few weeks that followed the Rising. However, God's help is never far from the door, for it was this cold-blooded action by the British Government that probably gave us our freedom, for Ireland found, in the men who fought and died for her, a new sword for her spirit.

'In my childhood I could remember the whole week a damn sight better than I can now,' he said, as we walked back down the street again, 'for all my family were in the Rising. And they told the stories to such good effect that I was in there with them. There was nothing remote about it. For the matter of that, I grew up to be rather surprised by and condescending to any grown-up person who had not taken part in it.

'I was with Tom Clarke and his 1,500 men in the Post Office when the tricolour flag went down, and I marched to the Rotunda' (he pointed to a building round the corner from O'Connell Street as he spoke) 'with them in defeat, and even heard Tom Clarke's gleeful remark: "God, it was great to see them run."

'Now I have learned enough arithmetic to know that I could not possibly have taken part in an event which happened seven years before I was born, and it saddens me.'

At the corner of O'Connell Street and Parnell Square Brendan stood silently waiting for the traffic to let him cross to the other side. I kept a discreet distance not wishing to intrude on his recollections, but when he reached the middle of the road, he called back over his shoulder to me. Didn't I have a share in the honours too, he shouted, for I knew Aunt Maggie and his mother, who were feeding the messengers and keeping a stopping place for despatch carriers, and Valentin Iremonger, whose father-in-law, Paddy Mannin, had been in the garrison up at Jacob's factory?

One or two of the passers-by glanced at me in surprise and it was my turn now to feel embarrassed. Quickly I caught up with him and shepherded him over to the pavement. 'Brendan, I am proud of being English,' I said quietly, once we were across. 'You know that. Nor would I want to change my nationality. But I am not that much of a heathen that I don't think the English have a lot to answer for in Ireland.'

We had our backs to the Gresham Hotel, and Brendan took hold of both my arms and turned me round in a half-circle to face the building.

'This is as good a place as any to tell you that not one of us is free from having to answer to somebody for something. On Sunday, November 21st, 1920, in that hotel a perfectly innocent man from Texas, here to buy Irish animals to improve his bloodstock back home, was shot dead, suspected of being a British secret agent. Instead of cattle, he got a load of lead and a coffin for his pains.'

I would have liked to have asked him more, but he was already at the taxi-rank opposite telling me we were going to meet Rory Furlong, his half-brother. Brendan's relation lived in one of those beautiful Georgian houses for which Dublin is famous. The front door was open, though the place appeared deserted except for a ladder and tins of paint and paint-brushes scattered around the hall. The ground floor was obviously in the process of being redecorated and on seeing the ladder, Brendan scampered up it, paint and paint-brush in his hand. His skill at his former trade had not diminished and I said so, a remark that brought him hurrying down and out into the street and into the nearest pub where he could discuss his experiences in the painting line in greater comfort. For an hour or two he talked calmly and amiably about his days as a house-painter and was touchingly proud of his father's position as President of the Painters' Union. It was a pub in which he was not well known and although he occasionally nodded his head in response to recognition, he still wanted privacy and enjoyed the anonymity offered him. He missed the companionship of the fellow-workers in his former trade, he explained, who shared, in the main, the same background, the same left-wing views politically and the same degree of poverty. He was not a communist, although he supported the party financially, and would not care to be labelled one for fear that *bona fide* members might sue him for libel. Recently a Dele-

gation had been sent to the Soviet Union as representative of
Ireland's culture, but the local reds had not included him on the
grounds that he was too rough-and-ready and had too strong a
Dublin working-class accent. Of the ten men who were chosen,
all were university graduates and seven of them landowners or
sons of landowners.

Later we returned to Anglesea Road for a meal and to collect
Beatrice to accompany us for what was left of the evening. The
talk now was mostly trivia, light-hearted and gay, as we toured
the pubs from one end of the city to the other. For me, Dublin
became alive as it was never to do again. Finally I was forced to
admit defeat in exhaustion and I left them for a solid night's
sleep.

As soon as we had breakfasted the next morning, Brendan
moved into the front room and asked me to set up the machine.
His large face radiated activity without the slightest sign of
fatigue and although by now I was getting used to the incredible,
his limitless stamina astounded me. Prodding myself into action,
I gave him the list of Paul Hogarth's illustrations, and allowing
himself the customary moments in which to collect his thoughts,
he indicated that he was ready to record.

It would always have been an experience to listen to Brendan
talking about the city that cradled him, for his family and families
before them came from Dublin, and his fantastic memory and
passionate interest enabled him to remember in minute detail
every story handed down from generation to generation. Added
to which, he had an extraordinary gift for words and was happy
to have the opportunity to use it. For myself, I truthfully forgot
that the purpose of the operation was to produce a book and I
became immersed in the history of Dublin, in her splendour and
her poverty in past and present days. In a way, it was the ideal
set-up for Brendan because he enjoyed monopolising the stage
and his role as entertainer was an essential and delightful part
of his character when he was not cocooned in worthless adulation. At the same time he was fulfilling a commitment and
functioning as a writer, for the use of the tape-recorder is not

uncommon by even less eccentric authors. Brendan knew that I regarded his work seriously and although the sessions were conducted in a free-and-easy atmosphere and his uninhibited singing punctuated most of the facts that he was relating, his approach was always professional without a trace of the clown. In my delight I moved to play back the tape, but Brendan would have none of it.

'Much as I like the sound of my own voice,' he chuckled, 'I'll stand no competition from it.' Nor did he ever. Throughout the morning there had again been a stream of callers to the house; people wanting to meet him; cadgers, journalists and others eager to take him out for a drink; and I realised more clearly the difficulties he was facing as a gregarious man and the strain he was under for having become a world-famous character. As long as he could work, he would be able to resist the temptations.

That evening Brendan and Beatrice took me to the R.A.F. Club situated in the fashionable part of Dublin. We came into the main room where a wary-eyed group stood at one end of the bar while all along the rest of it were scattered the shocked, panic-stricken faces of what I presumed to be the Anglo-Irish upper-crust wearing checked suits and old-school ties. Brendan immediately sensed the dismay that his presence was causing and, delighting in their discomfort, he bustled around the room pointing out first the Duke of Edinburgh's portrait which would have been impossible to miss, and then the wooden painted squadron shields, emblems of the British few to whom we owe so much. A dreadful feeling that something was happening removed the shock from the members' faces and they spoke in loud, false tones rather as one does at a dinner-party when the host's dog has made it abundantly clear that he would be better off outside. But their voices could not cope with Brendan's when he put his mind to it, and he told the assembled company in anything but a whisper that he had a brother in the Royal Air Force which 'makes me sort of eligible here.' His words were received with pompous disdain which did not quite hide their uneasiness at waiting for the balloon to go up.

I do not know why Brendan ordered a whiskey, unless it was
he needed one to release his pent-up emotions at so stultifying a
reception. But he must have known it would not stop at one,
and it was ridiculous to allow the occasion to spark off a bout of
steady drinking. He started to sing and the annoyance in the room
became palpable; he followed this with more songs and more
drink until finally after much coaxing, gently but firmly, we persuaded him to leave the place before he was ejected. Out in the
street, he grumbled and complained that we had taken him from
a party which he was just beginning to enjoy and insisted that we
pile into a horse-drawn cab and hoof our way round the pubs of
Dublin. There is no stopping a volcano in eruption, and for a
while he was the loud life of the evening, but by the early hours
of dawn he had slumped back into the cab, crumpled, dishevelled
and exhausted to pass out cold not a few minutes later.

After sleeping off his hangover in the morning I found
Brendan morose, but nevertheless he assured me that he intended
to work on his book. Strangely, the session started well as he
launched into a long and far from rabid discourse on the similari-
ties between Northern and Southern Ireland, but soon his reaction
to my questions became slower and the silent periods longer as
he recollected and reshaped his answers. Beads of perspiration
formed on his brow and his hair in the front became damp and
matted, and he stammered and stuttered out the elusive words,
rephrasing his sentences many times before he would let them go.
More and more his attention was diverted by the noise of the
front gate opening, and twice he tottered to the hall to offer his
personal welcomes. As his concentration weakened, so did his
enthusiasm, and after a while he gave up the struggle.

Throughout the week he continued in this manner, but as day
followed day, he drank a little more and ate a little less, and our
tape-recording sessions dwindled in accordance. All I could do
was to watch helplessly as his mental wheels ground to a stop.
Despite the fact that, by now, Brendan felt really ill, he was
determined to drive himself on and refused either to see a doctor
or to go to bed. Each day we would go out, but they were sad

excursions and ended with Brendan just making his home before the inevitable collapse. The only time I remember him getting the faintest enjoyment out of these trips was at the Phoenix Park Zoo where by chance he met the son of the poet Yeats, and allowed himself to be photographed with a tawny python from the snake house coiled around his neck. Even at Leopardstown races (he was an ardent follower of the horses and had been known on occasion to deputise for the racing correspondent of the *People*) he found the atmosphere more congenial in the bar than on the racecourse and returned to the Stands only to insist that I back Irish Coffee instead of Daily Telegraph, 'that f—ing limey rag.' As it happened there was little to choose between the two horses; they were both on the floor before the completion of the first circuit. Throughout he was despondent, bad-tempered and mentally and physically sick, and the will-power to do anything about it lessened the further he penetrated the tunnel of alcoholism. Whether it was from the schoolgirls who sniggered and pointed at him, the nun who called at the house for alms ('They won't accept me, but they'll take my bloody money') or a chance remark from Beatrice, he always found some reason to continue on his lonely journey. It was useless to try to stop him for he was beyond the barriers of communication; only a fear of having pushed his luck too far would bring him to his senses.

On February 9, his thirty-seventh birthday, I had invited Beatrice and himself to a celebration dinner and we left Ballsbridge early in the evening to give me time to cook it. I had a few bottles of Guinness in the flat and I hoped that Brendan would be content to sit and drink them until the meal was ready. As we neared O'Connell Street it was plain he had other ideas for he insisted that he have a few jars at the I.R.A. Club around the corner, and he stopped our protests by an assurance that he would join us before I had even peeled the potatoes.

By eleven o'clock he had not returned and we had our dinner without him. Gradually our concern changed to alarm, but it was relieved by the ring of my bell from the front door below. As I ran down the first flight of stairs I did not notice at once the woman standing on the landing, but when I came within touching distance of her she was not long in telling me that she was the widow who occupied the flat below mine and more, she would not tolerate disturbances from the likes of Brendan Behan.

I opened my mouth to utter some comment and received the full force of her next blast. She had just come home to find him on her doorstep and not alone had he fouled it, but he had used language on her that had her cold with it yet. And if this wasn't enough to send her to an early grave, hadn't she the police circling round her building as well, making a whore-house of the place?

At the mention of 'police' I was down in the hallway quicker than gunpowder could blow me to find Brendan crouched on the doormat. He must have slipped in with the woman but, hearing her diatribe, had wisely decided that the best ploy was to stay where he was. I whispered 'Shshsh' and put my finger to my lips, and as he turned to look at me I noticed a splurge of blood on the left side of his face. By now Beatrice had joined me, and together we helped Brendan up the stairs, thanking the Lord God in all His mercy when we were safely past the widow's door.

Brendan was beginning to sober up and was extremely frightened. He had no recollection as to how he had received the cut under his eye, but knew he had gone to the I.R.A. Club to celebrate not only his birthday but the twenty-first anniversary of his arrest in Liverpool for bomb-planting activities. He remembered singing and could only assume that some of the fellows hadn't enjoyed it and he must have got into a fight. I did not tell him that the police were looking for him, but whispered to Beatrice that I would go downstairs and see if they were still about. I was immeasurably shaken and at a loss to know how to handle the situation and not a little scared myself. Renewing my courage with a tiny glass of whiskey, hidden in the kitchen cupboard, I tiptoed downstairs uncertain which was the greater hazard, the police or the elderly widow.

As I reached the bottom step of her landing I saw with relief that her door was closed, and I snaked along the side of the iron banisters past the danger zone, down the remaining two flights of stairs and out into the street. There was not a person in sight and if the police had been there before, they were not in evidence now as I waited in the bitter air of the night delighting in my solitude.

As I returned upstairs, my way was barred by the widow who, arms akimbo, made further progress impossible.

'It was you he was asking for, you know,' she said, and the smile on her face revealed the pleasure this knowledge was giving her, but faded immediately as she reeled back from the smell of the whiskey from my breath. 'I see you suffer from the same weakness,' she added, screwing up her face in disgust.

Before I could offer my explanation, she was screaming that she would not be a party to such unpleasant goings on, and as a right-minded, clean-living, Irish citizen, it was her duty to telephone her landlord, despite the unseemly hour, and have me evicted forthwith.

Hearing the shouts, Beatrice put her head over the banisters above us. 'What's up, Rae?' she called. Shaking with rage and righteous indignation, I effected the introductions from this distance, putting undue emphasis on the words, 'Brendan's wife,' and I did not wait for the widow's reactions but stalked grandly up the stairs accompanied all the way by her profuse apologies.

We bathed Brendan's eye. The wound was only superficial. I spoke sharply to him for causing so much trouble, carefully mentioning our concern over the presence of the police. Hardly had I done so, however, when my doorbell rang and the hunted look in Brendan's eyes showed clearly what was on his mind. Terrified, he pleaded he was going to straighten up, finish the book and never touch another drop. If I would see him through this lot, he would not let me down. Throughout the length of three flights of stairs I repeated what Brendan had said in an imaginary conversation with the policeman I expected to find on the doorstep, but as I opened the door, geared to deliver my speech, the face of a friend met my startled gaze, and dimly I heard him ask if he could come up for a night-cap. As he spoke, my eyes caught sight of his car parked by the kerbside; he was more than welcome to a pint in exchange for taking Brendan home afterwards. Half an hour later, Brendan walked down the stairs under his own steam, and if he did raise his voice a shade on the first landing, it was from over-excitement at his lucky reprieve and a belief in having the last word.

His recuperation began at once and in earnest. He agreed to see the doctor and with medical aid his marvellous powers of recovery reasserted themselves. During the day, he would lie on the couch in the front room of his home reading or sharing his dreams of a future without the curse of drink. I do not remember his exact words, but I recall clearly him saying that the success of *The Quare Fellow, The Hostage* and *Borstal Boy* was poor compensation for the harm it had done to him personally. He found it difficult to sleep without sedation, and he met every dawn with great fear. He was anxious to start working again for that and that alone took his mind off his troubles. Throughout his convalescence, I remained with him (except for the nights, when I returned to sleep in my flat), waiting for his magical words of 'set up the machine.' Even so, I did not imagine that he would be able to record for very long periods or that his efforts would be comparable to our earlier sessions. When the day came for us to resume taping, I realised my mistake.

With no prompting, and without playing back the tapes, Brendan picked up the threads from where he had left off as if the intermission had never been and the daily routine uninterrupted. Nor was there any repetition as he spoke effortlessly of gerrymandering in the Six Counties; of a former proprietor of the Bluebell public house in Sandy Row who once refused to allow the Duke of Edinburgh to play the Orange Drum on the grounds that he wasn't a member of the Orange Order, and it was too sacred a business even for him; of the warm reception given to *The Quare Fellow* in Belfast; and of the time when he treated the students of Queen's University to his views on prisons and political prisoners. He loved Belfast, believing it to be the land and heart of proletarian Ireland and was certain that, in the end, it would be the Belfast worker who would upset both the Orange and the Green applecart.

He had a very special place in his heart too for the West of Ireland and the Aran Isles, as the tapes reveal. By the hour he spoke of the historical attributes of Galway ('once one of the biggest ports in Europe and the last that Christopher Columbus saw on his way to discovering America'); the wild beauties of Carraroe where he spent many holidays ('purely Gaelic speaking and a favourite haunt of many writers, artists and actors, including Stefan O'Flaherty who remembers Sir Roger Casement coming to visit his school and giving him a shilling because he had the best handwriting'); and Inishmore, one of the Aran Islands off the west coast from which he had been banished for locking up a policeman in his own cell before throwing away the key. He was perhaps more subdued, and the songs he sang of a gentler nature during our second bout of recordings; and the rest of his day would be spent either in the local or sitting quietly at home over a pint; otherwise I noticed little difference in him.

When the book was finished, Brendan insisted that his last words should be shared with his tortoise-shell cat. Sitting Looney O'Toolle on his lap, he spoke to her in terms of affection which she reciprocated in loud purring, and the tape ends with his words, 'Thank Jaysus, thank Jaysus,' set to musical accompaniment by a contented cat.

Before I left on the boat at Dun Laoghaire, we had a celebration dinner at the Royal Yacht Club with Christopher Gore-Grimes, a friend and a Dublin solicitor. Unlike a former evening at the R.A.F. Club, but in precisely the same atmosphere, Brendan behaved impeccably and Christo did not have a moment's qualm that his membership would be questioned in the morning.

The whole project had taken a little over three weeks, and I returned to England with the slightly ravelled air of having myself been wound through the tape-recorder. Although the forty thousand words may not have been captured entirely in soda-water sessions of untrammelled tranquillity, as *Brendan Behan's Island* they were to be worth the effort.

VIII

BACK IN HOSPITAL

As his friends had hoped, working with a tape-recorder inspired Brendan to write again on his own, and within a week of my departure he completed the first draft of his third play, *Richard's Cork Leg*. Each morning he would rise early and shut himself away in the room above the one we had occupied for the recording sessions, where his daily routine would be less likely to be interrupted by visitors. He was an extremely quick writer, typing his words straight on the machine and made few, if any, pencilled notes beforehand, but whereas earlier he would type and retype before he was satisfied, he was now beginning to adopt an 'anything will do' attitude.

Dublin is a small city in which news travels fast and while people began to talk about Brendan's new play, they commented too on the fact that Dominic, his brother, was shortly to have his first play, *Posterity Be Damned*, performed in the West End of London. For his own reasons, this news upset Brendan and I'm sure he was determined at this point that the first night should not take place without him. Simultaneously, he heard that Gerry Raffles and Joan Littlewood were flying over from England to spend the week-end with him and, his ego boosted, he arranged a party in their honour.

Unfortunately, on the appointed day Gerry Raffles was ill and the visit cancelled, but not the party which ended several days later with Brendan methodically touring any bar in Dublin and beyond still willing to serve him. Undaunted by his dwindling health, he drank merrily on until, less than a week before the opening of Dominic's play, he returned to London. I had no previous knowledge of his coming before he and Joe McGill, with whom he was staying, arrived in the office. Outwardly, he didn't look too bad, but his over-loud voice, his too hearty laughter, his accentuated grimaces and his broth-of-a-boy buffoonery gave me the impression that I was facing the saddest man in Europe.

At the same time, although I could not put my finger on it, I sensed an uneasiness between us and he seemed reluctant to look me straight in the eye. He said he was going with Joe to the Salisbury public house in St. Martin's Lane and asked me to come too, but when I refused he became aggressive and demanding, and I gave in meekly to prevent a scene. As we reached the pub, he took me to one side and told me what was troubling him.

'There's a man back in Dublin,' he confided, 'who was after telling me how good you are to me, and I snapped back at him, "Why wouldn't she be? She's my publisher, isn't she?" Honest to God, daughter, I don't know why I said it, and no sooner were the words out of my mouth before I was wishing to cut off my tongue.' He stared strangely into a far-away vacuum, and then continued: 'If it's any consolation to you, I've not been easy in my mind since.'

Afterwards, when I came to know him even better, I was to discover that this trait was highly characteristic; he was never at ease with anyone of whom he had spoken ill until he had truthfully squared the matter with them. He seemed quite sober then, and I contemplated telling him that while the tapes of *Brendan Behan's Island* had been transcribed and the typescript was waiting to be edited by him, it was still in its raw form of question and answer and needed a great deal of working over to put it into shape. But once he was at the bar of the Salisbury in the middle of the theatrical clientèle who drank there, he determined not to be tranquil, accepting every drink and having nothing to eat. His previous weeks of imbibing, however, had already taken their toll, and the life in his body now was drawn from the strength of the alcohol. He shouted that he had come to London for the opening of his brother's play, and if it lacked nothing else that came from *The Hostage*, it would have to get along without Joan Littlewood's direction. A woman behind the bar called for less noise, and Brendan charged over to tell her that, contrary to anything she may have read in the papers, it was he, and not Dominic, who was paying the trip over for his parents to see it as well. Spilling drink over himself and everyone else as well, the rambling, difficult and sick Brendan of this day bore little resemblance to the ebullient and entertaining man I had last seen in Dublin. Several times Joe and I asked him to leave, and even tried to lure him away by promises of drinking in a fresh environment, but although his answer was always 'in a moment,' that moment did not come. Helplessly, victims of despair, we watched him stagger and retreat to a state of appalling drunkenness, a figure of ridicule for strangers who would not know the goodness which lay behind the barriers of his stupid self-indulgence. At closing-time, we heaved him into a taxi and took him home to bed.

Brendan's parents were arriving from Ireland the next day, and although he had expressed his intention of meeting them at Euston station, I was certain that his hangover would now prevent it. I was surprised to find him waiting for me in the office early the following morning. He was standing in the middle of the room, his body drooping in a sort of doomed resignation, his head sagging on his shoulder while his eyes pleaded silently for someone to take care of him. Somehow he had managed to shave and put on a suit, but in the process he had forgotten to take off his pyjamas and the cords of the bottom half were hanging down the front of his trousers, while the jacket of his suit did little to hide the fact that the green and white pyjama top was a stand-in for his shirt. He was barely articulate, not so much from drink, but from physical sickness, and the brief efforts he made to be sociable only served to increase the coma in which he was now encased. He was not fit to meet his parents. This I knew. But

I knew too that, in his stubbornness, he would do so and that I would have to help him because I could not ignore the feeling of protectiveness which Brendan in trouble always put upon me. Nevertheless, to guard myself in case I did not have the strength, literally, to hold him up, I prevailed upon the offer of a journalist friend to lend me both himself and his car.

I was certain that the press would be milling round Euston for the meeting of the Behans, and while I could not hide from them Brendan's dazed and exhausted manner, I could ensure, at least, that he arrived respectably dressed. On our way to the station we stopped at an outfitter's in a side street off the Euston Road, and although the clothes in the window had little in common with Brendan, we went in. As I busied myself informing the immaculately dressed assistant that we wanted an overcoat, shirt and a tie, I did not notice that Brendan was preparing himself enthusiastically for the fitting until, too late, he stood in front of us with not a stitch between himself and his Maker, his suit and his pyjamas bunched in a pile by his tiny bare feet. With a dignity that is essentially the mark of a perfect English gentleman, the assistant did not raise an eyebrow as he helped Brendan into his new shirt and back into his trousers as though the sight of a naked customer in his shop was an everyday occurrence. Brendan did not say a word. The effort of undressing and dressing had made him sweat, and the eyelids fell heavily over his eyes as though they would never open again. I took hold of him by the arm and slowly he shuffled out of the shop and into the car.

'Brendan,' I pleaded with him, 'let me take you to a doctor. This isn't simply a hangover. You are sick, truly sick.' Pathetically, he nodded his head in agreement, but he said quietly, 'I'm not feeling too bad, not too bad at all,' and he slipped back into a daze to mutter a few moments later, 'I must see the ould one, I must see the ould one.'

At Euston, when we first arrived, he summoned up the will-power to chat with reporters, photographers and friends who were collected on the platform, but he was too ill, too deeply tired to keep it up for long. By the time his parents arrived, he could do

no more than embrace his mother in silence and allow the jubila-
tions to pass him by. There are no words to describe the quiet
from this noisy man as, like a robot, he pushed one leg in front of
the other to walk down the platform, out of the station and on to
the street where he clung to each car parked at the kerbside,
looking for the right one. He did not feel safe and he wanted to
sit down.

After a quick consultation it was generally agreed that lunch
should be taken in a pub next door to the Metropolitan Theatre
in the Edgware Road, where a rehearsal of Dominic's play was
being performed in the afternoon. The short car journey appeared to revive Brendan, for he walked into the pub with more
confidence and sat down at a table with a group which included
his parents and Dominic. A little relaxed within myself now, I
was able to sense the animosity which existed, at any rate on the
surface, between Brendan and his brother and made up my mind
too that my nerves were not strong enough to cope with the added
tension. Standing behind Brendan's chair while he swallowed a
plate of soup (the first nourishment he had taken since his arrival
in London) I whispered in his ear that I was leaving him with his
family.

Immediately, he struggled to his feet. 'Where are you going?'
he cried. 'Where are you going? I must come with you.' I had
intended to disappear without drawing attention to myself, but
suddenly I was the focal point of several pairs of eyes whose
expression clearly accused me of trying to break up the party by
dragging Brendan away. Irritated and confused, I mumbled I
had some work to do, and I hurried to the door feeling the beam
of their gaze centred on the small of my back.

Later that night, I met Brendan again at Joe and Kathleen's
flat to hear what happened during the afternoon. He had attended
the rehearsal as arranged, sleeping peacefully in a seat next to
his mother in the middle of the stalls, until Dominic's shouting
from the stage that the I.R.A. were murderers woke him up and
brought him to his feet to dispute the allegation. 'It's a lot of
rubbish,' he bawled across the empty row of seats, 'there were

no murderers in the I.R.A. The whole play is a load of muck.'

Dominic retaliated almost as if he had rehearsed the words. 'What are you saying, man? 'T'is you who was the worst of the lot.' The interchange filled the air before Brendan stormed out to leave his mark on the bar tops of hotels, clubs and pubs and finally to collapse back in the flat.

For the next three days, Brendan spent his mornings drinking, his afternoons back in the flat, holding his head and groaning that he felt like 'death itself,' but fulminated alarmingly each time I mentioned getting medical help. Every evening he slipped further into a diabetic coma which was steadily overcoming his slender resistance to it. Making the decision myself, I summoned Bob Lusty's personal physician, after Bob had kindly offered to telephone and warn him of my call.

Dr. Allison's prognosis was not surprising. Brendan had diabetes, was suffering from advanced cirrhosis of the liver and must be admitted to hospital at once, but preferably in Dublin where his case history would be known. Unfortunately, the morbid press publicity which Brendan's illness had attracted frightened Aer Lingus and B.E.A., and neither airline company was prepared to fly him without the supervision of a member of the medical profession. For hours I searched London in vain for a free and willing participant, but the answer was always the same; the notice was too short. Dr. Allison made arrangements for Brendan to be admitted to the Middlesex Hospital early the following morning.

That night, with my journalist friend, I returned to the McGills' flat. Brendan's condition had deteriorated and he appeared to be unconscious. During the day, in his few waking moments, Kathleen McGill had tried to feed him with spoonfuls of egg and milk, but he had vomited them up immediately and pleaded for a drink of whiskey instead. Worried and alarmed, we sat by his bedside. I do not recall how the conversation started, but I remember saying that Brendan had once told me Parnell pronounced his name with the emphasis on the first rather than the last syllable.

'That's what my father always said, and he should know,' came a voice from the bed.

In Brendan's own words, I knew Aughrim was not lost.

Although he slept fitfully in the night, by morning he was considerably better and began to take notice of what was happening around him. I explained the position regarding the airline companies and told him he was going into Middlesex Hospital, and he accepted the situation placidly. He did not want to be carried out of the flat on a stretcher, however, and as he looked so dishevelled and grubby, we set about smartening him up. After we had shaved, washed and dressed him, he sat on the bed drained of what little strength he had by the effort of it all.

I do not know what prompted me, unless if was lack of sleep and a total weariness of seeing him reduce his mind and his body to a flabby amoeba-like substance, but I heard myself telling him sharply that he was going into hospital on the National Health, though I failed to see why we should pay for him to get better just to do the same thing all over again as soon as he was.

My harshness surprised and shamed me but it appeared to put new life into Brendan. Heaving himself to his feet and forcing his body to its full height, he said he did not blame me for the outburst. He accepted the fact that he was very ill, appreciated that everything was being done to get him better, and determined that very day to begin to do something about it for himself. And to prove the truth in his words, would I now please telephone David Astor and tell him the same?

I knew David Astor only in his capacity as editor of the *Observer*, and was unaware that Brendan had any personal connections with him. To me, he was a member of the press, however illustrious, and the idea of giving the *Observer* an exclusive story did not please me at all. 'Ah, Brendan,' I answered sadly, 'haven't you had enough publicity? Do you really want the world to know every move you make?'

His face wrinkled by folds of irritation, he explained crossly that he wanted nothing of the sort, and didn't I realise that he would want to avail himself of David Astor's offer to help cure

him of alcoholism? One of the many difficulties of becoming
Brendan's friend was not only that he expected you to read his
mind, but also to possess the ability to know, without being told,
what had transpired in your absence.

Infuriated, I asked no further questions but from David Astor's
response to my telephone call, at least *he* was not perplexed.

Joe and I rode in the ambulance with Brendan to Middlesex
Hospital, and Joe calmed his fears about being incarcerated. In
the meantime I was beginning to have doubts about the motives
of my journalist friend. I had already thanked him profusely for
all the help he'd given, but although he had the chance to return
to his own way of living, he refused to do so, preferring to follow
us in his car. I did not cherish the thought that perhaps I, in the
end, would be responsible for the details of Brendan's illness appearing in print.

At the hospital Brendan, like a child and as insecure, insisted
that we go with him to the ward and stay as long as was permitted. This time I was adamant that only Joe and I should accompany him and we took the lift to the third floor, walked along
a corridor in silence except for the clipping of my high-heel shoes
on the stone floor, and through glass doors at the end which
led to a large public ward. Brendan's bed was at the other end of
the room, and while our entrance naturally aroused the interest
of the patients, they gave no intimation that they recognised the
face of their new inmate. Indeed, he would have been hard to
recognise. Shot to pieces by alcohol and bodily pain, he was
trembling as much from fear for himself as of his surroundings
and without a single layer of protective covering for the sensitivity
of his nature. We helped him into bed and he begged Joe for one
more tot. When Joe refused, he flung back the bedclothes, raised
himself to his feet and charged down the ward like a man in
search of his salvation. A nurse gently brought him back, while
another more elderly one gave him an injection, and he fell on to
his bed defeated and deflated.

We decided to go, using the excuse that I had to meet
my daughter, Diana, from school, for Brendan had a great affec-

tion for children and would never wittingly cause them distress. His interest was aroused at once, and heaving himself up to sit comfortably against the pillows which were propped behind his head, he promised to do what the nurses asked if I would bring Diana in to meet him.

My journalist friend was waiting in Admittance and hurried forward on seeing us, anxious to know the end of the saga, but he was fussed and bothered because he had run out of small change to make the final phone-call.

'It's true, then?' I asked him coldly. He seemed astonished that I could think it would be otherwise. He had sold the entire story to a daily newspaper. I went home in utter disgust with myself for my lack of discretion.

I was invited the next evening to a cocktail party at the offices of the *Spectator* in Gower Street. My inclination was to hide my head for ever. From the moment I entered the crowded room, I received, alternately, rebuffs and praise and conceived an idea of the torments of Hell. I did not protest, but persecuted myself further by allowing the offenders to think that my character was as base as their fury or congratulations were deserved. Later, I visited Brendan and as I walked the length of his ward, I felt his eyes scrutinising my every step until, by the time I had reached his bed, he was regarding me with hostile suspicion.

'Have you seen this?' and he waved in front of my face the newspaper in which the offending article had appeared. I lowered my eyes and bit my lower lip as I felt the hot tears scald my eyeballs.

'Did you know it was going to be in there?' he asked again, but softer. Steadying my voice, I told him quite truthfully that it was only the night before that I realised the situation, and by then it was too late to do anything about it. I apologised most sincerely, related my discomfort at the *Spectator* party and emphasised that I neither asked nor expected him to forgive me. All the while his face interrogated mine, but when I had finished speaking his anger of a moment before had dissolved in a mixture of pity and understanding.

'You'll not be apologising to me. I would have done just the same,' and he lay back on his pillows and slid down under the bedclothes as if this action would divorce him from the whole nasty business.

'It was my fault, Brendan,' I replied, pulling back the sheet from his head. 'It was naive, ingenuous, and stupid of me to confide in a man who makes his living by writing for the newspapers. I put an exclusive story in his hands.'

He sat bolt upright in the bed, pivoted his big head to an angle of thirty degrees and grinned broadly. 'I would not be wanting you to lose your simplicity,' he said. 'It rather becomes you.'

As soon as Brendan was fit enough, David Astor visited him and together they discussed the various cures for alcoholics, although the decision was left entirely to Brendan as to which method be considered most likely to succeed. David, at the time I think, favoured Alcoholics Anonymous, but while Brendan was extremely anxious to accept the help offered him, he knew he was not the character to stand up in a crowded room and bare his soul, an essential part of this particular treatment.

There was the added complication too that Dr. Nabarro, in whose care he had been placed at Middlesex Hospital, wanted him to enter the psychiatric wing where he would still be under the strictest medical supervision, but David did not favour the idea and felt he could not be a party to it. Obviously Brendan could not serve two masters, but he failed to appreciate that both masters in this case were genuinely sincere in their desire to see him well, and how he achieved this was relatively unimportant. Quite wrongly, he believed he had been placed in the unfortunate position of having to offend one of them.

Dr. Nabarro's position was a tenuous one. He had already carried out a series of preliminary tests on Brendan, the results of which had made him doubt whether his physical condition was entirely due to excessive drinking, and while he was certain Brendan would live longer if he gave it up, he was not sure he would ever enjoy old age. The doctor's first consideration was to get Brendan well physically, and having been warned of his habit of discharging himself on the most slender of pretexts he did not welcome any interference which might upset his patient.

There the matter was left in abeyance, but after Beatrice had come over from Dublin to see Brendan and had spoken herself with David Astor, Brendan made up his mind that he would place himself in David's hands, while he still had the common sense to want to be cured. The official note was given to Dr. Nabarro who accepted it without the slightest resentment.

I agree that David Astor should supervise medical treatment for me and I authorise him to prepare such measures as he sees fit. April 2nd, 1960. (Sgd) BRENDAN BEHAN

David immediately set the wheels in motion in readiness for the day when Brendan would be discharged as medically fit. He approached Dr. Glatt of St. Bernard's Hospital, Southall, and asked his advice on the most suitable hospital or nursing home for an alcoholic of Brendan's type who would not respond to any method comparable to Alcoholics Anonymous. Dr. Glatt suggested Dr. McKeefe of Warlingham Park in Surrey, a large private house standing in its own grounds and situated not too far from London should Brendan feel the need for city lights.

Dr. McKeefe had read a great deal about Brendan in the newspapers, had been interested in his case from afar and was agreeable to accepting him as his patient, but only on the condition that they met first and were temperamentally attuned. As I visited Brendan daily, it was left to me to arrange the meeting at a time convenient for them both. Brendan had, of course, been kept fully informed of every development, but as his health improved I detected a certain disinclination on his part to listen when I mentioned the subject, and I trod warily as a result.

True to my word, I had taken Diana to see him and though, to begin with, she was a little in awe of his reputation, it was not long before his love of children and his ability to put everyone at ease had removed her shyness. Before she left, he signed his name on an Irish pound note which, after protest, he persuaded her to take. Nothing short of starvation would ever induce her to spend it. It was the start of a touching relationship.

Brendan's health improved rapidly and each day he was allowed to get up for longer periods at a time. Fully dressed he would wander about the hospital without taking advantage of the freedom which this offered him. He was never short of visitors and to my knowledge he neither asked for, nor tried to bribe anyone to bring him in a drink. On the rare occasions when visitors were not allowed, he would pull up a chair and sit at the bedside of other patients, and I was told by more than one of them that his lightheartedness and his effervescent personality turned the dreaded fading daylight into the moment they were waiting for.

Throughout his convalescence, I had made several allusions to his expected meeting with Dr. McKeefe, but Brendan always managed to manœuvre my words up a sidetrack and I had not been able to arrange anything definite. Unable to defer the matter longer, on his last day in hospital I decided to be more direct in my approach. I was packing up his belongings into a selection of battered cardboard boxes when he blew down my ear that he wanted to talk to me privately in the anteroom outside. Assuming that he was going to bring up himself the question of Dr. McKeefe, I followed eagerly. The incredibility of Brendan was something I had come to expect, but his opening remark surpassed my preparation for it.

'Some people call me a genius,' he began, embarrassed. 'What does this mean?'

'Oh, I don't know, Brendan,' I answered quickly, to hide my confusion. 'Someone, I suppose, who can make us believe we are seeing, hearing and feeling for the first time in our lives.'

He thought on my words and then spoke again.

'Do you think I'm a genius?' He was still embarrassed.

'I'm not here solely because I like the colour of your eyes or the curls in your hair,' I replied, laughing.

He grinned back at me. 'Well, tell me this and tell me no more. Do you ever think of me as a man?' His face wrinkled in puckish delight as awkwardly I shifted the weight of my body from one leg to the other to try to hide my discomfort at being asked the question.

'You don't catch old birds with chaff, Brendan,' I said finally. 'I don't know about you as a man, but I do know you've got a genius for drowning your genius under gallons of liquid.' Before he could say more, I asked him bluntly when he was going to see Dr. McKeefe.

He was waiting for my question. Without a second's hesitation he replied that he was not seeing anyone. He was going home to Beatrice.

'I want to try and work this out in my own way, and I'll write and swim and go for walks again as I used to do. If I fail, perhaps I can come back and ask Dr. McWhateverhisnameis, if he will take me then.'

I knew better than to argue with him; the cure could only be effective with Brendan's complete co-operation. As I left, my footsteps, heavy as my heart, pounded on the stone floor, not so much with irritation at Brendan's stupidity but more from the frustration of knowing that the plans and hopes of the last weeks had come to nothing. I do not know what prompted Brendan to refuse the treatment, but there was no doubt that he genuinely believed that he could manage to beat the drink bug on his own.

It is all part of the sadness that this time he so nearly did. Apart from one lapse in America, he did not touch a drop of alcohol for nine full months.

IX

AMERICA: TRIUMPH AND DISASTER

Almost immediately after his return to Dublin, Brendan took Beatrice on a rambling tour of the towns in north-west Ireland. The prolonged period away from alcohol helped him to adjust to the new aspect of himself, and he now had a reason for living. While publicly he remained reticent, he was delighted that he had presumably found a way to come to terms with the monster in his back yard, and although he recognised that his reputation as an outrageous uprooter of protocol had taken him more quickly to the top of the literary mountain, now he was determined to be appreciated solely for his achievements on a Remington. And it was not short stories that he had in mind. But his flimsy hold on victory frightened him, and he wanted no more battles with his avid thirst lest he be bulldozed, not only down the mountain, but into six feet of earth at the bottom of it.

Sensibly he remained away from the immediate temptations of his friends in Dublin, but his continued absence gave rise to rumours that he could no longer allow himself the luxury of sitting in a pub, a ridiculous assumption and without a grain of truth. Public houses were Brendan's life-blood, not for the drink that they sold but for the people who frequented them, and it was upon these characters that he based much of his writing material, particularly in the articles which he wrote for the *Irish Press*. Added to which people were always his chief interest in life, for he needed their touch more than most of us. He could manage by

a word to bring together easily the oddest assortment of characters. He did not keep out of the pubs when he was on the wagon;
he probably frequented them more, and when he was sober the
customers crowded round him with the fervour of disciples.

While he was away, Brendan learned that he had been invited
to America for the opening on Broadway of *The Hostage* in
September, and he came back to Dublin to obtain the necessary visa; a feat he accomplished with extraordinary ease considering the previous attitude of the U.S. immigration authorities.

For several weeks, he had had the transcript of the tapes for
Brendan Behan's Island, and although Iain Hamilton had written repeatedly to plead with him to complete the editing, his letters had remained unanswered and each time he talked to him,
either by telephone or personally in London, Brendan had been
evasive. Iain decided to fly over to Dublin and sit him down
with the manuscript before he disappeared 3,000 miles across the
Atlantic.

Brendan was delighted to see him, but was too excited over
his impending American visit to concentrate for prolonged
periods on the business of editing a book. He admitted that he
had been working on a new play, but excused the priority as
being one nearer to his heart. Iain returned to England hardly
cheered by Brendan's promise that he would take the manuscript
with him to the United States where under Beatrice's persuasive
eye, the editing would be done without fail and posted back
directly.

A few days before he left, I telephoned Brendan, partly to tell
him that the paper-back rights of *Borstal Boy* had been sold to
Corgi books for £5,000, but also to warn him of the pitfalls he
would be likely to meet through the overwhelming hospitality of
the American people. Hundreds of acquaintances had warned
him of this, he assured me, and for that reason he did not think he
would accept the many lecture tours offered him as they were
purported to be pretty hard boozing expeditions.

He was pleased to hear about *Borstal Boy,* but was much
happier about the progress he was making on *Richard's Cork*

Leg. 'Mind you,' he stressed, 'the sixty-four pages of manuscript are no more than notes for it as yet.' It was set in wartime Dublin and raked in everything from the Spanish Civil War to brothel-keeping. The heroine of the piece was a young girl called Deirdre, and it was at this stage of the conversation that I exploded.

'Brendan, it's *the catacombs* all over again. Are you really going to stretch one plot to the lengths of a novel and a play?'

For a moment I thought the line had gone dead, but before I could get back to the operator, Brendan was agreeing in a mere whisper that that *was* his intention, but could see no harm in it as the titles were quite different. The title he had chosen for his play was not without interest. When James Joyce was in Paris, in the early thirties, he wrote a play around a character called Richard, and it was rejected because the sponsors thought it was too gloomy. He never submitted it again, but confided in Sylvia Beach, Joyce's original publisher in Paris, that perhaps if he had jollied the story up a bit and given Richard a cork leg, his play might have been accepted.

'Now I have nothing against jollying things up,' Brendan gave a short, half-suppressed laugh, 'so in honour of James Joyce, I am calling my play *Richard's Cork Leg*.'

In fatherly fashion, he asked me to tell the press that it was about sex, religion and politics as nothing else was worth considering anyway. He believed that it might make people angry and hoped that it would, and emphasised that he did not need to tell me how much he enjoyed stirring up trouble. But he liked to make people think too. He did not know if he would stir anything up in America, but he had heard that there was some doubt in the minds of the American branch of the I.R.A. as to whether they would accept a charity performance of *The Hostage*, or bomb the theatre instead. He followed his instructions by a peal of song, 'It's my old Irish tomb, I'll be in there soon,' and while I did not attach any great significance to the words, he assured me that this was only a line of verse from his new play, and not his swan-song.

'But if it wasn't for you, Joe, Kathleen, David and a few more like you,' he said, 'it might very well have been.'

He did not hear my reply for he was hurriedly telling me he would be back for Christmas and would send me a postcard of Marilyn Monroe to keep me in trim. Then the line went dead. This time he had replaced his receiver.

Few people believed that Brendan would remain on the wagon in America, and he flew into a New York which had been bracing itself to witness at first hand the reality behind his colourful reputation. As soon as he and Beatrice had been processed through customs, they were met by a barrage of reporters, photographers and TV cameramen anxious, in colloquial language, to 'catch the scene.' Straight away they were taken into the airport bar where, for an hour, Brendan drank milk and posed for the click of the cameras and replied to the bombardment of questions until he gave up on the grounds that he wasn't a politician; he only had one face, and he wasn't a calf; he could not swallow another glass of milk. But he made his point. He intended that his American visit should be dry.

It was inevitable that Brendan should fall in love with New York, for it was nearer to his dream of the Never-Never-Land than he would ever find elsewhere: a city which never appears to go to sleep, and a fancy fair of brilliant lights where at any time of the day or night he could walk without fear of being lonely. His restless and inquisitive personality found a thousand avenues to explore, and always a friendly face to accompany him, to sit and enjoy a cup of coffee or a glass of orange juice whenever he felt the need.

'I think New York is a fabulous place,' he said in a broadcast shortly after his arrival. 'I think it ought to be investigated by a committee—the whole town, the twenty million people in it— for being jolly.'

In a letter to *The New Yorker*, he made a list of the things he most wanted to do:

I would like to see the Rockefellers' paintings by Diego Rivers.

I would also like to see in New York the Rockefeller who said that he would like to see me in Ireland. I would like to see and pay my respects to Big Daddy Burl Ives, Lee Tracy, Studs Lonigan, Billy Graham, Tom Lehrer, the Empire State Building, the Saint Patrick's Day Parade on Fifth Avenue, Costello's saloon on Third Avenue, Robert Frost, Marilyn Monroe, back and front, the most unforgettable character you know, the Mafia, the Mizrachi, the Daughters of the American Revolution, the Ivy League, Niagara Falls, Nick the Greek, the Governor's pitch in Albany, William Faulkner, the Yankee Stadium, a love nest, a hot dog stand, a jam session, the Golden Gloves, and the candidates for the presidential election.

Brendan had arrived in New York in the middle of the election campaign and naturally, as a fellow-countryman, he was ardently pro John F. Kennedy. At the frequent parties to which he was invited, the conversation usually drifted to the merits and demerits of the two candidates concerned, and Brendan's set piece was to tell the amused guests that they would never get back into the old country if they didn't vote for Kennedy.

It was inevitable too, that the Americans should fall in love with Brendan. Unlike Dylan Thomas, who had lived up to, and strengthened, the legend which preceded his coming, they were introduced to a Brendan who had not been drinking for six months, and showed no signs of doing so. And contrary to popular opinion, lack of alcohol did not depress him, nor lessen his ability to fountain his inexhaustible fund of stories and *bons mots*. Even in his last months of trauma, drink only served to push him further from tangibility and certainly did not cheer him up.

But on this first trip, his hosts and their guests came under the spell of his personality. His riotous conversation and his bursts of song which cascaded over them made him a one-man cabaret show to which they listened with devotion.

The Hostage hit New York by storm. Under Joan Littlewood's direction and with most of the Theatre Workshop cast, it opened at the Cort Theatre on September 20th, 1960. In the tradition of Broadway openings, after the show Brendan made the pilgrimage to Sardi's restaurant, where he modestly commented that the first-nighters had 'seemed to like it.' Giving his well-wishers a happy toothless grin and ignoring the champagne corks as they popped on every side, he moved to Downey's Steak House on Eighth Avenue where a party of dual purpose was in progress for the two best-known Irishmen in New York. Frederick Boland had just been elected president of the UN General Assembly; Brendan shared the honours with him. Until the early hours of the morning, a tide of champagne and stout enveloped the celebrating Irish and the cast of *The Hostage* and their friends, but Brendan remained with his glass of soda-water. When the early copies of the newspapers arrived, he read the reviews of his play. The Six Butchers of Broadway, as they are traditionally named, confirmed what everybody knew: *The Hostage*, which had run for two years in London, was a hit in New York. 'A grab-bag of wonderful and dreadful prizes,' said Howard Taubman in the *New York Times*. 'A man of extraordinary talent,' wrote the *New York Post*, while Walter Kerr in the *Herald Tribune* described the opening as 'a wild night and a welcome one.' If it was not the sort of wild night usually associated with Brendan, it was one he was never to forget.

The pressures imposed on the unknown and the inexperienced in America are considerable. But for a world-famous playwright, there are no scales large enough to weigh them. Iain Hamilton, who was in New York shortly after the opening of *The Hostage*, stayed in the same hotel as Brendan and Beatrice, and he told me the floor of their suite at the Algonquin was carpeted with unopened mail. Primarily, he was interested in extracting the manuscript of *Brendan Behan's Island*, but he found it almost impossible to catch Brendan on his own for he was surrounded by publishers, agents, and magazine and newspaper editors who were anxious to sign him up. For $3,000, he contracted to produce for G. P. Putnam a photographic book on himself and each illustration was to be captioned by Behan witticisms; and he promised Bernard Geis that, in return for $12,000, he would write a sequel to his autobiographical *Borstal Boy*.

With no head for business and probably less interest, Brendan ignored the fact that one day he would have to honour these contracts, along with the small consideration that he was already legally bound, through the publication of *Borstal Boy*, to offer his next book to Hutchinson and Alfred Knopf. For his plays, however, he remained consistently faithful to Methuen and Grove Press. Beatrice did her best to cope with the entanglement of appointments and endless correspondence on her own, but the task was too much for one person.

The lionising was beginning to have its effect, and Brendan's determination to stay on a milk diet weakened. One morning he and Beatrice quarrelled over a minor domestic matter which appeared to sour his humour. Later they were lunching with two friends at the Monte Rosa restaurant, next door to the Cort Theatre, when Brendan ordered the waiter to bring a bottle of champagne. Beatrice objected vehemently, but Brendan overruled her with such force that the waiter did not have to be asked again. For the rest of the dreadful afternoon he sat drinking eight bottles of champagne, one after the other, out of a tumbler.

Maddened by alcohol after so long a period of abstinence, he charged into the theatre where the house was packed and the curtain had already risen. Lurching on to the stage and shouting, 'My show is good, and if you don't believe me, I don't give a damn,' he gave a repeat performance of the shameful episode at Wyndham's Theatre in London, and he brought down both the curtain and the house. This time, the repercussions were more serious. Whilst the audience enjoyed Brendan's impromptu appearance, Perry Bruskin, the stage manager, smashed a photographer's camera in order to keep the story out of the press and was arrested for assault. It was Brendan's only lapse, and appalled by the harm he might have done to Perry Bruskin, he did not repeat it.

Shortly before he sailed home on the *Saxonia*, Brendan had agreed to return in the spring to compère a series of jazz concerts for $3,000 a week, which were planned to take place in numerous cities across North America and parts of Canada too. A mad idea at best, and a gruelling test of stamina, it was hardly the assignment which a writer should accept. Added to which, Brendan still had not touched the manuscript of *Brendan Behan's Island*. *Richard's Cork Leg* was only in draft, and he was committed to Putnam and Geis for two further books.

To do him justice, when he first returned to Ireland he did resume working. Despite the fact that he had been invited officially to John Kennedy's inauguration, an invitation of which he was inordinately proud, he did not accept it, partly because Beatrice felt, and he was inclined to agree with her, that he might not be able to celebrate on soda-water, but more, I believe, because he sensed the changing man inside him, and was resisting the adulation which fostered the change.

Joan Littlewood flew to Dublin to encourage Brendan to complete *Richard's Cork Leg*. She wanted to stage it in London in the spring, but when she read the draft she was not convinced that the play would be ready for production so soon and felt it was lacking in plot. Brendan was disappointed but hid his chagrin by telling a friend that he was busy searching the *Encyclopaedia Britannica* for one. He began to translate it into Gaelic, and hastily adapting it as a one-act play, *A Fine Day in the Graveyard*, he submitted it to Gael Linn, the Gaelic organisation who had originally commissioned *An Giall*. This was a fatal mistake. Believing that everything which carried his name was bound to be a success, Brendan forgot that Balzac and Conrad, to name only two fairly experienced and well-known literary figures, used to rewrite their work about ten times, and then cover the galley proofs with corrections. Gael Linn informed him that extensive revisions would have to be done before they would accept it, and he bitterly resented their audacity at criticising his writing. I am certain that in his heart Brendan concurred absolutely with the rejection, but this would only make him more distressed with his own surface conceit.

At any rate he fell off the water-wagon, and the impact was such that it involved him in a fight in a Dublin shop, cost him two black eyes, two appearances in court and a fine. And from then on, apart from isolated patches like scattered showers in April, he remained in varying degrees of intoxication until the day he died.

From the beginning, Beatrice had been against Brendan's return to the States. Now that he was drinking again, she became even more so and accompanied him knowing full well that, in a country which encouraged him to publicise a false version of himself, the task of reminding him that he was not a tin god was going to be twice as difficult. I do not intend to enlarge in detail on the events of his second trip, except to mark it chronologically as the end of Brendan as his true friends enjoyed him.

Banned from taking part in the St. Patrick's Day Parade in New York as a 'disorderly person,' Brendan crossed the border for the pre-Broadway run in Toronto of the jazz show, *Impulse*, which he was supposed to compère. After a single appearance, he was arrested in his hotel where he had created a rumpus because the management would not obey his order to send up a bottle of whiskey to his room. He assaulted two detectives, spent a night in the cells, was released on bail of $100 (which he borrowed from Bernard Geis) and the jazz revue folded. He was in another fight after belligerently telling a native: 'Ireland will put a shillelagh into orbit, Israel will put a matzo ball into orbit, and Liechtenstein will put a postage stamp into orbit, before you Canadians put up a mouse.'

But instead of appearing in court he had an alcoholic seizure and was gravely ill in hospital with a diabetic and heart condition. In two months he had managed to destroy the good of nine months' sobriety. When his case finally came up, instead of returning to Berney Geis the money he had borrowed, he sent him the fragmentary manuscript of *the catacombs*, hastily renamed in a gesture of appeasement, *Confessions of an Irish Rebel*, the autobiographical sequel to *Borstal Boy*.

The pattern repeated itself throughout the eleven thousand miles he travelled across the Union. In Hollywood he was arrested for disturbing the peace when refused a drink in a pizza parlour and went to gaol again. He suffered a second alcoholic seizure and was once more admitted to hospital.

But the most serious aspect of his second visit to America was that he now believed his behaviour, however unworthy, should be condoned and he both demanded and expected adulation and acceptance. From henceforth his periods of genuine intent to pull himself together would be few and far between.

X

TO CURE OR NOT TO CURE

Brendan's return to Dublin was heralded by the statement that he was 'off the gargle—a retired alcoholic,' but distance could not change his new conception of himself. Very soon his name was in the newspapers again, and he was up in Court for drunk and disorderly behaviour. I wrote to Beatrice to ask if there was any way in which I could help.

27th September, 1961

Dear Rae, Very many thanks for your kind thoughts, and your letter, which I was very pleased to get. These days, concern about Brendan and myself is a rare thing—I mean genuine and constructive. At the time I received your letter I had just got Brendan into a nursing home by ambulance in a state of complete collapse. He stayed two days—and then did his usual trick of running out behind the doctor's back. Ten days later, B.B. is off again on the beer. He is today still bashing away regardless, money flying in all directions. Perhaps if he comes out of this bash—say in about ten days' time, David Astor would write him a letter 'playing it cool' as the Americans say—about considering a cure, or treatment—without directly mentioning it. You know the sort of letter I mean, and as Brendan has I know a high regard for him it might have some effect. I don't really know how to manage him any more. I just leave the house when he starts and live with my parents as much as I can to avoid rows. Then when his friends (?) get tired of him he is sent rolling back to me in a state of collapse. I hope you will come to Dublin soon. Brendan I think intends to head for warmer climes this winter—whether I go or not —depends. My very best love and thanks, from Beatrice.

The letter saddened me immeasurably. Through all the trials
and tribulations, Brendan and Beatrice had always been happy
together but the bad in Brendan was slowly swallowing up the
good and their respect for one another was affected accordingly.
More than anyone, Brendan needed the stability of a successful
marriage, and I was disturbed by the thoughts of where it all
might end.

David Astor was upset by Beatrice's letter too, and generously
wrote at once to Brendan:

6th October, 1961

Dear Brendan,

It seems years since I last saw you and I am very sorry not to
have written before. I gather from newspaper reports that you
have travelled a lot, but one learns little from these reports. If
you ever feel inclined to take up again the question of attempting
a serious re-conditioning programme here, you know I would be
as keen as ever to assist in any way. This time I would see that we
avoided the mistake of the last attempt, when only some kind of
group treatment could be obtained at short notice. Given a little
time, I could find out the best possible way of going about the
problem. I have just come back from visiting Warsaw, where I
was at a conference of journalists attended by the editors of
Pravda and *Izvestia*. I think you would find Warsaw very congenial—it has a wonderful atmosphere of audacity and friendliness. Do let me know if you are ever over here with time to spare.

With best wishes, David

For several days the letter lay unopened on the hall chest at
Cúiz, but each morning Beatrice would place it in a strategic
position at the top of the mounting pile. At an opportune moment, she mentioned casually that it might not be a bad idea if,
some time, Brendan attended to his correspondence. Disgruntled
by being asked to do anything, he stumbled out to the hall where
he picked up a few of the letters and aimlessly flipped through
them. He noticed the word *Observer* printed on the back of the
envelope, and putting the others down he opened it. Like a
miracle, David's letter worked. He agreed to go to London and
accept his offer of assistance. David immediately set about

making the necessary arrangements. He wrote to me:

11th October, 1961

Dear Rae,

About Brendan, I have got the medical correspondent of this paper, Dr. Abraham Marcus, to go into the question of what best could be done for him. Apparently, the best man on curing alcoholism *is* Dr. Glatt. He has long been following Brendan's career from afar and hoping that some day he might get an opportunity to help him. To be quite ready to cope, it is necessary that Dr. Glatt should know as much as possible in advance about Brendan's physical condition. This would enable him to get the most suitable type of accommodation and the appropriate kind of consultant lined up in readiness. It seems to me that the best way of going about all this would be for you to get in touch direct with Dr. Glatt so that you can keep him informed of the present situation and of anything that may develop. If you introduce yourself as Brendan's pal and say that I asked you to do so, I think you will find Dr. Glatt keen to co-operate.

Yours, David

I gave Dr. Glatt, to the best of my ability, all that I knew of Brendan's case history, and after repeated talks with David it was decided that a nursing-home in the East End of London—an area of which Brendan was particularly fond—would provide the best accommodation for this type of treatment. Not only was Brendan pleased to go along with these arrangements, but he was in a hurry to begin the cure. He was worried, however, that the press might come to hear about it, and I gave him my word that I would do everything in my power to prevent sensational publicity. Whilst self-advertisement appealed to him in far more degrading forms, there was once again this feeling of shame that he was actually taking steps to modify his drinking.

Quietly he slipped into London with Beatrice, and I met them at Euston station. I had not seen him since his American trip and I was so shocked by the change in his appearance that I found it difficult to cover up my alarm. His face was puffy, his skin blotched with purple and grey, his lips painfully cracked, and his eyes, which had sunk into his head, were without a vestige of expression. He went through the motions of being pleased to see me, but rather in the manner of a mechanical toy which, at the turn of a key, wags a rigid tail or raises an arm stiffly to attention. I tried to persuade myself that he was probably petrified at having to go back into hospital, but in my heart I knew it was something more serious.

Leaving their luggage at the station, we taxied to the York Minster public house in Soho, where Brendan wanted to lunch before being admitted. He ordered something special, but when it arrived he picked at it, complaining, and ate practically nothing. None of us spoke much, for our separate worries prevented light conversation, but when Beatrice left the table for a few moments, Brendan burst out his long tale of woe. He wanted to return to America, he said. There he was understood, but Beatrice did not like the idea. She would rather he remained in Ireland an invalid. I interrupted to remind him that as long as he craved for publicity, there was little hope of him recovering his health. Treatment in hospital now was exactly what he needed.

There was no time for me to tell him more before Beatrice rejoined us. Without warning, Brendan suddenly announced that he was not going to bury himself in the East End of London unless Beatrice remained with him all day and all night. Dumbfounded, her eyes questioned me as to what she should reply, and framing her answer with care, she told Brendan angrily that he was just making excuses for he knew his request was an impossible one. All at once I became determined that Brendan would not disrupt, so easily, our schemes to get him well, at any rate physically. Excusing myself from the table, I telephoned the matron of the nursing-home to see if she could make an exception in Brendan's case and allow his wife to be with him. To my amazement she agreed, but added the proviso, 'apart from actually sleeping in his room.' When I returned, Brendan and Beatrice were scowling at one another across the table, and when I relayed the matron's words, Brendan's scowl deepened. He was furious with me. For half an hour I played cat and mouse with him, spoiling each fresh excuse before he had collected it, until finally he played the trump card. He did not think this type of cure was right for him and there was no point in attempting it. He would like to make another effort for himself.

Beatrice had little to say throughout the drive back to Euston station, but after we had piled the luggage in the taxi and Brendan had decided on a hotel, her patience, strained beyond endurance, could no longer be contained. Did Brendan ever consider, she asked, what life was like for her under these circumstances? If he was not mindful of his own well-being, perhaps he might consider, sometimes, the state of her health. She was sick and tired of carting him in and out of hospital. My sympathy went out to her, but in a flash Brendan retorted that she was not forced to live with him; he would settle for a fifty-fifty split if that was agreeable to her.

Benumbed, I witnessed the rising tensions and prodded my brain to come up with some diversion. By sheer luck I was successful. For the rest of the taxi-ride to the Holborn hotel, a discussion took place as to who would be the best person to give David Astor the gloomy news. Calm and soft-spoken now, each of us explained our obvious reluctance to be chosen for the job, and it was not until the pair of them had registered as guests and we had trodden the puce-coloured stair-carpet to their sparsely furnished bedroom, that I decided, as Brendan had put us in this unenviable position, it was up to him to carry the can. Like a naughty school-boy waiting to be reprimanded, Brendan picked up the telephone, and although tactfully Beatrice and I busied ourselves talking, we could not help over-hearing his plea to David for 'just one more try.'

He remained in London for about a week and did make serious efforts to steady up, but he was too low for overnight reparation and continually feeling wretched depressed him. At his suggestion we went to Frank Norman's *Fings Ain't Wot They Used T'Be*, now playing in the West End, and while he enjoyed it as much as he was capable of enjoying anything in his present state, he was fidgety and unhappy at being hemmed in. During the interval, we sat talking in a pub, mostly about Eden Phillpotts, for whom Brendan had great admiration, not on account of his plays or his books which he had not read, but because he had survived to the ripe age of ninety-eight. Eden Phillpotts had died in the previous year and Brendan was fascinated by my story of meeting him in his home outside Exeter. I had gone there with John Betjeman who was to interview the old man for the B.B.C. television programme, *Panorama*, the only public interview of any sort he gave. I asked him about the younger generation of writers, really having in mind John Osborne and 'the angry young men' school of authors, but Eden Phillpotts was adamant that L. A. G. Strong was the most promising he had read. He grumbled continually that he was no longer able to see and was having to go into hospital shortly for the removal of a cataract. However, during tea, his wife accidentally knocked one of the tiny, delicately cut cucumber sandwiches to the floor, and while she did not notice her mistake, her husband, who was a considerable distance from the table, boomed out: 'Robina, you have dropped a sandwich. Kindly pick it up.'

It was the only time during this week that I heard Brendan laugh freely. When the time came to return to the theatre, he was reluctant to do so, and we lingered on for a while before he left with Beatrice for a long night's sleep.

Early next afternoon, he came into the office where he spoke to Iain about the editing of *Brendan Behan's Island*, but his bored attitude towards the book alarmed us. Iain suggested that perhaps an outside editor night be persuaded to tackle the job for him, and while initially Brendan was overjoyed at being relieved of his responsibility, the possibility occured to him that a member of his family might be chosen for the task, and he became unreasonably upset. Instead of voicing aloud his thoughts, he left Iain bewildered as he charged out of the office, dragging me with him and into the Mason's Arms where he promptly ordered a whiskey. Propping himself on the counter, he mumbled that all the world was against him, that his writing was being mutilated without his consent and that it was no longer even considered necessary to invite an author to the film première of his play.

After many setbacks, *The Quare Fellow* had finally materialised as a film and was showing at the Rialto Cinema in Leicester Square. For reasons which I never quite understood, both Blondefilm and C.B.S., who earlier had been squabbling over the rights, had backed out, and for £2,000 they had been bought by Arthur Dreifus. At the time, Dreifus was under contract to Columbia, but when he failed to persuade them to make a film, he had had to wait a further two years before an independent company, backed by Bryanston Films, Pathé in America and the Irish Film Finance Corporation, agreed to accept the project. Originally, Brendan had been asked to write the script but had failed to do so by the required time and Arthur Dreifus had written it himself, but with additional dialogue by James McKenna, author of *The Scattering*. Unfortunately, the film version bore little resemblance to Brendan's play, for most of the action was set outside the prison walls and sex had been injected between the young warder, Crimmin, and the condemned man's wife.

As Brendan moaned and fumed about the changes, I began to convince him that the same thing would happen to *Brendan Behan's Island*, if he did not do the editing himself. If only he felt well, he said, things might be different. He had tried taking nothing but tea and milk, and this hadn't worked. Now he took nothing but abuse. Perhaps if I returned to Dublin with him, together we might be able to knock the book into shape. The suggestion did not please me. I did not feel I should have to importune him to work when this was simply a matter of his having sufficient will-power to sit down at a table and reconstruct his own words. Added to which, I knew nothing about the history of Ireland, and my only use would be as a body-guard standing by to remind him of what he had to do, or worse, a kill-joy hanger-on to listen to his drunken chatterings which both infuriated and saddened me. While I still enjoyed his company and was glad to do anything to modulate the alcoholic tenor of his life, I was certain that our relationship would be damaged if I allowed my role as midwife to become one of wetnurse. Moreover, I had my job to consider; there were other authors on the Hutchinson list who needed publicity.

Brendan understood. When I said good night he said he would surprise me yet, for he intended to edit the book himself before the month was very much older.

I am convinced that, had it not been for Perry Bruskin's letter informing him that *The Hostage* was opening in the Village in New York at One Sheridan Square, Brendan would not have gone back on his resolution to remain in Ireland and finish his book. As it was, the excuse came too readily to hand. With his head fired with burning emotions, laced with 70 per cent proof spirit, he could only think of the renewed publicity. Alone, he flew to America.

The visit was disastrous. Through the usual friends, Beatrice heard of Brendan's every move. He was rarely sober, had been thrown out of the Algonquin and the Bristol Hotel, and was now living in an apartment with two mutual friends. She was desperate, for she did not think that either of his companions would put up with him in his present condition, and then he would be out in the street and left to die in the gutter. At once she wrote to Perry Bruskin to implore him to use physical force if necessary to get Brendan home on the next plane, and she begged me to telephone him and use my powers of persuasion also. At first I was not anxious to comply with her wishes, for mediating between man and wife is always a hazardous occupation. But I was worried too by the truth in what she said, and I did have very good reasons of my own for getting in touch with him.

Iain was leaving Hutchinson to become editor of the *Spectator,* and he suggested that I should edit *Brendan Behan's Island* with the help of Valentin Iremonger, whose knowledge of Ireland was certainly comparable to Brendan's. It was to be a lightning job, for the publication had been delayed long enough, but when we came to assemble the text, we found we did not have sufficient words to fill the required number of pages for the drawings. We needed Brendan's permission to include two of his previously published short stories, 'The Confirmation Suit' and 'A Woman of No Standing,' two of his poems, 'Thanks to James Joyce' and 'Oscar Wilde' which Val had translated from the Irish, and his one-act play, *The Big House*. At the same time we wanted to extend the section on Dublin to include an amusing story he had written on greyhound racing, 'Bogmen and Dogmen', commissioned and published by *Twentieth Century* magazine several years earlier. I put through the call.

He answered the telephone himself and from the tone of his response, I sensed he was suspicious as to how I had traced him. I would not say he was drunk, but either he had been drinking and was suffering from a hangover or else he was ill. I explained that Val and I were editing his book and he whispered 'That's good,' or words to that effect. Briefly, I mentioned the lack of text and listed the pieces which I hoped he would allow us to include. He would leave the choice entirely to me, he replied wearily, and he sounded so sad and depressed that I asked him why he didn't leave New York and take the next plane home.

'How's Beatrice?' I heard him say, trying to put some cheer-fulness into his words.

'I don't know, Brendan,' I retorted. 'Shouldn't I be asking you that question? She is your wife, you know.'

He ignored the barb, and becoming dismal again, he pleaded that I should tell her he was asking for her. Putting down the phone I felt the absurdity of it all. His concern for Beatrice was completely genuine. It was not many days afterwards that he arrived back in Dublin.

Brendan's exhaustion now was not entirely the result of con-tinual hangovers. It was something more serious. But despite his dog-tiredness, his guilt at going to America against Beatrice's wishes made a sober homecoming impossible, and his devouring unhappiness could not be obliterated in creative work. For a while the turmoil launched him into orbit more successfully than the astronauts hurled into space, before it landed him back in hospital.

Meanwhile I was having my own troubles in trying to produce a book by a living author who, for all intents and purposes, might as well have been dead. Although I had managed to trace the owners of the copyright in the numerous quotations, verses, and songs which were scattered throughout the tapes, I could not satisfy myself that the text was free from libel. I had sent the typescript to Michael Rubinstein, of Rubinstein, Nash, a firm of lawyers who have an international reputation for dealing with such matters, and Michael had pointed out the dilemma of knowing, without Brendan's help, what might be fact and what fiction in a book of this kind. He did, however, list three passages which he considered dangerous.

While rumours and press cuttings brought depressing news of Brendan, I knew it was hopeless to expect him to deal sensibly with the seriousness of the problems facing me. But when I heard that he was in hospital, I decided to wait for a few days for him to dry out, and then fly to Dublin with the offending pages and sit by his bed to ensure he applied the proper attention to each passage. The day before I intended to leave, I telephoned Anglesea Road just to check with Beatrice that I was not wasting my time, to be confounded by Brendan's voice at the other end of the line. He had done his usual trick of discharging himself but was quite sober, and asked of his own accord how the book was coming along. Even in this briefest exchange of words, I could hear his cheerfulness and encouraged by his jovial approach to my call, I mentioned the libel queries. I knew I was jeopardising his good humour by doing so, but the matter was too important to miss the opportunity of discussing it with him while he was receptive.

At once he grasped the gravity of the situation and suggested I tell him more, so I read Michael's letter to him in its entirety. When I had finished, I heard him say coolly and precisely that he was sure Mr. Rubinstein knew better than himself, and he thought it would be wiser to remove two of the passages, but the third could remain unchanged. I again reminded him of the necessity of being absolutely sure about this, and he replied crossly that as he had written the f—ing story, he should know. We turned to other aspects of the book—the dust-wrapper, the blurb, the dedication and technical details—and while he was happy to leave most things in my hands, he hoped that David Astor would be offered first refusal of British serial rights, and Bernard Geis the American rights. The contract he had signed with the latter was very much on his conscience. He prayed that, by the publication of this book, the Lord God in all His mercy would persuade Berney to lengthen his patience. Amidst half-hearted apologies for his inadequacies to myself and Michael Rubinstein, for he was sure Michael at that very moment was on his way to Gray's Inn muttering, 'Jesus, a hangover, *and* more of that f—ing Behan this morning,' he laughed and put down the receiver.

As it was my responsibility to steer *Brendan Behan's Island* through every stage of production, I was constantly in touch with Brendan during these days, and every time I telephoned (it was out of the question now for him to answer letters) he was professionally responsive to my calls.

The spring and early summer passed uneventfully, and except for an inaccurate report that he was to read the works of Séan O'Casey from a Dublin stage Brendan's name did not appear in print for several months. Four years previously, Séan O'Casey had quarrelled with the Dublin Theatre Festival organisers, and as a result he had refused to allow his plays to be produced in Dublin. The news of Brendan's intentions naturally upset him.

'Brendan's all right,' he is reported to have told one newspaper. 'Sometimes he's done foolish things. But he has very great talent. I simply don't want my work publicly elocuted from a Dublin stage.'

Fortunately Brendan did not let the tarnish of his words sink in deeply. Telephoning Séan O'Casey to his home in Cornwall, he managed to convince him that he would never be guilty of the impertinence of reading from his work without first asking for his permission to do so.

At the time, I am bound to admit that I was worried as to the effect this misunderstanding might have on Brendan. His book was scheduled for publication in September, and I had already committed him to several engagements which required a modicum of conformity. The B.B.C. television art programme, *Monitor*, wanted to interview him and the *Yorkshire Post*, which held monthly literary luncheons, had dedicated September entirely to authors published by Hutchinson, with Brendan as one of the chief guests. The impending publication of his book after so long a delay was causing a certain amount of excitement and, much to Brendan's delight, Bernard Geis had acquired the American rights, and David Astor the British serial rights for the *Observer*.

Although Brendan's absence from Dublin would make immediate contact with him virtually impossible, I was relieved when Beatrice wrote that they were going off on a short holiday to the peace and quiet of the west of Ireland.

June 1st, 1962

Dear Rae, We will be going to Carraroe on Monday for a few weeks. Things are brighter on the front than they've been since January. So I hope the play will be finished at last, to say nothing of all the other work that's been piling up. Much love, Beatrice.

And it was in Carraroe that Brendan heard not only that *Brendan Behan's Island* had been chosen by the Book Society as their October choice, but that his play, *The Hostage*, had been elected by the French Theatre Critics' Association—*Le Syndicat de la Critique Dramatique*—as the best play of the season in Paris.

Accordingly, Hutchinson postponed publication of the book until October and Bernard Geis agreed to do likewise. But the *Yorkshire Post* were unable to alter their plans for the luncheon in Harrogate as the invitations had already been sent out. Brendan was to come to England, as arranged, at the beginning of September for the luncheon and to face the cameras, once more, for Colin MacInnes to interview him on *Monitor*.

I wrote to Brendan in Carraroe and informed him of the arrangements, but since I was used to not hearing from him by letter, his silence did not bother me. Shortly after his return to Dublin, the first instalment of *Brendan Behan's Island* appeared in the *Observer*, and I was so childishly excited by the proof that his book had finally left the assembly plant and was now out on the road that I telephoned him to see what he thought of it. His elation was almost as great as mine, not on account of having read the pages, but because they were there at all. Then I heard him say that he had no intention of spoiling my hard work on his book by making a public spectacle of himself during any of his engagements.

A week later, the *Observer* ran the second extract, but this time our pleasure was to be short-lived.

XI

A LUNCH TO REMEMBER

The first shots were fired on the anniversary of the outbreak of World War II. On that date, a Dublin solicitor wrote a letter to the *Observer* in which he complained that his client had been libelled in an extract from *Brendan Behan's Island* which had recently been published in their newspaper.

When Tristan Jones, manager and director of the *Observer*, first telephoned the news, I was not unduly alarmed. Naively I assumed if Brendan went to see the solicitor in Dublin, he would be able to placate both him and his client. But when I phoned Brendan from London, I realised that he had been a shade optimistic when he said the third passage could be left in. He then agreed to come to London to discuss the problem as soon as a meeting could be arranged between Michael Rubinstein, the lawyer for Hutchinson, and P. F. Carter-Ruck of Oswald Hickson, Collier and Co., who acted for the *Observer*.

At the beginning of the next weekend, Beatrice arrived in England on her own, leaving Brendan to follow on Monday morning in time for the scheduled conference at 11 a.m. I had invited her to stay with me for the two days at Uckfield, and taking the train from Victoria she arrived at Haywards Heath station where I met her. On the thirteen-mile drive to my home bordering on Ashdown Forest, she told me with extraordinary calm that Brendan was no longer in the best of health. He had been upset by the whole business and had taken refuge in his hobby, the nature of which she did not need to enlarge upon. This news I could not regard lightly, but when I questioned her as to whether Brendan would make the journey at all, she assured me that she had arranged for him to be collected from Anglesea Road early on Monday morning, taken to the airport and put firmly on the plane. At the same time, as she and Brendan would be staying with Max Sylvester and his wife, whom they had known for many years, she had persuaded Max to meet Brendan at London Airport and drive him straight to my office in Great Portland Street. If her plans materialised, we could all go on from there to the meeting of the lawyers in Chancery Lane.

On Monday morning we waited hopefully for either Brendan or a phone call from Max, but when neither came, we started out for the conference without him. We had barely settled ourselves in the taxi however when, through the window, we saw the unsteady figure of Brendan weaving his way up from one side of the pavement to the other, in the direction of the office. Whilst Max Sylvester was nobly supporting him, he could not manage to steer him on a more positive course. Beatrice and I hurriedly conferred as to whether we would intercept them, but deciding that Brendan in this condition would add nothing to the dignity of trained legal minds, we drove by unnoticed.

Solicitors' offices have always terrified me, and despite the fact that I should be well versed in the trade, for both my father and my brother are members of the profession, I find the legal language utterly incomprehensible. As I sat with Beatrice in the waiting-room of Rubinstein, Nash & Co., the same fear enveloped me and I did not pay too much attention to the girl with the long brown hair who was standing at the window. A few moments later, Michael Rubinstein breezed in and out again to usher us into his impressively furnished sanctum. To my amazement, the girl followed. Once in the room, however, she introduced herself as Mr. Carter-Ruck's daughter and articled clerk, and explained that as he had been called out of London quite unexpectedly, she had been asked to attend in his place. When I heard this, I was relieved we had made our decision, for I was

sure her tender years would not have permitted her to understand Brendan in the state in which I had last seen him. Without
going into detail, I apologised for his absence, but said that
Beatrice had agreed to accept the responsibility of speaking for
him.

Like birds collecting for migration, we sat in a line opposite
Michael at a large mahogany table. Politely, he offered us
cigarettes, but hardly had I taken one before Brendan's voice
could be heard from outside, shouting oaths, if nothing else.
Michael and Miss Carter-Ruck raised their eyebrows; as the
noise came nearer, their eyebrows lifted higher; by the time
Brendan reached the outer door, they had joined the hairline
on both their heads.

With a certain degree of humour, Beatrice observed that
Brendan had, after all, decided to come to the meeting, and we
hurried out with the idea of stopping him before his abuse became violent. He was swaying in the arms of a startled clerk
named Paddy. On hearing his brogue, Brendan burst into song
and Paddy was trying to restrain him from entering the office. As
we joined them, the clerk, embarrassed, relaxed his hold on
Brendan and whispered to Michael why he was using force.
Meanwhile Brendan began devoting his freedom to loud complaints about the f—ing concrete steps he'd had to climb to get to
the main door, and left little doubt that, as far as he was concerned, no solicitor worthy of the name would contemplate doing
business from such an establishment. Miss Carter-Ruck reacted
to his rampagings in the manner I had suspected. Her face
drained of all colour; an encounter with Dracula in the dead of a
winter's night would not have sent her scurrying off more quickly
as she fled to the sanctuary of Michael's room.

But Michael, annoyed by Brendan's raving protests, grabbed
him by the arms and shunted him backwards towards the exit.
For a moment I was transfixed with horror as Brendan, hurling
abuse, wrenched one arm free and hurled that too in Michael's
direction, missing contact by centimetres. I knew I had to do
something to prevent a scene, and speaking the first words that

came into my paralysed brain, I commented that it was not every day in the week that one would catch a solicitor in the act of evicting his client. I was nervously talking for the sake of talking and had not intended to be funny or clever, but the sparring-partners were so flabbergasted by the inept timing of my remark that they interrupted their mêlée. Suddenly Brendan's ugly expression changed, and his mouth stretched to a grin as he held out his hand to mine. For his part, Michael had his first indication of Brendan's irrational nature and now, more sympathetic than angry, he suggested we all go back into his office and discuss calmly the reason that had brought us together in the first place.

As we stepped inside the door, Miss Carter-Ruck came forward apprehensively and introduced herself. I doubt if Brendan appreciated, at this stage, her function at the meeting. We sat down in a line at the table again, Brendan sandwiched between Beatrice and myself, Miss Carter-Ruck as far from him as socially possible, while Michael took the chair. But the moment the threatened libel action was mentioned, Brendan, gripped by anguish, ranted on, and little sense could be gleaned from him as to what course of defence he would take. He was in personal torment and although his words were slurred, disconnected and somewhat incoherent, he made it clear that his world was no longer fit to live in.

Between Brendan's bouts of despair, Miss Carter-Ruck bravely outlined her instructions from the *Observer*. There was to be a printed apology in the next issue of the paper, after which it was hoped the opposition would accept a modest settlement. Michael approved the proposal in principle, but as Hutchinson were not yet involved with the libel and had received no letter of complaint regarding the offending article, he had to reserve for consideration with them the advice which he would give, if they later had to instruct him. Throughout the conversation Brendan was still mumbling in a maudlin fashion, but all at once and with remarkable steadiness, he rose to his feet and, sweeping the features of each one of us with a searching sharpness, he settled his gaze on me and began to speak.

It would be over his dead body, he said, before a penny would leave *his* pocket. I lowered my eyes so that I could not read the implication of traitor in his expression, and Michael made it clear that Brendan's intentions vitally affected the wish of the *Observer* to apologise. The meeting broke up inconclusively. As we left, the cold, dispassionate nature usually associated with the law was strangely missing and Michael's parting remark, 'Take care of him,' told Beatrice and me that he saw beneath the rough surface.

After the meeting, I had intended to return to my own work, for there were still a few details that required my attention in connection with the *Yorkshire Post* literary luncheon taking place at the end of the week. Brendan made it plain, however, that without bothering to eat, he was going to spend his time drinking in a pub, and Beatrice wisely adopted the policy that if Brendan intended to drink, he could do so just as easily and more safely in the Finchley home of Max Sylvester and his wife. Surprisingly Brendan agreed to her suggestion, but only on the condition that I accompanied him, and after a brief struggle with my conscience, I smothered my desire to leave and obeyed his request. Apart from the excuse my departure would give him for becoming more drunk, I was afraid it might add to his belief that all the world was against him.

Mrs. Sylvester greeted us warmly, and under the circumstances most good-naturedly. I asked her if I could use her telephone to let Margaret, my assistant, know where I was, and she ushered me into the dining-room where I could operate my business in peace. To my dismay Margaret informed me that Penelope Mortimer, who was to have been one of the guest speakers at the literary luncheon, had been taken to hospital and the firm were busy searching for a last-minute replacement. I was convinced that now two replacements would have to be found, for it appeared unlikely that Brendan would be able even to attend the function. In a panic I returned to the sitting-room where Brendan, reclining on a couch, was drinking gin by the glassful, and issuing orders to Beatrice and Mrs. Sylvester like a sergeant-major drilling his squad on the barrack square. I tried to convey to him that I would have to go at once, but he was far away and out of connection and I left without being positive that he knew who was speaking to him.

Next morning we met at the York Minster for lunch. Brendan was still recovering from his hangover and was moaning and groaning about his ill-health. As we sat down to lunch, he complained that he could not eat, but after going through the menu several times, he reluctantly agreed to order a plate of cold meat. He began fretting again about the threatened libel case, but broke off to call over a waiter to bring a bottle of red wine. I was quickly on my feet. It was no business of mine, I said coldly, if he wished to drink himself to death, though I could suggest tidier forms of suicide. But unless he made some effort to straighten out, I would not be responsible for taking him to Harrogate for the luncheon. As I spoke, I felt my temper rising and by the time I had finished the sentence I was shaking and my face was flushed in anger. The sudden outburst surprised Brendan, and in sulky tones he cancelled the wine and suggested I sat down and told him some of the plans. Actually he did not need my permission to go to any luncheon, either in Harrogate or Kalamazoo, and thankful for his graciousness in not reminding me of the fact, I quickly restored my humour and did as I was asked.

Briefly I outlined the arrangements. The function was being attended by a galaxy of well-known authors and the speakers included, apart from himself, Kenneth Allsop, Frank Swinnerton, who had kindly consented to take the place of Penelope Mortimer, and Ursula Bloom. At the end of the luncheon, Kenneth Young, then the *Yorkshire Post*'s editor, would be proposing the health of the guests, and Lord Boothby had been given the task of replying to his toast. Many of the authors would be travelling up by train to spend the previous night at the Swan Hotel, but I had arranged with Geoffrey Howard, Hutchinson's sales director, that we should drive up in his car and thus avoid the temptations of drinking on the journey. Two honorary guests were also to be included in the train contingent;

Val Iremonger, as secret editor of *Brendan Behan's Island*, and my daughter, Diana, for no other reason than her dogged determination not to be left out of it.

Throughout my proposals, I noticed that Brendan was toying with the meat on the plate in front of him, picking it up in his hands and nibbling at it half-heartedly. The fact that he was trying to eat at all gave me the first sign that he wanted to participate in the event. As we lingered over the plans and schemes, he became clearly interested, but after a while, certain doubts came into his mind and his interest waned. Literary events of this nature, he said, reminded him of the intelligentsia whose prissiness and snobbishness had done nothing but put years on him, and who talked glibly about his work although their information was gleaned solely from the pages of the *Sunday Times* or *Observer*. I tried to convince him that the luncheon would not be like this, but he seemed gloomy and despondent again. Suddenly he said he felt awful, and pushing back his chair from the table, he hurried out of the room and down the stairs to the bar below us. A few minutes later he had become one of the boys, lugubriously displaying his talent for exhibitionism in front of a group of wide-eyed admirers. I determined to remain outside the circle, but Brendan drew me into the centre by shouting offensively that as the chief guest, he would certainly come to Harrogate, though whether he appeared on the television programme, *Monitor*, depended on the fee the producer had in mind. Meekly I agreed with him, for I wanted no active part in the gruesome scene I was watching. But in my mind I was now seriously debating whether Brendan was not too precarious a proposition for me to handle at the luncheon. As much for his own sake as for my own, I felt it might be foolish to risk the balloon going up on the distant moors of Yorkshire where it would be difficult to get him into hospital at short notice.

Inevitably, at closing time, he was reluctant to leave, and sick of his giggling companions who, whilst encouraging his stupid behaviour, I knew would be strangely absent the moment he became out of hand, I walked out on my own, blinking into the sunlight of a lovely Indian summer's afternoon. Weary and confused, I paced my way back to Great Portland Street recapitulating Brendan's immediate engagements. His television interview with Colin MacInnes for *Monitor* was scheduled for the following morning, after which we were due to drive to Harrogate in time for dinner at the Swan Hotel. Whilst I earnestly desired to cancel both and thus be relieved of my anxieties, unaccountably I could not dispel my suspicion that the pleasure of Brendan's company exceeded my fear that I would end up with a nervous breakdown.

Bewildered by my dilemma, my uncertainties and a thousand conflicting emotional pressures, I returned to the office no clearer in my mind as to what decision I would make. Hopefully, I waited for Beatrice to telephone and force me into action, one way or another, but when this did not happen, I went home in the evening with my problems unresolved.

Early the next morning, Brendan arrived at the office looking as though he had slept for a week in his clothes, but apart from this, his general demeanour had improved. Greeting me with his usual half-spoken apologies for yesterday, which I had now come to recognise, I quickly learnt of his intention to become part of the Hutchinson evacuation to Harrogate. Indeed, he was so excited by the prospect of it that his good humour prevailed throughout the television interview with Colin MacInnes. Colin MacInnes had recently published in the *London Magazine* an article on Brendan in which he claimed the author of *The Quare Fellow* to be one of the greatest writers of the century. I had tried to persuade Brendan to read it, but after the first couple of pages, he had dismissed it as being a load of rubbish. As a result of his attitude to Colin's literary opinions, I had been somewhat apprehensive about the meeting, and was delighted when Brendan answered the questions sensibly and seriously without indulging in lampoonery.

Afterwards, I invited Beatrice and Colin to join us for lunch at the York Minster, but explained it would have to be a quick one as we were off shortly to Harrogate. Once settled at the table,

Brendan became difficult, and although he ordered rollmops, he refused to eat it or anything else instead. He drank nothing in our presence, but as he was continually disappearing out of the room, it was a fair assumption that the bar downstairs was becoming his headquarters. I sensed the danger signals, and hurrying through the meal I suggested to Beatrice that we leave at once for the office.

We started off well enough with Brendan hailing the taxi himself, but as soon as he had climbed inside it, he sprawled across the back seat complaining dismally that he could not face the long drive to Harrogate unless we allowed him a half-bottle for succour on the way. Our cries of 'No' sent him into silent gloom, but just as we reached our destination, and punctuating his words by an exaggerated fit of coughing, he spluttered out that he was going to buy one at the off-licence opposite, and was off before we could stop him. I did not expect to see him again that day, and was happy at least that the difficult decision had finally been made for me.

Ten minutes later, Brendan reappeared like a welcoming committee in his attempts to cover up his guilt. But he could not hide the tell-tale glow of his eyes or his slightly unsteady footsteps. He was not damaged beyond repair, however, and at Beatrice's bidding, he stumbled along the corridor to have a wash and tidy up. Unfortunately, his somewhat dishevelled appearance had not gone unnoticed as he made his way to the lavatory, and very soon consternation and dismay were sweeping away the customary calm of the office. Bob Lusty and Harold Harris, who had replaced Iain Hamilton as the firm's editorial director, intimated with regret that Brendan must now be left behind.

Even at the time the humour of the situation did not escape me, for the devil himself could not defeat Brendan at the game of pandemonium. And for those whose knowledge of him was confined mostly to the newspaper columns, his physical presence alone, drunk or sober, was quite alarming.

Patiently I waited outside the lavatory door, whilst others better equipped for the use of the gents buzzed in and out to report back on the latest state of Brendan's undress. I endured the suspense for several moments, but after I had called his name and received no answer, my curiosity overcame my female inhibitions and I burst into the room. He was standing in the middle of the linoleum-covered floor, his limp shirt draping the wash-basin, and while his trousers remained in touch with his body, they had dropped in a heap to his ankles.

Covered with embarrassment, not so much on Brendan's account as at the almost certainty of being discovered in an all-male privy with a near-naked man, I hastily dressed him. The object of my distress remained quite unconcerned, however, and apart from reminding me caustically that a gentleman's lavatory was hardly of my size, had little else to say.

As luck would have it, we had the place to ourselves, and I handed him his jacket with relief as he trundled out of the door. Standing at Reception, kindly but firmly, I reiterated the directors' resolution not to take him to Harrogate. My words appeared to stun him briefly before the contours of his face crumbled into folds of disappointment and dejection. Like a small boy who is forbidden his favourite treat, his eyes filled with tears. The *Yorkshire Post* luncheon really mattered to him, and in one small sentence I had taken away his chance of a little pleasure.

I did not try to appease him, but grabbing my luggage, I ran down to the street and sat in Geoffrey Howard's car where I could review the position in more dispassionate surroundings. I knew the *Yorkshire Post* would be disappointed because Brendan's name on the guest list had produced an overwhelming demand for luncheon tickets, and I knew, too, that if he did not have anything more to drink, despite the mangling of my nerve tissues, he would still add to the enjoyment of the affair. I determined to hold myself responsible for his behaviour, and I winged my way back up the stairs again to try to persuade the directors to accept my word for it and revoke their decision.

As I burst into Harold Harris's room, Brendan ran forward to embrace me warmly, but something hard in his pocket crushed into my ribs and my breath was hurtled from me like a deflated balloon. Sheepishly, he retreated a few paces, but as he realised I had guessed his guilty secret, he did not protest when I removed a half-bottle of whiskey from the inside top pocket of his coat. I spoke to him—not gently this time—and pronounced that I had intended to vouch for his good conduct, but with the proof of his intentions clasped in my hand, I was not going to be used solely for his advantage. My words hurt him sharply, but he had come to accept the limits to which I would go in order to help him, and knew he could not push me further than I was prepared to go. He pleaded with me to give him a chance, and I weakened. After much deliberation with Harold, Bob and Beatrice, Brendan piled into the car and we were on our way to Harrogate.

Apart from one small break to stretch our legs, we drove to Yorkshire without stopping, and as Brendan slept soundly throughout the journey, he arrived at the hotel showing little signs of his previous drinking. Shortly afterwards, the train contingent appeared and joined us in the dining-room where we had already started our meal. Brendan immediately spoke to Val in Irish and beckoned to Diana to come and sit next to him. (Later I was to hear from Val that Brendan's first words were to thank him for his work on *Brendan Behan's Island*.) Harold and the rest of the authors who had travelled up by train crowded at the large table.

For a while the conversation was thrown backwards and forwards, shared equally between the assembled guests. But soon Brendan attempted to become the ring-master, and cracking the whip loudly and deliberately, he tried to dominate the party. There had been a time when he could have held his audience entranced for days and nights, but now repetition and halting words, not spontaneously spoken but prised out from his tired brain, revealed the damage of years of indulgence. Those of us who knew him well, whilst pitying it, loyally tolerated his deterioration, but others were less inclined to be charitable. Slowly the numbers at the table dwindled to a handful as, one by one, the visitors excused themselves and formed a party of their own at the opposite end of the room, until Brendan, dissatisfied with the few who remained, trundled across to join them.

To begin with, their irritation was expressed only by silence, but as Brendan took the floor once more, words of barbed hostility underlined their resentment. At last, but only after he could ignore it no longer, he was forced to acknowledge that he was the cause of their animosity. Deeply wounded, he repaired to the cocktail bar, not for the purpose of drinking, but to find a more receptive audience. Soon he was immersed in conversation with a doctor who had seen *The Hostage*, and his upset forgotten, he went to bed sober and contented.

He was up early the next morning, congenially at ease and flitting from one public room to another, chatting alike to his own party and to other guests in the hotel. He admired Paul Hogarth's drawings from his book which were on display in the main hall, but said he was scared to touch the volume itself because 'it had been got up to look like the Bible.'

The press were busy interviewing the authors, of whom he was the main attraction, but surprisingly, with them, I noticed he was less free in his manner and, if anything, tried to avoid being cornered and questioned. When he beckoned to me from the corner of a group in the coffee room I joined him, and he took me to one side to confide that, although he had been a journalist, he could never make up his mind how to react to the interviews; with eagerness, indifference or reluctance. I do not know what prompted me, unless it was the word journalist, but as he spoke I remembered Val telling me that Brendan had written a series of weekly articles for the *Irish Press* which he considered worth preserving. On the spur of the moment, and rudely interrupting his confidence, I asked Brendan if he would allow his articles to be published in a book. Forgetting his former worries over the press, Brendan eagerly agreed to my suggestion, but could not remember the exact years in which his column had appeared other than the fact that Jim McGuinness was the editor at the time. It was not the best moment for a discussion of this nature so I let the matter drop, but the idea remained in my head.

By midday, the luncheon guests were beginning to arrive for

the large cocktail party which was taking place beforehand. The chief patron, the Earl of Harewood, was unable to preside, but his place had been taken by his wife, the Countess. Since everyone was curious to know how both parties would react to their meeting, Brendan's introduction to the Countess was watched with interest. The encounter was an immediate success and the Countess openly admitted that she liked his simplicity and easy humour. She complimented him on the Mexican turquoise tie he was wearing, and Brendan was so delighted with her praise that he spun round the room like a top showing it off to all the guests, before settling finally in front of the only tieless man present.

'What's your business, matey?' he asked of the Bishop of Knaresborough.

'Not so profitable as yours, I'm afraid,' came the answer.

And Brendan, who was never slow to give credit where credit was due, acknowledged the older man's wit by a hand-shake which caused His Reverence to wince under the pressure. At the same time, his wild and uncontrolled laughter so shattered the nerves of the less composed at the party that they quickly fortified themselves with the contents of the glasses which they held in their trembling hands. For a while the atmosphere was filled with electric currents flashing warnings that something was going to happen each time Brendan moved towards the drink, but nothing did, and we filed into lunch.

I was seated next to Brendan at the top table, and coaxed him to eat, which he did spasmodically. He seemed to rise out of himself and respond to the occasion. We shared a jug of ale between us, while the rest of the assembled company drank wine. Shortly before he was due to make his speech, the waiter brought him a scribbled message from Val, who was sitting further along the table, to remind him to moderate his language as there were children at the gathering. Brendan raised his hand to indicate that he understood, braced himself, stood firmly on his feet and began to speak to the now hushed audience.

It was one of the few pure pleasures of his life, he said, to be the guest of honour at the luncheon, and although he had been in Yorkshire before, under very different circumstances (he was referring to his time in the I.R.A. when he had been on the run in the county) he found, even then, extreme loyalty among the natives. Not alone had they hidden him, but they had fed him as well and given him ammunition. 'Money, not guns,' he chuckled. He talked about his days in America, told an amusing story connected with Harpo Marx whom he had met briefly, and concluded his speech by words of praise for Frank Swinnerton ('He gave me the only lesson I have ever received in writing from his book *Literary Taste*') whose talk was due to follow his own. He had spoken for ten minutes, and while at times he seemed to lose the thread of his words and paused as he struggled to find it again, it was a brave effort. Even in his true days, his broad Dublin accent had been difficult to understand on first acquaintance, and considering that the bulk of his listeners had never met him before, their response was gratifying.

His ordeal over (and for a man who was all too aware of his own deterioration, this must have been one) Brendan sat down to listen to the orations of Frank Swinnerton, Ursula Bloom, Kenneth Allsop and Bob Boothby.

After the luncheon, the authors were shepherded into an adjoining room to sign copies of their books for the patrons queuing to buy them. Each author was allotted his or her separate table placed at vantage points in a room which otherwise had been cleared of all furniture. As the Book Society Choice for October, *Brendan Behan's Island* could not be sold, but an advanced order list had been prepared and Brendan and Paul were expected to autograph their book in the presence of anyone who put their name on the list. A group soon collected round their table, but while Paul was kept busy penning his signature, a search party was sent out for Brendan who was nowhere to be found.

Two hours later, he walked through the revolving doors leading to the hotel with Diana, obviously unaware of the consternation his absence had caused. He had become fed up, he said, with the literary and academic atmosphere and with being treated like a time bomb. He had been walking round the town with Diana, but this had hardly cheered him, for judging by the looks of them, the community who assembled in Harrogate did so for no better purpose than to call-over their gloom. He admitted that under different circumstances, he might have been tempted to relieve his depression in other ways, but with Diana, he felt this would not have been proper. Now he was ready to leave a place where the odds on damnation appeared to be at least a million to one on.

I could hardly blame him for his bad humour, for the previous twenty-four hours had imposed a considerable strain on him. But he had kept his word. He had not let me down. Geoffrey Howard lived in Hertfordshire and as Brendan and Beatrice were still staying in Finchley, to save Geoffrey the necessity of driving into the heart of London, I came back by train. Later I was to learn that their drive had not been a success and that Brendan had ended the day very drunk.

A dreadful week of drinking followed and although his body stood up valiantly to the pressures he put upon it, the stamina was on overdraft now and could not be repaid in the normal period of rest. He had begun to live on borrowed time. Utterly illogical, he appeared to believe that if he drowned himself long enough in a sea of alcohol, one day a miracle would happen and he would emerge to a new life of golden memories. Added to which, he was so ill physically that drinking was a defence mechanism from the pain he was feeling.

Inevitably he ended up in hospital, semi-comatose and barely able to recognise even Beatrice. For the first time his life was in danger and the doctors and nurses who attended him constantly at Westminster Hospital left no doubt that his condition was critical. Before Beatrice and I left the hospital the house doctor spoke to Beatrice shortly, and asked her all she knew of his diabetic history and of his previous illnesses. When she had answered most of his searching questions, the doctor promised he would telephone any change in Brendan's condition to the McGills' flat where she had now moved to be closer at hand.

The first page of the manuscript of *Richard's Cork Leg*,
Brendan's unfinished play

(1)

This is an Irish cemetary. There are the usual crosses, headstones, and tombs. There is an arch with the inscription:"I am the Resurrection and the Life," and beside it a board reading,"Greenwood Dawn (USS.A.) Credit Cards honored here.There is a large statue of the Sacred Heart, to the left. Behind, there is a chapel on the hill.

Two shawled figures sit, either side of a Celtic cross in bowed attitudes of what appears to be deep mourning.

After a moment, the silence is broken by a burst of loud jazz, played by Mr. Maynard Ferguson and his disciples, if they will be so good. I cite Mr. Ferguson because his music is noisy and clearly defined.

———

Maria Concepta: (Rises and throws back her shawl wich is seen to be
                     an ordinary topcoat): Turn that off, can't you?
                     (She has to shout to be heard above the music)
                     Turn it off can't you?!

Rose of Lima: (Rises, takes a portable radio from under her coat,
                     and switches it off) Me little Japanee transistor.

Maria: I like a bit of music, myself, but there's a time an
                     a place for everything. Not in a cemetary.You might
                     get us barred.

Rose: Thats one place they won't bar us out is the grave-
                     yard.

Maria: They say this is one of the healthiest graveyards
                     in Dublin.On the shores of Dublin Bay. Theysea air
                     is very healthy____the ozoon,you know.

Rose: And there's a lovely view.(She points) Lookoverthe
                     there to the South side of the Wicklow Mountains,
                     and Bray and Killiney and the Sugarloaf.

Maria: Ah,Killiney Strand.

Rose: I was had be a man,there.The first time. I lost me
                     virginity. He was the Lay Brother in charge of th
                     Working Girls' Protection Society. He said he'd sh
                     me what I was'nt to let the boys do to me.It was o
                     an outing.

Rare examples of Brendan's handwriting. Above—a letter to Iain Hamilton and below—a typical postcard to the author

The crisis passed. Somehow out of nowhere Brendan found the strength to pull through the critical hours, and by morning he was considerably better. Because of his undoubted influence, we called upon David Astor once more to try and persuade Brendan to accept treatment for alcoholism while time was still on his side. But when he visited him, he was so shocked by his appearance and by the impression that Brendan did not recognise him that he did not touch on the reason for his coming.

A few days later I visited Brendan on my own. He was screened from the other patients in a general ward, and the moment I pulled back the curtain he began a long spiel about his treatment in the place. There was not enough food; he had nobody to talk to; and during the hours spent lying on his back staring at the ceiling, he had become certain that drinking was not the main cause of his troubles. While he could not find contentment in a life without Beatrice, there was little happiness for him living in Ireland. Fortunately, he was in a position financially to be able to choose where he lived, but Beatrice was determined that this should not be in America. And with sorrow and anger he stressed that she would rather see him in sickness than help him walk in health on the only path which he knew how to tread.

It was useless to remind Brendan of the many sacrifices Beatrice had made on his behalf, or that she would gladly live in America if she felt this might check his thirst. As it was, there was no evidence that Brendan drank less in that country, with or without her.

Instead, I merely pointed out to him that he was drinking heavily long before he met Beatrice, and the responsibility for his weakness could not be laid at her doorstep. 'You know, Brendan,' I said, 'there is no place man enough to stop you drinking. This is up to you and you alone.'

I discerned a new face peeping behind the curtain, so I ended the unhappy conversation and left Brendan with the fond hope that a stranger might be more successful in cheering him up. It was a forlorn hope.

That night, I stayed in London with Margot Walmsley, the

assistant editor of *Encounter*, and naturally worried, I talked late into the night about Brendan's instinct for destroying himself. Margot had not met Brendan, but she realised that by encouraging me to speak about him she was freeing me from the tensions I had brought with me in the first place. We had not been in bed long before the telephone roused us again. It was Brendan. He had discharged himself on the spurious excuse that the night staff at the hospital had deliberately abused the I.R.A. in his hearing. Throughout what was left of the night, I worked my teeming brain to find a way to get him back into hospital, for I knew he was under drugs that would make drinking extremely dangerous.

Early in the morning I telephoned David Astor who promised to arrange a meeting with Brendan within a few hours, but this time it was to be in his office at the *Observer* and with the aid of Dr. Abraham Marcus, the paper's medical correspondent. Brendan and Beatrice started out happily enough for Fleet Street and Brendan greeted both David and Dr. Marcus as though he was genuinely pleased to see them. As soon as we were seated, David explained the purpose of the delegation and Brendan nodded his head to indicate he understood. But the moment David mentioned he would have to go back into hospital at once, Brendan became ebullient and rude. Dr. Marcus told him bluntly that he would be dead within the year unless he made some attempt to help himself, and Brendan banged his fist on the table and told him to mind his own business. With the sweat from his brow pouring profusely down his face, he snarled further obscenities at Dr. Marcus, sarcastically complimented David on surviving the nature of his mother's womb, insulted Beatrice for no other reason than that she had opened her mouth, and then left the room.

We hurried after him, and David most generously offered us the use of his car and chauffeur in the unlikely event that we could persuade him to go back into hospital.

Once seated in the car, I told Brendan positively that we were driving to Westminster Hospital, and cunningly he agreed to the plan, but pleaded that he should be allowed to collect copies of

Borstal Boy from Hutchinson's city warehouse, so that he could give them to the nurses in return for his rudeness of the previous night. I made this concession, but as soon as he had accomplished his mission, I fiercely counteracted his order to the chauffeur to drive to the York Minster, and we reached the hospital entrance without any more diversions.

But having got him there, to persuade him to do more than deposit his books at Reception was a task of a different calibre. He ingratiated himself with as much charm as he was able, and our hearts melted under his entreaties to lunch with us before being subjected to the indignities of hospital life. The hotel we chose for the purpose was not far distant and the quietness that pervaded the deserted restaurant applied equally to Beatrice and myself. Stupidly, Brendan mistook our silence as a sign that we had given up the struggle, and expansively, while he looked at the menu, he ordered the waiter to bring over three glasses of brandy. He had pushed his luck too far.

Sick at heart, something burst inside me, and in the explosion that followed I have no recollection of my precise words. But their meaning must have been clear, for by the time I had finished speaking, Brendan was coarsely telling a bewildered waiter that only fools in puzzle factories were unable to differentiate between the meaning of the words brandy and water, and it was the latter that he'd ordered.

For the rest of the meal, of which he ate practically nothing, he smothered his desire to have a drink under a greater fear of provoking another outburst, but when I left the table for a few minutes, he asked the same waiter to pour a brandy into his coffee-cup. He did not have time to drink it, however, before I returned, and he looked at the cup so guiltily that he might just as well have told me what he had done.

I did not say one word, but picked up my bag and my gloves and gave a convincing performance of a person who is about to leave a room in anger. Brendan's eyes darted to the coffee-cup and back to me before, in silence, he handed Beatrice the offending article.

Later that afternoon, after an interminable time coaxing,
wheedling and cajoling, we managed to deposit Brendan safely
back in the hands of the nurses. Our brains and our bodies were
now reduced to a pulp, and we returned to the office in eager
anticipation of a night of promised peace. Not an hour after our
arrival, Brendan telephoned for Beatrice. He had discharged
himself once more, and in vile humour, he announced that he
was never going back. At that moment I knew I had reached
breaking point. Hanging on desperately to my own existence and
instinct for survival, I deserted Beatrice and left immediately for
my home in the country.

On Monday, October 1st, 1962 *Brendan Behan's Island* was
published simultaneously in England and America, and the reviews on the whole were favourable.

'One immediately likes Behan,' wrote Cyril Connolly in the
Sunday Times. 'He has more than charm, he has instinctive kindness and charity, a verbal grace, an unforced assertion of a strong
personality that may even have a touch of greatness, a demonic
energy that notoriety has not entirely dimmed,' while Nigel
Dennis in the *Sunday Telegraph* described Brendan as 'a real
Irishman,' and his book as 'absolutely packed with funny stories
about nuns, priests, whiskey, Englishmen, bloodshed, and fairies,
and will do much to revive the old-fashioned view that the Irish
are not ripe for Home Rule.'

Louis MacNeice, writing in the *Observer*, was enthusiastic too.
'As for Behan's text, anyone who has read *Borstal Boy* will know
what to expect; he writes like a talker talking, with plenty of
hyperbole and emphasis,' and appreciated his 'humanity, gusto
and formidable wit.'

Anne O'Neill-Barna in the *New York Times* described the
book as 'a rare gem. Like a flash of insight, it jumps a thousand
hurdles and immediately takes the reader into the essential Ireland,' while S. K. Oberbeck in the *Sunday Post* felt it abounded
in 'salty observations of all the major Irish cities, counties and
tiny islands, taking readers everywhere: through North Dublin

slums and through state houses into fisherfolk cabins, country barns and numerous alehouses . . . a delightful romp and a sensitive trip through the Emerald Isles.'

When in health, Brendan, like most established writers, was interested in both praise and criticism of his work. But in this instance I doubt if he knew that his book had even been published, for the day prior to publication he had accidentally taken one of the most important steps in his life. He entered a home for alcoholics.

XII

THE CURE THAT FAILED

It had happened quite simply and with the minimum amount of fuss. Dark oppressive Sabbath days in England and their ungodly licencing laws had always been anathema to Brendan, and on the Sunday following his walk-out from hospital he had left Beatrice early in the morning to visit an Irish acquaintance who kept a superior boarding-house at the back of Victoria. The attraction of the journey lay not in the lodgers, but in the amount of drink his friend kept in the place. Over a pint or two he hoped he would be able to pass the hours until the pubs opened at midday.

Unfortunately, in the haze in which he found himself and in the similarity of the London houses, he had approached the house next door and assuming the nurse who answered his ring on the bell to be one of the lodgers he stumbled in unsuspectingly. Never can she have seen a patient better fitted for admission. Before Brendan realised what was happening to him, he had been given a strong sedative and put firmly to bed.

It was an established nursing-home for alcoholics under the patronage of one of the leading experts on the subject in the country. As the man himself was away in Rome for the Ecumenical Congress, Brendan was placed in the care of Dr. B., his partner, who for twenty-four hours did little more than watch Brendan recover from a monumental hangover.

Although the Doctor was unaware of the mistake that had

brought Brendan into the nursing-home, he was not prepared to treat him for alcoholism before Beatrice had been fully acquainted with the details of the cure. But Beatrice did not want to go to the meeting on her own, and she persuaded me to accompany her. Nervously we sat in his Chelsea consulting rooms while he outlined the procedure for us.

The 'aversion treatment', as it was called, required the use of the drug apomorphine which was given in large quantities of alcohol, and the two combined produced appalling bouts of vomiting. In the beginning the apomorphine was administered in small doses, but it was increased gradually each day until the recipient was so violently sick that he was down on his knees pleading never to have another drop. Later he was given pills which would acclimatise the cells in his body to solid food, but he would need several weeks in bed to recover from the physical exertion of constantly vomiting on an empty stomach. Later still and following his discharge from the home a nurse usually accompanied him for a while, so that when his aversion to alcohol weakened a pill would be slipped into his glass to cause him momentary unconsciousness, and he would be so frightened by the experience that he would never wish to repeat it.

The doctor had spoken these words so often that he delivered them as though he was conducting a tour round a picture-gallery, but by the time he had finished the curriculum I was consumed by doubts and fears whether Brendan had the physical strength to stand up to so drastic a regime. He confirmed my silent suspicions by admitting that, in the light of Brendan's diabetic condition, he was not prepared to accept him as a patient without Beatrice's assurance that she would be on hand throughout the first days of treatment when decisions of the utmost gravity might have to be taken. I raised my eyes to the ceiling in horror and back again to look at Beatrice, but whatever her inner reaction she met his words with statue-like composure.

Quietly she pointed out that this was not possible. She had shut the front door of her house in Ireland in the belief that she would be opening it again within a few days. She would have to go to

Dublin and make the necessary domestic arrangements for prolonging her absence. At the same time, since God had moved to take a hand in Brendan's affairs where everyone else had failed, she was not anxious to let the opportunity slip by postponing treatment until her return. As she spoke she glanced over at me, and wide-eyed I heard her ask if I would shoulder the responsibility for her. Alarmed by the thought of what my acceptance would mean I wavered, and for a split second my indecision troubled the air, but as quickly I realised that I could not reject her request. Meekly I agreed and as Dr. B. appeared contented for me to take her place, Beatrice gave her written authority for me to do so.

1st October, 1962

To whom it may concern. This is to say that Mrs. Rae Jeffs is to act on my behalf, as I will be away for a few days. She has my full permission to represent me on any occasion in my absence. Signed, Beatrice Behan.

That night I tried to relax under the weight of my new responsibility and was relieved when the nursing-home phoned the next morning to say that, as Brendan was better, it was planned to start the treatment at once. I was to come to the nursing-home to discover whether Brendan wanted to avail himself of the cure and was conscious of the Herculean efforts he would have to make.

I met Dr. B. in Chelsea for a preliminary discussion, and we drove to the home together. As soon as we arrived I was ushered into a room to the left of the hall and not many paces from the front door. Brendan was alone, lying inert in his bed with his back to me and facing the window opposite. Assuming him to be asleep, I tiptoed softly over and whispered his name. The bedclothes stirred first, and then he moved his huge frame slowly round in my direction. He looked grey and ill and his hair was moist and tangled. For a moment his eyes appeared sightless but as they focused on me, suddenly they filled with tears. Straining every inch of his body he tried to raise himself up further in the bed, and silently formed my name on his lips as though to speak aloud would tip him over the edge and he would lose all control of himself. He had been obviously bewildered by his surroundings and the recognition of a face must have convinced him that he was not, after all, in *delirium tremens*. Speaking softly, I told him that Beatrice was coming to see him soon, and that I would stay with him for a time. He pondered awhile over this information, but then as the fog in his brain cleared and his equilibrium returned, he asked me humorously to unfathom the mystery of what he was doing in a strange house.

Gently I told him that, of his own accord, he had taken himself into a home for alcoholics, and while I appreciated that he had done so by mistake I considered that he would be well advised to take advantage of the error. I explained the cure to him to the best of my understanding, but while at first he showed little reaction to my words, gradually he became more and more agitated, until by the time I had finished speaking he had stumbled out of bed and was tottering round the room naked, bawling for his clothes.

Having searched the only cupboard in the room and dropped to his knees to peer under the bed, Brendan forgot about his clothes and aggresively ordered me to go and get him a drink. But his previous exertions had exhausted him and perspiring freely he eased his shaking body into the nearest chair. He was a very sick man and although he knew it, I could see no harm in reminding him of the fact. He had to make a choice, I said, whether he wanted to live or to die, for he would certainly die within a year the way he was travelling. If he chose to live, he was in the right place for immediate help to do so, but if he wanted to die, he had only to get up out of his chair and ask for his clothes which were of little use to anyone else in the nursing-home.

Brendan had now come to a total acceptance of me and my directness did not upset him. He was aware too that I considered him well able to make decisions for himself. I would not pander to his eccentricities. He had to do what he had to do, and if he was to survive it must be without pleading and by his own wish. Added to which, he had a streak of obstinacy in his make-up which could not be bettered by any mule, and if he felt he was being pushed he would go in the opposite direction for no other reason than cussedness.

In grating distress he growled out his dislike of being confined once more to the four walls of one room, but after a while he became less belligerent and, contemplating the alternative, he came to the conclusion that he was less likely to die from treatment for alcoholism in London than from the liberal sprinkling of the Holy water to which he was subjected in the hospitals in Ireland. Chuckling freely at his own joke, he admitted that he had had pneumonia as a boy and had no wish to experience the illness again.

I do not think that time could ever erase from my memory the first week of Brendan's treatment. Despite the fact that he was under the constant supervision of two male nurses and Dr. B. took every precaution to avoid his slipping into a diabetic coma, on the second night he became so deeply unconscious that it took all the medical resources and what seemed an eternity to bring him round again. Indeed, the fight for his life had been so intense that there had been no time to call for a priest to administer the Last Rites. As Brendan had been excommunicated from the Catholic Church for I.R.A. activities while he was in Walton prison in Liverpool, and had always pleaded that he should be taken back into the church of his calling before his death, this was not a wish that would have been discarded lightly.

To make matters worse, in the midst of the crisis Brendan's impending libel case was making headlines in the newspapers. Not only had applications been granted in the High Court, Dublin, for leave to serve summonses on Hutchinson and the *Observer*, but an application had also been granted 'for an injunction until Friday week stopping Mr. Behan, his servants or agents from writing, circulating or otherwise publishing the matter complained of, or any other words similarly defamatory.' Leave too had been given 'to serve notice on Mr. Behan that on Friday week an application would be made for a continuing injunction pending determination of the actions.'

A more inopportune time for so serious a matter would be hard to imagine. Brendan was in no state to meet anyone, let alone be served with a summons. But to keep his whereabouts from the opposition and the press who were combing London for him posed a problem which, even with my fairly varied experience of helping Brendan out of jams, left me floundering in a quagmire. Dr. B. both shared and understood my dilemma, but to move Brendan to a less approachable place at the height of his treatment would be extremely dangerous to his health. As the telephone wires vibrated with the eagerness of those who were trying to locate him, I stood helplessly watching the net draw in ever closer.

The following weekend Beatrice returned to London and I went home to enjoy three nights of untroubled sleep. Throughout the next week Brendan's whereabouts miraculously remained undiscovered and I was able to get on with my work at Hutchinson reasonably undisturbed. Soon, however, he was offering the two eyes in his head in order that he might never catch sight of another drink and it was felt he was now in a position to be moved to a new address, and to be told of the web of intrigue which was spinning around him.

His delight at being the centre of a Scarlet Pimpernel drama, coupled with his consuming relief that the treatment was over, was sufficient for him to thoroughly enjoy the clandestine atmosphere which accompanied his move as he was smuggled out to a waiting ambulance to be driven to Redcliffe Gardens in Chelsea. After a few hours in bed, and in the dead of night, once more he was spirited away, this time cocooned in a blanket, to a nursing-home in Cromwell Road, South Kensington, where he emerged from the chrysalis as plain John Brown, well able for and loving the impersonation. Incredibly, this simple disguise was to foil all but a few friends, and for the length of his recuperation he remained incognito.

Meanwhile, the libel case came up again in the High Court where a further application had been made for an injunction against Brendan, but the judge, Mr. Justice Murnaghan, found it hard to believe that so notorious a character could really be mislaid, and indicated that perhaps the efforts to find him had not been taken seriously. As a result a London firm of solicitors were instructed to join in the search, and the extensive hunt for him across the two cities took in the most unlikely places, including an approved school for girls which had a name similar to that of a non-existent hospital in which Brendan was reported to be a patient.

As the days progressed and his health improved, I began to discuss work with him, but when I showed him the reviews of *Brendan Behan's Island* he seemed strangely reluctant to read them for himself. Assuming he did not wish to be reminded of the circumstances which surrounded the book's publication, I again brought up the subject of his articles in the *Irish Press* which we had first discussed in Harrogate. In the interim, I had conceived the idea that Beatrice should illustrate the pieces, for she is an artist of no mean repute, and had earlier exhibited her work in the Royal Hibernian Academy. Whilst Brendan said he would like me to go ahead with the plan, he seemed to want to remain apart from it, and I was sure he had something on his mind that prevented him from adopting his usual professional attitude to his work. Our talk wandered on to other topics, inconsequential and light-hearted, before I heard Brendan say clearly that although he believed he had been helped with his drinking problems, he was experiencing difficulty in reading and was in fact seeing double. I could see that this knowledge was so troubling him that there was little joy to be found in contemplating new writing material.

Later that evening I telephoned Dr. B., but I was only telling him what he had discovered for himself, and already he had arranged for a further series of pathological and neurological tests to be carried out on Brendan to try to find out the cause of the trouble.

Once Brendan had aired his ugly secret he appeared more at peace with himself than he had been for many months. It was not that he was shielded from his troubles, for he concerned himself a great deal as to the best way of handling his libel case. As he had finally come down in favour of proving justification for the supposedly defamatory words in his book, and Hutchinson were pleading innocence to the charge, it was necessary for Brendan to be legally represented by a different solicitor. Accordingly, Christopher Gore-Grimes had flown over from Dublin for his instructions, and at the meeting in the nursing-home, both in his calm manner and in the fashion with which he prepared his statement, Brendan revealed a stability that had been sadly lacking in his previous appointment with Michael Rubinstein. Nor was he unduly disturbed when G. P. Putnam's, the American publishers with whom he had contracted in New York to produce a photographic record of his life, used me as a go-between for the return of the advance. He was sorry, of course, to lose $3,000, but was thankful that the photographs he had seen, admittedly only a few, would not permanently depict him in his less attractive moments.

I believe he would have been perfectly happy to remain in the home but for the disquieting result of his tests. Dr. B. surmised that Brendan's difficulty in focusing correctly was due to slight pressure on his brain, and he recommended that Brendan should undergo an operation to remove whatever was causing it. For Brendan, who at the best of times was never blessed with a great amount of common sense, this was more than a straightforward diagnosis requiring straightforward attention; it was a severe blow. He had a stubborn fear of becoming mentally deranged and threatened repeatedly that, should he ever be committed to an asylum, he would drink himself to death the moment he came out. As far as he was concerned the operation was but the thin end of the wedge of insanity and nothing would induce him to agree to it. From that moment his rational approach disappeared and his one thought was to remove himself as far away as possible from the threat of the knife.

When the libel case came up for the third time in Dublin, and only hours after Mr. Justice Murnaghan had been informed that Brendan was still missing, he was out of the nursing-home and giving an exclusive interview to the *People* newspaper.

'He seeks me here, he seeks me there,' he boasted, 'but I'm damned if I know what the fuss is about. I didn't leave Ireland to escape from the law. I came over here to be cured of the drink, but I am going to fight this case tooth and nail.'

At the time of issuing his statement Brendan had not actually received his summons, but within twenty-four hours it was served on him and he was given twenty-one days in which to file the answer he had already prepared with Christo Gore-Grimes.

For a while, but always in the company of his nurse, Joe Garratty, Brendan hunted out the people he continually needed around him, and while he naturally gravitated to the pubs, he did not take advantage of the opportunity to drink. It looked as though the cure was going to work. But the most disturbing feature of his total abstinence was his sudden interest in girls and an obsession with sex. He had never before shown any promiscuous inclinations and the change in him both surprised and alarmed us. But his repeated conversations on the subject were no less boring than when he had been drinking heavily, and once again he became a man to be avoided.

For some time, there had been no mention of work, but as I had managed to have photostat copies of all his *Irish Press* pieces in the office, I thought Brendan's attention might be drawn to more constructive business by suggesting that he paid daily visits to Great Portland Street to pick out those which he considered most suitable for inclusion in the book. His face contorted by irritation, he went off into raving protests. Didn't I appreciate that his eyes were giving him a hard time? And even if they weren't, reading his own words was a form of mental incest to him, and he wouldn't be bothered with it. I reminded him sarcastically that it was not unusual for an author to read his words as well as write them but, without actually saying so, he dismissed the argument in a way that seemed to indicate that as he had been decent enough to write the articles and given his permission for them to be used, the least I could do was to cope with the rest. For one dreadful moment I seriously wondered whether

Brendan, the alcoholic, with his creative ability to fall back upon, was not preferable to Brendan, the teetotaller, who appeared
no longer interested in using his talent.

Feeling shut-off, he now decided to leave London and spend
a few weeks in the sun with Ralph Cusack, the Irish author, and
his wife, Nancy, who lived in the South of France. He had in
mind a remote village in the mountains, twenty miles inland from
the Riviera coast, and he was looking forward to a gossip with
his friends about mutual literary acquaintances and an occasional swim in the sea. Monetary considerations scarcely
bothered him, and it was left to Beatrice to obtain the necessary
francs to cover the unspecified period. She was to travel on ahead
and await his arrival a few days later, for he wanted to stop off
in Paris and show Joe Garratty some of his favourite haunts.

After she had left, Brendan came into the office to say goodbye. I had not seen him since our contretemps, and he looked
contrite and a trifle ashamed but had little to say. Somewhere in
his subconscious, he was becoming aware that if lack of drink
was to have this effect on his attitude to work, the consequences
would be no less serious than if he had remained an alcoholic.
Embarrassed, he picked up one or two of the books on my table,
absent-mindedly fingering the pages, and I, uncomfortable in the
uneasy communication between us, made some disparaging remark about a crime novel which Brendan was holding in his
hand. All at once the tension dissolved, and enthusiastically he
asked me if I knew that he had written a detective story too. It
had been published as a serial in the *Irish Times*, he said, during
his happier if less prosperous days.

'I wrote it under the phoney name of Emmet Street, which was
the name of the street opposite the one where I was reared in
North Dublin. And I wrote it under a phoney name for the simple
and sufficient reason that, at the time, I was quite well-known as
a poet and a writer, and whereas up to this date the Dublin intelligentsia had been favourably disposed towards me, unfortunately they had now seen the pieces of pornography I had
written for French magazines—in English of course—when I was

in France and this didn't exactly endear me to them. As I was short of the readies, I didn't see why the little matter of a name should come between me and my needs, so I decided to write it under a phoney one.'

He had called his story *The Scarperer*, and treading his ground gingerly while he scrutinised my face for every reaction, he mumbled that if I liked to have it republished, I could give him £450 outright and take the rest for myself. I did not need to answer. Brendan knew I thought sufficiently of his work to want to see it published. Immediately he had gone, I mentioned the proposition to Bob Lusty and, ignoring his most generous offer to myself, I arranged for a contract to be drawn up between himself and Hutchinson but giving him the advance of £450 that he required.

When he finally arrived in the South of France his irascible temper, combined with his guilt at having kept Beatrice waiting while he enjoyed himself in Paris, resulted in him having his first drink. I do not think that he either wanted or needed one, and although he said he had been frightened by the effect of the pill which Joe Garratty had neatly tucked into his glass, his fear was not strong enough to prevent him from trying again.

Meanwhile, back in Dublin, his case had come up for the fourth time, but when it was known that he was in France it was adjourned once more and the temporary injunction against him extended until his return. Lamentably, this came sooner than was expected. Since Brendan's one lapse, I had had no news of him, directly or indirectly, and taking the quiet to be a good omen, I was unprepared for Beatrice's phone call when she telephoned from Nice. She had just seen Brendan and Joe Garratty off on their way to London. Earlier, Brendan had been approached by Eamonn Andrews and had been persuaded to appear on the B.B.C. television programme, *This Is Your Life*, which was shortly to feature his father. Joe Garratty could do nothing with him; he was completely out of control and had been drinking heavily ever since he had accepted the assignment. Would I arrange to have him met at London Airport and seduce him back to the nursing-home before it was too late? Nonplussed as to how Brendan could be inveigled into doing anything if he was as drunk as I suspected, I nevertheless wrote down his flight number and the time of his arrival and promised to do whatever I could.

He was due within the hour and an immediate business appointment made it impossible for me to meet him. I telephoned Dr. B. who agreed to despatch someone directly in an attempt to intercept him. The mission failed, for by the time the dragoman had arrived, Brendan had already come and gone. The following day he slipped the net entirely and flew to Dublin, a bacchanal on the wing.

With a sense of despairing hopelessness, I realised that not only had the cure failed but it had used up much of Brendan's fast diminishing physical strength. It was a disastrous ending to weeks of hope; his path of good intentions was strewn with the weeds of defeat and our minds were blank as to how to help him pull them up and start again. But while I was forced to admit that the candle was burning perilously near to its end, I still refused to believe that there was no more talent to be salvaged from Brendan.

I had had a letter from Bernard Geis who, having heard of my part in the taping of *Brendan Behan's Island*, suggested I employ the same method to capture Brendan's long overdue, but promised, autobiography. And still under the impression that his 12,000-word manuscript, *the catacombs*, was an integral part of the book, he sent that along as well. But taping a man's life story was a very different proposition to a travel book even if Brendan had been fit, and whilst I did not want to reply definitely in the negative in case Berney should add to Brendan's troubles and ask for the return of his advance, I delayed my decision by explaining that, as he had been ill, I did not think he was ready to face so arduous a task. I was sure, however, that when he felt able to do so, he would let his intentions be known.

Actually I had in mind that a better way in which to ease Brendan back into working harness would be the editing of *The Scarperer*, his *Irish Times* serial which I had eventually managed

to trace. But 1962 was by now nearing its end, and I decided I
would wait until the turkeying and the comings and goings of the
holidays were over before I would go to Dublin and encourage
him to make a start.

Soon after Brendan's return to Dublin, the case came up again,
but this time Mr. Justice Henchy refused the application for a
continuing injunction against him on the grounds that, by agreement with Hutchinson, he had signed over all the rights in
Brendan Behan's Island and therefore had no control over its
publication. Remembering clearly the day when we had tried to
get Brendan back into Westminster Hospital and his insistence
that he must collect copies of *Borstal Boy* from the warehouse
to give to the nurses, I could not help smiling when counsel for
the plaintiff mistakenly assumed that this was the book concerned in his libel case. Brendan's defiance of the injunction was
typical of his irresponsible behaviour, he said.

Early on Christmas morning I was awakened by the telephone.
It was Brendan calling from Dublin. Incredibly, he sounded as
though he had never touched a drink, and his voice travelled the
distance clearly and without effort, echoing his good humour. He
wished me a happy Christmas with flagons of booze to go with
it, asked me to listen while he read out a letter he had written to
the *New Statesman* complaining about a review of a book, the
title of which escapes me, and conveyed his delight at the result
of the recent Court hearing. As the time pips kept ringing in my
ears, I suggested we end the conversation, but he told me to 'hold
your hour.' The expression had always amused me, and it flashed
into my head that it would make a wonderful title for the book
of his *Irish Press* articles. Brendan agreed but added, 'and have
another,' and *Hold Your Hour and Have Another* was christened
on the spot.

He mentioned my coming over, for he was thinking of working again, if only to prevent competition from Beatrice who, each
day, was studiously at her drawings for the book. I said I would
bring *The Scarperer* with me, and while I distinctly detected a
sigh of boredom he did say he supposed he would have to edit

it himself. Anxious not to be reminded further of work, Brendan asked to speak to Diana, and whilst I could only hear one side of the conversation, her loud guffaws and joking answers assured me that his efforts to amuse her were successful.

There was no real point to his telephone call; such acts of friendship were as much part of his character as his less appealing qualities, but never received quite the same publicity. It was to be several months before I either saw or spoke to him again.

Despite Brendan's optimism over his libel action, the constant threat of it worried him and made Ireland more and more a place to be avoided. Above everything he wanted to return to America, but knowing Beatrice's passionate resistance to the idea he neither had the strength of will nor the inclination to overcome his unhappiness unless he was perpetually befuddled. Continual dissension made his home uncomfortable and he began sleeping out. As a result, while Beatrice made every effort to keep in touch with him, there were many days when she did not have the faintest knowledge of where he might be.

To make matters worse, on one of his few visits home he had tried to telephone New York, but when the operator failed to understand his croaking voice he abused her so vilely that his name as a subscriber was permanently erased. The difficulties of tracing him were now immensely increased.

In the last days of February 1963, carrying nothing more than the clothes on his back, Brendan took off for America. He telephoned from London Airport an almost incoherent message to Beatrice at her parents' home in Dublin to tell her what he was doing. Then he unsteadily boarded the plane that was to take him across the Atlantic.

Within two weeks, I received a letter from Bernard Geis.

Mrs. Geis and I received a very unexpected caller at our home on Sunday, March 10th. We heard a husky voice over the phone and, while at first it didn't sound like Brendan, it was nevertheless he. At first I thought he was calling from Dublin. It turned out that he had been in New York for several days and wanted to drop in. When he arrived, he appeared to be in about as bad shape as I've seen him, and that's saying a lot. He asked for a drink almost before he said hello. We of course refused him. He practically got down on his knees—but nothing doing.

We had some conversation in his rambling discursive way. He claims he is going to finish *Confessions of an Irish Rebel* soon but I'll believe that when it happens. I'm going to give him the initial portion of the ms [again *the catacombs*[1]] and try to set him up in the office so that he can work on the book every day. While he heartily agrees to this plan, it will be a small miracle if it materialises. Yesterday, for example, he called me to say he was on his way to the office, but he never showed up. I've been trying to reach him at the Bristol Hotel, where he is staying, without success.

At the stroke of one on Sunday, Brendan shot out of our apartment as if he were jet-propelled. It then dawned upon us that we had no reason to be flattered at his visit. The bars in New York are closed on Sunday until 1 p.m. and he had hoped to sustain himself at our house until they opened. I'll keep you posted on his activities. He had a very rough day or two, he tells me, in Harrison, New York. All the best.

If Brendan could not be happy with Beatrice, the contents of Berney's letter gave little encouragement that he had found contentment without her. Soon he was asked to leave the Bristol Hotel, and Katherine Dunham, the dancer and choreographer, who happened to be in Berney's office at the time, suggested that she should take Brendan under her wing. She was living at the Hotel Chelsea on New York's unfashionable West 23rd Street, between 7th and 8th Avenues, a hotel consisting of one-room and larger self-contained apartments where Dylan Thomas had spent the Walpurgis Eve of his life. Berney booked a suite for Brendan on the tenth floor, where he could enjoy a wide vista of most of Manhattan, and Katherine Dunham arranged for Lucille, one of her troupe of dancers, to act as his housekeeper.

Not long afterwards I received a telephone call from Berney which was to relieve me, once more, of my duties as publicity manager. Brendan was asking for me and I was to join him in America. He had decided finally to tape-record his autobiography.

[1] Author's note.

XIII

REUNION IN NEW YORK

If I had been apprehensive over my first tape-recording jaunt to Ireland, I was now in a mortal funk. I had never been to America before, had no American friends and, as I had not spoken to Brendan myself, was not even sure that he really intended to write his book. More than likely, I thought, he was merely trying to appease Berney who was paying for his board and lodging and expected some return for the financial outlay. I had visions of either waiting for Brendan's inevitable collapse in a strange country or sitting by myself in a hotel bedroom. But I had said I would go and I was determined to take the leap in the dark in the forlorn hope that he was not spoofing.

Diana, however, regarded my trip with envy, and on the spur of the moment I asked her if she would like to come with me. She jumped at the chance. Her education was finished, she had not yet taken a job, and furthermore, as she had never seen Brendan totally drunk, she regarded him as a lovable and huggable teddy-bear. I persuaded Hutchinson to lend me the money on the quite genuine grounds that previously she had had a most steadying influence on Brendan, and I booked a double berth on the *Queen Elizabeth*. As on my earlier mission, I had again decided that my living quarters should be separate, and we registered at the Hotel Governor Clinton on 7th Avenue which, I was informed, was within easy walking distance from the Chelsea.

On Tuesday, April 9th, 1963, Diana and I sailed into New

York shortly before dawn, and we stood on deck to watch thousands of kaleidoscopic lights twinkling and blinking merrily across the harbour. By 8.30 a.m. we had disembarked, and passing through Customs remarkably quickly, we peered at the crowds pressing against the wooden barriers which, without a visitor's permit, was the nearest point of their meeting with the passengers. But there was no one to welcome us, and while our porter took our luggage on a truck through a different exit, we piled into the elevator feeling strangely alone and unwanted in the middle of a thronging, noisy mass.

Down in the street the sun was beginning to shine through the morning mist, and as we stood waiting for our baggage, basking in the warmth, we were pushed and buffeted unmercifully by a host of shouting people. When the porter arrived he explained that we'd have to get our own cab as it was against the union rules for him to do so for us. The question of small coinage bothered me, and not wishing to appear mean I felt I was quite safe in handing the man a dollar bill. He fingered it as if perhaps there might be two of them, looked at me, hovered a moment, made as if to say something, thought better of it before he dimmed into invisibility in the teeming mob, leaving me with the impression that I was the stingiest woman he had ever encountered. We had stepped into a new world, and as yet were not accustomed to it.

Our first glimpse of New York was too overpowering to be appreciated on a cab drive from Pier 90 to 7th Avenue. Silently we stared out at Manhattan and its skyscrapers, formal and dignified but outwardly devoid of heart or soul; a Daedalian city both beautiful and frightening. And even our driver, whilst functional and efficient, chewed gum with clockwork precision and seemed without identity.

We converged on the Governor Clinton Hotel where we were immediately ushered up to our double room on the second floor. Sad and depressed, we began to unpack but, as there were no hangers in the wardrobe, I telephoned Reception and asked for some. Within a few moments there was a knock on the door and

I was confronted by a buxom, jovial, coloured woman, her hair concealed under a kerchief with large, scarlet spots and her mouth stretched, from ear to ear, in a grin.

'Here you are, doll,' she drawled, as she handed me an armful of coat-hangers, and she rolled off down the corridor again singing loudly, 'Puff the magic dragon.' Suddenly our fears and loneliness left us, and we sat on our beds rocking with helpless laughter. Inconsequential though it may seem, the sight of an uninhibited person made us at ease, and I felt ready to test for myself the sincerity of Brendan's intentions.

His phone was answered by a voice who introduced herself as Lucille. Brendan was indeed expecting me, she said, and would I come round to the hotel at once. Diana and I set out like jungle explorers, but as soon as we turned the corner from 7th Avenue to 23rd Street I recognised, from description, the old-fashioned red-bricked building and the ironwork balconies of the Hotel Chelsea. I noticed a plaque on the wall which commemorated its many distinguished visitors from the world of art and literature: Arthur B. Davies, James T. Farrell, Robert Flaherty, O. Henry, John Sloan, Thomas Wolfe, Dylan Thomas, Edgar Lee Masters and Henry Miller. Brendan was in good company. We pushed open the wide glass doors, incongruous in this setting, walked across the marble floor and announced ourselves at the desk. A telephone check brought the information that Mr. Behan would be with us in a moment and we sat down in the lobby to wait. The floor was bare except for a small carpet upon which stood a glass-topped table, and apart from the leather upholstered sofa which we chose, the only other form of seating was two gilt ormolu chairs. Hanging on the wall was an enormous engraving of what I took to be angels and devils except that their positions were faintly compromising.

I had expected Brendan to appear from the direction of the elevator and was surprised when he joined us from the street. He was coatless but looked neat and tidy in a dazzling white shirt and crumple-free trousers. As he trotted forward happily to greet us, I was struck by the change in him for he bore little resemblance to the shuffling and distraught figure I had imagined I would see. Almost at once he became The Host again, and insisted that he would have to take us to a celebration lunch at Downey's Steak House, in his opinion the best restaurant in the city.

While he devoured raw steak, he began to talk about his book. He had every intention of starting work directly, but his hospitality would not allow him to do so until he had shown us some of the fabulous sights of New York. He made no mention of his recent drinking bout other than to refer, without the slightest resentment, to an incident which had taken place in his bad days when he had been rolled, while drunk, off 3rd Avenue and robbed of his overcoat, air ticket, passport and $280.

'The pleasantest part of that affair,' he chuckled, 'was when I applied for a new passport, an Irish Embassy official wrote on the form: "No proof of Irish nationality required." Now there's a friendly remark.'

We dropped Diana back at the Governor Clinton to finish unpacking while Brendan and I returned to the Chelsea to talk a bit about our plans. He introduced me to Lucille, for whom I felt an immediate warm regard. She was obviously fond of Brendan, but was firm with him and detached, and I could see he accepted her orders without resentment. We opened two bottles of Miller's High Life ale, but after only one gulp Brendan began to tell me how much he was missing Beatrice.

Habit was the thing that bound people together, he confessed. He sat silently for a few seconds before he told me, sheepishly, that he had taken off for America without even telling Beatrice and this knowledge now shamed him. 'Each man hurts the one he loves,' he added, sadly. Now he wanted news of her, and he was sure I could give him some.

Before I left England, I had sent the printers the forty-six *Irish Press* articles which I had chosen for inclusion in *Hold Your Hour and Have Another*, and Beatrice had promised that as soon as she had completed the drawings, she would join us. I told Brendan this and he was delighted, but before I could go into any details, Katherine Dunham came into the room and the subject was changed. She explained that she had just broken away from her rehearsals in the studio along the corridor to meet me, and to find out if I would be replacing Lucille as Brendan's housekeeper. Hastily I replied that while I would be with him most of the day, at night I would be returning to the Governor Clinton and my daughter. At the mention of Diana's name Brendan became agitated, insisting that she had been alone long enough. New York was not London or Paris, he stressed, and it was not a safe place for a young girl to wander about in on her own. He had been invited to a Jewish festival later in the evening, and he suggested we all meet early the next day when he would show us around.

For the next few days Brendan introduced us to the city which he had come to regard as his second home, pointing out the famous landmarks with an air of lairdship. He took an almost childish pleasure in Diana's excitement and wonder. Whether he was giving us the background to the building of the Statue of Liberty, showing us his favourite churches and their links with his own country, walking down Broadway praising the neon lights and the friendliness they generated, or speeding through the Bowery—a district he particularly detested as he had once been marooned in it—he was a rare companion, and his main thought was always that we should be enjoying ourselves.

After our Harlem visit we sat in Costello's, a favourite saloon of Brendan's on 3rd Avenue. We talked leisurely over a pint, and I asked him to tell me more about the Black Moslems, for I knew he cared a great deal about the Negro problem. Their whole approach disturbed him, he said, for he could not condone violence. Well he could remember an Easter Day I.R.A. Commemoration Parade at Glasnevin Cemetery in Dublin, when his own violent resistance to the police, who were trying to break it up, achieved nothing but a fourteen-year prison sentence.

'It was not such a big deal,' he admitted, honestly, 'and in many ways I am what I am on that account.' And all at once he was hurrying on to a different topic; he did not wish to be reminded further of an incident he had long since endeavoured to forget. On the whole he was eating well and drinking mostly apple juice, milk or beer, and I was content to wait for him to tell me when he was ready to work. But as ever, this came when I was least expecting it.

One morning, I was awakened early by the frantic ringing of my telephone and, shaking myself out of sleep, I fumbled for the receiver to hear Brendan's wide-awake voice. He was in the lobby downstairs, he said, and as it was the sort of day that you knew God was in His heaven, would I ever get up and make a start on the old tape-recorder. He was sweeping the carpet when I joined him while an elderly coloured man stood by, amused. We had a large breakfast of bacon and eggs in a deserted restaurant adjoining the Governor Clinton, and later walked down 7th Avenue to the corner of 23rd Street, where we waited on the sidewalk for the Silver Rail to open at eight o'clock. After a quick one, we returned to his apartment, much to the surprise of Lucille. I whispered to her that this was the moment and, tactfully, she disappeared to leave us on our own. I had hired the tape-recorder from a radio dealer on 7th Avenue, and as I set up the machine and accustomed myself to the various buttons, Brendan sat on the sofa next to me and talked about his book. He was heartily sick, he said, of law suits.[1] *Confessions of an Irish Rebel* would be a respectable book, for family reading and Quaker meetings on Friday nights.

He appeared entirely at ease, but I was tense and apprehensive. Recently an article had appeared in the press which claimed that he would never write his autobiography as he was now 'simultaneously soaked and dried up.' Three years had elapsed since we had taped the *Island*, and a great deal of alcohol had been absorbed into his system in the meantime. I wondered myself whether there might be some truth in these hard words. His opening sentence was hardly encouraging.

'It was Deirdre who actually mentioned giving the party for

[1] The libel action, so far as Brendan was concerned, died with his death, and the other parties apologised, withdrew and settled the action.

me . . .' I heard him say. Hastily I stopped the tapes.

'Brendan,' I exclaimed, astonished. 'Are we recording *the catacombs* or *Confessions*?'

He reddened and stammered out his impatience. 'For the love of Jaysus,' he snapped, 'it's *Confessions* we're at, isn't it? Or has New York gone to your head to such an extent that you've forgotten the purpose of your coming?'

Scared that he would now abandon the whole operation I let the tapes roll again without answering, but he sat glaring at the microphone in silence. I do not know how long the dead-lock would have lasted, but the telephone rang and Brendan, delighted to be out of it, seized upon the opportunity and answered the call. By the time his conversation ended his humour had improved.

Once more I switched on the machine, but before the tapes had turned one circuit, Brendan shook his head for me to stop them. 'You know, daughter,' he said, 'you are a friend of Beatrice, and I am hoping that she will be coming over soon. But you know what the matter is. I am ashamed of the way I walked out on her and I cannot get it out of my mind. I do not mean to get it up for you.'

He extended his hand to mine and a shy smile flickered his apology for his previous irritability. Again I moved to start the machine and again he prevented it. It was driving him insane, he said, not to be able to work in *the catacombs*. Twelve thousand words took a great deal of writing, and he would have liked to fit them in somewhere. I resigned myself philosophically, but when the recorder finally hummed into life, it was for the birth-pangs of *Confessions of an Irish Rebel*.

Haltingly and unhappily at first, he searched for the words to tell of his last days in Borstal, but as the session progressed his speech became less laboured and his account of his short period of freedom in Dublin before the fateful incident at Glasnevin Cemetery was considerably more fluent and colourful. While it would be true to say that in the beginning the tapes showed little deterioration in his remarkable powers of description, after a short time his mind began to wander, and I was having to prompt him. Later I noticed his stuttering increased and he was having difficulty in delivering his words; as a result, the spontaneous gaiety which had accompanied the taping of *Brendan Behan's Island* was now sadly missing. Nevertheless, he was neither soaked nor dried up, and if by the end of the session he had not covered as much ground as he had expected, he had made a start and this fact pleased him.

Throughout the afternoon, he sat in the Oasis bar stopping every customer to tell them how happy he was to be working again, and rather touchingly conveyed his relief at discovering that he was not, after all, washed up. When there was no one left to share his happiness, he insisted that I fetch Diana so that, while he would not listen to them himself, she could hear some of the tapes to prove that we had not been wasting our time. When she arrived, he became expansive and amusing, giving her fatherly advice on the dangers of falling in love and of the neces- sity of wearing clean underclothes. They had a childish joke be- tween them when, every time they met, Brendan would try to guess the colour of her petticoat and if he was successful, she had to show him a corner of it. Today, he proved correct and the ritual over, I played back a little of the tape while Brendan put on a clean shirt to take us out to dinner. Giggling like school- children throughout the meal in the Village, we lingered on until late evening when we parted for a night of carefree sleep.

Strangely, on Easter Sunday twenty-one years after the event, we were to record the incident that had taken place at Glasnevin Cemetery. When I arrived at Brendan's apartment, he was still in bed but cheerfully called through the partition which separated him from the living-room that he was glad I was showing our Lord a bit of respect, for if He had risen today he was certain it was earlier than himself. 'I haven't even been to Mass,' he chuckled.

He asked me to set up the machine in his bedroom. I did not question his decision but I was a little disturbed by his change of working habits, and felt he would not really concentrate while he was lying in bed. We began recording immediately. Loudly, and in a voice quite unlike his own, he threw out his words, not about Glasnevin but the period following in Mountjoy Jail. He continued for several minutes, his eyes piercing mine and defying me to interrupt, before his voice became softer, dwindling to a whisper and then fading altogether. In the pause, I reminded him of the I.R.A. Commemoration Parade in Dublin, and he covered his face with his hands.

'Oh, God,' he muttered bitterly, 'I don't want to think about it,' and he lay back on his pillow, sullen and brooding. Suddenly, and without his usual nod of warning, he sat bolt upright and began to talk of the gun-fights, killings, hatred and fear of his youthful years as a tough I.R.A. rebel, and his words fled from him in angry waves. It was the police who started the fracas at Glasnevin, he cried sharply, and as he was in their direct line of fire, he had snatched a revolver from the hand of an I.R.A. officer nearby in self-defence.

'They opened fire,' he insisted, 'I didn't. But when they opened fire, I fired back at them and still firing, I ran away.' For a moment his voice softened as he recalled the young girl who had sheltered him, but hardened again as he spoke of holding up at gun-point a gambling school for money while he was on the run. There had been an order out that he was to be shot on sight, but he had sent back a message to say that he could be shot in his absence too.

The recollection amused him, and with less distress he related his arrest, his period on remand with the threat of the death sentence over his head, his trial and the fourteen-year prison sentence (commuted to four years as a result of the political amnesty of 1946) which was to send him to Mountjoy, Arbour Hill and the Curragh Internment Camp. He had dragged everything out of himself that he had spent years in forgetting, and he was exhausted. Closing his eyes, he lay back on his pillow and I crept prudently away.

He did not contact me again for two days, and I was to learn from Lucille that during this time he remained almost consis-

tently in bed, disagreeable and edgy, and attacking his food
without appetite. This knowledge pricked my conscience and I
began to have serious doubts as to whether we should continue.
In the lull, Diana and I accepted an invitation to dine with Dr.
and Mrs. Merrill Lipsey whom I had met through friends in
London. At the dinner also was their daughter and her husband, Dr. Peter Harpel, who was practising at Bellevue Hospital
in New York, and before the evening ended, he handed me his
card and private telephone number in case an emergency should
arise concerning Brendan's health. Contacting a doctor at a moment's notice was perhaps not quite so easy as it might be in
London, he explained. While I thanked him warmly, I could not
foresee that eventually I would be in desperate need of his help.

When we returned to the hotel, I was surprised to discover
from one of the staff that Brendan had been looking for me;
'rather the worse for wear,' he said. As it was late I decided
to do nothing about it, but wait until he had had the chance to
sleep off his hangover. At six o'clock the next morning I was
again awakened by the telephone, and this time I knew whose
voice to expect. He had remembered an incident which he would
like to include in his book, he growled, and he had come round
to collect me so that I could tape it while it was still fresh in his
mind.

As soon as the elevator doors opened, he came towards me,
and although his eyes bore unmistakable alcoholic traces his condition had been improved by a night's rest. On our way to the
Chelsea he admitted that he 'had had a few jars,' but was 'none
the worse for that.' Indeed, I am bound to admit that once we
started to record, he *was* more animated and spoke without a
single stammer. The incident to which he referred was about
Lord Kitchener, and he had heard it from a priest—a namesake
of his though no relation—whom he had met when he was on the
job of repairing and restoring the home of Daniel O'Connor in
the South of Ireland after his release from the Curragh in 1946.
Father Behan had been a chaplain in the First World War and
had gone to see Lord Kitchener because the priests were being

hindered in attending to the Irish soldiers. During the interview
Lord Kitchener had explained to Father Behan the strange quirk
of fate that had led him to becoming Secretary for War. It was
an interesting story, but because it was slightly out of sequence,
I recorded it on a new reel of tape. As soon as he had finished, I
went through the normal procedure of a play-back, and Brendan
said he would use up the minutes by going to the jakes and re-
lieving his brain. When he reached the door, he stopped
abruptly; the silence from the tape-recorder was deathly and interminable. 'God bless us and save us!' he exclaimed as he
turned to me, bewildered. It was a faulty reel and not one word
had been recorded. While I fumed and fulminated, he repaired to
the bathroom lustily singing 'The Meeting of the Waters' and returned grinning all over his face. He didn't know why I was getting it up for the poor old machine, he said. 'Put on another
tape,' he ordered, 'and we'll do it again.' Patiently he retold
the episode, and it lost nothing by a second telling.

For the next two weeks, at intermittent intervals, Brendan continued to work daily, and although the strain of recording tired
him very quickly, by the end of this time he had managed to
complete 50,000 words of his autobiography. There were of
course the usual distractions; the Americans love a celebrity and
he was very high up on their list. But on the whole he resisted the
fêting, and, with one exception, avoided being interviewed by
the press. Kenneth Allsop was coming to America for the *Daily
Mail* and Brendan was anxious that he should be the first to hear
about the progress on his book.

Diana and I accompanied him to meet Ken at Idlewild Airport, but the interminable waiting for Ken to be processed
through Customs unsettled Brendan, and he became restless and
truculent. By the time Ken emerged, although Brendan literally
hugged him, his humour otherwise had deteriorated visibly.
Throughout the taxi-ride back to Manhattan he grumbled and
complained that he wanted a drink, but as Ken was tired from his
flight, he pleaded to be allowed to deposit his baggage at the
Hotel Sheraton first. Brendan gave in ungraciously, and suddenly

I detected he was jealous that somebody else might be absorbing his limelight. Deliberately, I began to devote all my attention to him and left Diana to gossip with Ken at the hotel. After a while he cheered up, but later, when we arrived at Downey's Steak House for a meal, he insisted upon paying for the cab and then made to walk away from us. I grabbed him by the arm.

'Brendan,' I whispered urgently, 'Ken has come a long way to see you. You are not being very hospitable.' He did not say anything but turned round and followed us into the restaurant.

Somehow Katherine Dunham must have heard of Ken's arrival, for suddenly she appeared at our table and immediately pulled up a chair, and Brendan retreated into his previous black humour. This time, however, he did not recover, but sat glowering at the uneaten plate of food in front of him, where we left him an hour later to get over his mood in the best fashion he could.

By morning all signs of the stresses and strains of the previous evening had left him as he sat answering Ken's questions in his room at the Chelsea. He was working these days under the economic lash, he chuckled, for he had tax problems. As a not very invisible export he had to support a population of people who couldn't recognise a potato and called themselves farmers, as well as a minister who said he earned fat profits from attacking him and his faith. Sombrely, he spoke of his new book, in which, he confessed, he had touched upon things that he had not spoken of before. 'I am not proud of them,' he admitted. 'I hate violence, but I was a soldier. Neither do I look back with remorse because, as Shaw said when he was asked what he felt about the Republican Army's methods of fighting the British Army, "A perambulator hasn't much choice of tactics against a furniture van." But only a lunatic boasts of taking human life. Essentially I'm a gentle and amiable person.'

Inevitably, Ken wanted to listen to the tapes. Brendan repaired to the nearest bar where we promised to join him. Later, in the saloon, his sombreness had passed, and he told Ken, between loud guffaws, that if he wanted a professional I.R.A. killer, he would have to look at another set of initials—not the I.R.A. but the B.B.C. 'There my brother Dominic is shooting Englishmen on the Third Programme at the expense of the British licence-holder,' he laughed amiably. It was a merry occasion and it did not break up until Ken left us several hours later for his meeting with Ray Charles, the blind coloured singer who was currently the rage.

Shortly afterwards I heard from Beatrice that she had booked a passage on the *Queen Elizabeth* and the news both elated and upset Brendan. On the day that she was due to sail, he insisted that I telephone her parents' home, and when he found she was really on her way his excitement was marred by the discordant note of guilt. Unable to face the meeting sober, slowly he blurred his horizon a little more each day until he was either suffering from a hangover or about to give himself another one.

Remembering our unhappiness when we arrived, unwelcomed, Diana and I were at the docks to meet her. She was gay and cheerful, had enjoyed her sea trip and was not the least surprised at Brendan's absence. Her first words when we were alone at the bar of the Governor Clinton completely astounded me. She was going to have a baby, she said, and she had decided to come to America in the quite genuine belief that things between herself and Brendan would now be considerably improved. She would tell Brendan as soon as the impact of their meeting had passed.

For several days I waited for Brendan to pull himself together, but once having started on a binge he could not wrench himself free. As I would never allow him to think that I had nothing better to do than watch his interminable drinking, I decided to return with Diana to England. On our last evening in New York he did manage to make the effort to accompany us to a farewell dinner at Downey's, and for a brief while his extraordinary personality came through the fog as he sang the 'Marseillaise', 'The Stars and Stripes', and in our honour, 'Land of Hope and Glory'. But he was too ill to keep it up for long and soon his voice croaked and his tunes became off-key.

The next morning he came to Pier 90 with Beatrice to see us

off, but like a bottle of champagne that has been opened too long, he was sour and flat and made no attempt to persuade me to stay. I promised that as soon as I was in England I would have the tapes transcribed and would place the material in chronological order so that, the moment he asked, I would be ready to return. Just before we embarked, Beatrice whispered that she had not been able to tell Brendan about the baby, and was nervous to be left with him in his present state of mind without money. I searched through my handbag and gave her £20 in dollars which was all I had left.

As Diana and I reached the top of the gangplank, we turned round to wave a final goodbye, but Brendan was already hurrying away from us and he did not look back.

XIV

ON AND OFF THE WAGON

Back in the office there was general surprise. My going to America had been a matter for gloomy speculation, and now it seemed as if the heavy gamble was going to pay off. I had been away five weeks but in that time Brendan had managed to produce a solid structure upon which to build his book. There were, of course, yawning gaps in his story and the skeleton needed dressing, but there was no reason to suppose that, having come this far, he would not accomplish the rest.

For some time, Hope Leresche, Paul Hogarth's agent, had been trying to set up a project by which a book on New York could be produced jointly by Paul and Brendan as a follow-on to the Irish book, but she felt it must be published in time for the New York World Fair of 1964. In the beginning Hutchinson and Geis had been opposed to the idea on the grounds that Brendan had other commitments, and indeed Berney had written despairingly: 'As far as Brendan is concerned, we have done little more than pour money down various bottomless holes. At the moment, we are not looking for more holes.'

Now there was a change of heart. After a long talk with Hope Leresche, Bob Lusty said he was quite happy for me to go ahead and tape Brendan's comments on New York providing *Confessions of an Irish Rebel* was finished first. As time was getting short I was to return to America at once, where Paul would join us for Brendan to show him the subjects he would like drawn.

I telephoned Beatrice to inform her of the plans, and while she admitted that Brendan was still drinking she believed that my presence would probably persuade him to get back to work.

With optimism, I sailed for America again at the end of May. Beatrice was at Pier 90 to meet me and had booked me a room at the Chelsea three floors below their own. David Bard, the Hungarian proprietor, and the staff of the hotel greeted me warmly and, unlike my previous visit, immediately I felt at home. Brendan was in the familiar Oasis bar next door where directly I had unpacked, I joined him. His first words of greeting, 'I thought you must have got drowned,' were scarcely friendly, and once more I detected an uneasiness between us to forewarn me that he had something on his mind. He looked ill and tired and his mental inertness gave me the impression that, without throwing in the sponge, he had somehow contracted out of the business of living.

I deliberately avoided mentioning work, chatting to Willie and Jean, the owners of the saloon, and various casual acquaintances who came over to our booth to welcome me. But when Beatrice asked me about *Hold Your Hour and Have Another*, I praised her drawings and discussed other aspects of the book with her as though Brendan had no part in it at all. During my short period in England I had corrected the final proofs, and the book was now in production and scheduled for September publication. While Brendan on the surface appeared uninterested in this knowledge, I knew he was listening intently, but until he had spoken aloud the thoughts that were troubling him, his slough of despondency would not lift. Establishing my rights as a separate and self-contained individual, I left him to keep a dinner appointment.

As I was certain that the success of our collaboration depended largely on Brendan's respect for me as a separate entity, I had instructed the management of the Chelsea that, while I could be contacted by telephone, on no account was Brendan to be given the number of my apartment. Of late, he had formed the habit of finding his way into the rooms of his friends where he would

sit talking endlessly or sleeping off a hangover. I was afraid as
well that if I allowed him to use my apartment freely, I would
not have the physical stamina to cope with the rigours of work.

The next morning Beatrice telephoned early. Brendan was asking for me, she said, and would I ever come up and breakfast
with him? I agreed, but when I entered their apartment I found
him still in bed, quietly reading a book. He looked up without
smiling, his grunts of good morning giving little indication that he
wanted to see me at all. I endured his silence throughout the
meal, and when Beatrice left us to shop for groceries, I decided
to go as well. As I reached the door, Brendan called me back. He
had something to tell me, he muttered cantankerously, and I
braced myself to hear the trouble.

Through an American agent, he had signed a contract with
Doubleday to write a history of the Irish Revolution, and while
he had carefully avoided mentioning the difficulties to Doubleday, he was worried that I might not want to be included in the
deal. In his roundabout way he was asking me to help him, and
while normally I would gladly have done so, it seemed to me that
in this instance I was powerless. Quite apart from his legal
commitments to Hutchinson and Geis, I was employed jointly by
them to produce his work for their sole publication, and while
the existing arrangements remained I could not possibly embark
on an assignment which would benefit a rival publisher. But to
complicate matters further, Brendan had already received and
spent $3,000 of the Doubleday advance. I tried to explain the
problem to him, but he became unreasonable and abusive and
laid the blame for my civil servant attitude fairly and squarely on
my petit bourgeois background. Not wishing to incur more of
his wrath by definitely refusing to co-operate, I suggested that we
complete *Confessions of an Irish Rebel* and *Brendan Behan's
New York* first and then think again about the Doubleday book.
He accepted the idea rather ungraciously, but he had been drinking too steadily to put my suggestion into practice, and the tape-
recorder remained with its lid firmly closed.

For several days afterwards he made great efforts to stem his

downward trend but he seemed unable to connect with life as it
bustled on around him, and the private world in which he moved
appeared frighteningly near the realms of fantasy. Even Beatrice,
who had told him repeatedly about the baby, was not really sure
if he had taken in the fact. Although the first months of pregnancy
had not troubled her, she was reluctant to involve herself in unnecessary burdens and so she refused most of the invitations that
she and Brendan received. They were not isolated, however, for
they had a small group of friends who understood the enormity
of her task, and protected Brendan, to the best of their ability,
from needless temptations.

One such friend was George Kleinsinger, the composer and a
permanent resident of the Hotel Chelsea. A bohemian like
Brendan, he had an incredible penthouse apartment which he
had furnished with tropical trees and plants imported from all
corners of the globe, fluorescent-lit aquariums of rare fish and
snakes, iguanas blinking out from the foliage, and paroquets,
finches, canaries, red-plumed Brazilian cardinals and mynah
birds fluttering freely amongst it. Brendan loved this miniature
jungle, and although George never allowed him a drink in such
delicate surroundings, he was content to sit and watch the wild
life while he listened to George's piano-playing. Also in the
apartment was a large photograph of Charlie Chaplin disporting
himself fully clothed in a bath, which took up the length and
breadth of one wall. Brendan was fascinated by it and I think,
secretly, would have liked to possess it. It had been given to
George by another guest of the hotel, Agnes Boulton, the widow
of Eugene O'Neill and mother of Oona Chaplin.

The photograph was a favourite topic of conversation, and one
evening we were all discussing it when George's telephone rang to
ask him if he would bring Brendan to a party. Beatrice did not
feel up to the occasion but, as a favour to George, I agreed to
take her place.

The hooley was held in an apartment on the other, more
fashionable, side of New York, and while I was a little put out on
arrival by the host's opening gambit that Brendan was to be

given no drink, I was even more dismayed by the sight of the china ornaments and priceless *objets d'art* which decorated the home on mantelpieces, sideboards, slender-legged tables and individual plinths. Unfortunately Brendan, who had spent days in hopeless lethargy, took one look at the room-scape and suddenly came to life. Pushing past his host, he snatched a whiskey and downed it before I could stop him. Having accomplished this feat to his obvious satisfaction, he then lurched towards a vast Chinese figure, picked it up, smiled across at my ashen face, and proceeded to whirl it full circle around his body before replacing it clumsily on to its tottering base. I could not move a muscle until, unabashed, he disappeared from view into the middle of a large group of admirers when I breathed again. The host did not share my relief and, grabbing me by the arm, he screamed hysterically, 'You must go, you must go,' and then stamping his feet, 'You must go at once.'

Infuriated that he should have wanted Brendan at his party and yet not be prepared for his unpredictable behaviour, I did not hurry to relay the orders, but waited for Brendan to finish his version of 'I'm Lady Chatterley's Lover' which he was singing to a captivated audience. To be quite honest, I was delighted to see the return of something approaching his old self, and as he was doing no harm, I did not want to end his enjoyment too quickly. The sight of my host nervously twittering in the background, however, so sickened me that all at once I decided to leave on my own. At an opportune moment, which did not come too quickly, I informed Brendan in an undertone that I had been asked to decamp and was warning him of the fact in case he should think I had purposefully deserted him. As I reached the entrance hall, behind me came Brendan, and he said good night to his host with a dignity that lost nothing by the implication that only traitors stay where friends are not accepted.

George shared our taxi but when we drew up at the Chelsea, Brendan asked us to have a drink with him at the Oasis. I refused for I was still smouldering and wanted only to go to my room, and Brendan went off alone. I was to learn the next morning that when he eventually returned he was very drunk, had fallen over the glass-topped table in the lobby, and had had to be helped up to his apartment by the night-porter. The bout was to be the final straw for his weakening constitution, and throughout the following day he lay in his bed moaning and groaning, and racked by constant vomiting. He was a very sick man and his sudden decision to come off the drink while he was unable to take any food produced too great a shock on his system. He began to sink fast.

The crisis came two days later, on Sunday. Unexpectedly his vomiting had ceased and, believing him to be better, Beatrice delayed her decision to contact a doctor. He appeared less distressed in himself too, and periodically he would open his eyes and join in with our conversation before slipping back into stillness. Beatrice, who had been confined constantly to the sickroom, felt she needed a breath of fresh air, and as soon as she departed Brendan began to speak almost apologetically about his earnest wish to try to cure, for ever, his appalling thirst. He had seen an advertisement in the *New York Times* which interested him and, handing me the paper, he pointed out the book concerned. It was *Anti-Alcoholism: Drink and Stay Sober* by E. R. Richardson and J. P. Woolfolk. He knew there was a bookshop open in the Village, he said, and would I try and buy the book for him? Although I seriously doubted whether he was able to read in his present state, his manner of asking me so resembled the plight of a shipwrecked man who is clasping at a life-belt that I could not refuse.

I waited for Beatrice to come back and as Brendan was now sleeping peacefully she said she would accompany me. We combed every bookshop in the Village, but without success, and we returned an hour later apprehensive as to how Brendan would accept the news. On first sight, everything appeared normal. He was sitting up in bed apparently unconcerned. A little closer inspection, however, revealed that he was reading from a book that was upside down and his complete indifference to the failure of our mission was puzzling. Furthermore, the pile of Sunday

papers which had been on his bed when we left were now lying
crumpled and torn in a heap on the floor and spattered with
blood-stains, and the bed in the sitting-room looked as though
someone had recently slept in it. Beatrice asked nonchalantly if
he'd had any visitors, but when he said no and was obviously
surprised by her question, she gestured with her eyes for me to
follow her out of his hearing. From unhappy experience of the
evidence, she disclosed, she was in no doubt that while we had
been out Brendan had had an alcoholic seizure and a doctor
must be summoned immediately. Without medical aid, there was
no stopping the attacks once they had started. I remembered
Peter Harpel's offer to help in an emergency such as this, and I
ran down to my apartment where I could telephone him without
upsetting Brendan.

Conforming to the customary pattern of every design connected with Brendan, the complications mounted. Peter Harpel
was away, and when I eventually traced him he grasped the
gravity of the situation but explained that by the time he had
driven back into New York it would be probably too late. He
offered to get in touch with Dr. Max Tasler, a friend of his, and
promised to telephone the moment he had done so. Within a
short while he rang back to say that Dr. Tasler was out, but he
had given his secretary my number and had impressed on her
the urgency of the case. For the rest of the afternoon I paced the
floor wringing my hands in suspended misery, until at nine
o'clock I left for a hurried bite at the restaurant next door. Incredibly, during this short period Dr. Tasler called. The telephone operator at the Chelsea, on finding no reply from my apartment, put his call through to the Behans'. Unfortunately,
Beatrice was out too, and Brendan answered the incessant ringing to thank Dr. Tasler profusely for troubling, but explained
that as he was now so much better, there was no need for the
doctor to come round. Mercifully Max Tasler ignored these instructions, and after finally contacting me he arrived at the Hotel
Chelsea.

He was only just in time. Hardly had he greeted Brendan before a series of agonising shouts, enough to freeze our blood, revealed the truth of Beatrice's prophecy: Brendan was having a second seizure. As his body writhed and twisted grotesquely on his bed, the seconds passed heavily as hours while Beatrice held him down from one side and Dr. Tasler from the other. Slowly his cries dwindled to a distressed whimper before he quietened and recovered consciousness. I was standing at the foot of his bed at the time, numbed by what I had witnessed, and as his bewildered brain struggled to come out of the dark, his eyes focused on me. But it was not myself that they saw. Suddenly, perspiration broke out on his face and, deep in his horrors, his hair stood on end and fear harrowed up his soul. Waiting in apprehension, I spoke my name, repeating the word over and over again, before the sound of my voice came through to him and his trembling hand extended to mine. 'Of course, daughter,' he muttered almost inaudibly. 'Of course it's you. I'm sorry, kid.'

The ambulance arrived shortly afterwards, and he was taken to University Hospital where, despite a third attack during the night, by morning he had improved. But when we visited him, he had no recollection of the previous day's events, and when he was told, he must have been convinced that his mental lapse was a sign that he was losing his sanity. He did not reveal his fears, but they smouldered within him until he was fit enough to get out of his bed, when he rushed out of the ward and attempted to discharge himself wearing only his pyjamas. Restrained by physical force, Brendan, an easily terrified man, was now certain that Beatrice had finally committed him to a dreaded lunatic asylum.

His raving fantasies brought us hurrying to the hospital. He was rampaging up and down the corridors in bare feet and pyjamas when we arrived, but catching sight of Beatrice, he approached her menacingly. In an attempt to calm him I took him into a room on our own, and whilst he became less violent he could not get it out of his head that he was in Grange Gorman, a mental home in Ireland. I persuaded a patient to join us, but even his insistence that he was being treated for a duodenal ulcer did not pacify Brendan. Dr. Tasler was summoned hastily but his efforts failed too. Brendan was given his clothes and allowed to leave. There is no doubt that he genuinely believed a conspiracy was afoot to get him locked up for, once he was out of the building, the pressure on his brain subsided temporarily and he joked that if all puzzle factories were similar to the one he had recently vacated, they were not bad places at that.

Once back in the Chelsea, however, his nightmare world returned and for the hour following, he sat on the ormolu chair in the lobby speaking to phantom listeners in frenzied delirium. As soon as we could, Beatrice and I helped him up to his apartment where he fell on the bed to drift into a heavy sleep from which he awakened at nightfall with his brain miraculously repaired.

The experience had frightened us profoundly and our one thought now was to get Brendan home as quickly as possible. I think Brendan was scared, too, for he was most amenable to our suggestion to return, but he was curiously reluctant to use his existing air ticket, leaving us with the impression that something heinous had occurred on the flight over, the nature of which he would not disclose. As the $12,000 advance on his unfinished autobiography had by now dwindled to $2,000, we could hardly ask Berney Geis for the money to cover his sea passage, so the three of us paid a hasty call on his bank manager. Kindly but firmly the man regretted that he could do nothing for us as Brendan's account was virtually closed. Brendan suddenly became frantic, charging up and down the highly polished bank floor to the amazement of the numerous clerks. All at once, Beatrice remembered a royalty cheque from *The Hostage* which she had put in her handbag shortly before she left Ireland, and handed it to the bank manager. We were cheered to find that the amount was sufficient to cover the fare. A taxi-ride to the Cunard Steamship Company on Park Avenue removed the final obstacle and we booked the last double-berth in Cabin Class for Brendan and Beatrice, and a First Class single berth for myself for the next sailing of the *Queen Elizabeth*.

It had not occurred to me that Brendan would want to work in his few remaining days, so I packed up the tape-recorder with the idea of returning it to the shop. Artfully he waited until I had completed the job before he told me, in sheer delight, that I had been wasting my time, for he was going to put *Confessions* behind him before he sailed for Ireland.

True to his word, every day and sometimes two or three times a day, we recorded for short periods, but the sessions were painful for him and he tired very easily. When I played back the tapes, his voice was dull and flat without a spark of animation. He was plagued too by a recurrence of his eye trouble and I had to read aloud the manuscript of our earlier recordings so that he could edit the text by dictation.

Strangely, it was during the editing that Brendan revealed he was aware of Beatrice's pregnancy. In the course of his autobiography he had mentioned borrowing the passport of a married man and a father, and when we came to edit the relevant passage, he looked at me quizzically, put his weary head to one side and said shyly: Did I know he had now made up for both malefactions? In truth he was soon to be a father.

As the days drew nearer to the date of our sailing Brendan's spirits lowered, until on the morning prior to our departure he lay on his bed looking at the ceiling in dejected silence. On the few occasions that he spoke, he made it clear that his chief regret at leaving the city of his heart was a persistent doubt that he would ever see it again. Indeed, the extent of his affection for New York was such that for the first time he made no attempt to drown his sadness, but preferred to savour and remember soberly his last remaining hours in the place. But if he was despondent Beatrice was not as, in her delight at returning to Ireland, she busied herself in and out of the apartment with the last-minute necessities connected with a journey. Brendan watched her happiness with alternating affection and sorrow. He could, without doubt, have inebriated himself to such good effect that our departure would not have been possible, but he had the good sense to realise that one day he would have to return, if only to attend to the libel case that was still pending. He knew, too, that his love for Beatrice would not allow him to disregard her wishes that their baby be born in Ireland.

On our last evening in New York, I had gone to George Kleinsinger's apartment to fulfil a promise to feed his menagerie while he was away in Connecticut narrating his opera, *Archie and Mehitabel*. In case I should be needed I had told Beatrice where I would be, but had not mentioned it to Brendan for I was afraid he might do some irreparable damage in George's absence. I had barely started my business, however, before there was a thud on the door, which I opened to admit the stalwart figure of Brendan. Without uttering a word, he pushed past me and made straight for the bathroom. Beatrice followed shortly but, before she could offer any explanation, the silence was broken by the noise of someone falling, accompanied by a frantic shout, and we rushed into the bathroom to discover what had happened. I could hardly believe my eyes. Brendan was sitting fully clothed in the middle of the bath but at right angles across it, so that while his backside rested on the base, his little legs dangled petulantly over the side and his head appeared firmly wedged between the taps. To add further to his misery, cold water from the tap was pouring down his shoulder and he was already quite wet. Despite the efforts he was making to heave himself out of the bath, the violent movements of his limbs were achieving no more success than the kickings of a big woolly sheep that has had the misfortune to fall over on its back.

'Help me, help me,' he bleated pitifully as Beatrice turned off the tap. When we tried to lift him, his body went along with the extent of our pulling, but his head remained behind, hopelessly and irrevocably stuck. Panting, we paused for a moment to regain our strength for a second attack. Out of the corner of my eye, I caught sight of Charlie Chaplin's photograph and I knew I could no longer control the laughter that was welling up inside me. But if I considered Brendan's abortive attempts at imitation a subject for mirth he did not appreciate my humour, and he roared out his rage.

'It's not so f—ing funny being stuck in a bath,' he bellowed,

and although I pulled myself together sufficiently to mutter that
it wasn't so funny either trying to lift him out, his increasing indignation sent me off in an explosion of laughter even worse than
the first time, and now Beatrice became infected by my convul-
sions. With the tears helplessly rolling down our cheeks we
finally managed to extricate him, and as we guided his dripping
figure down a flight of stairs to his apartment, our hysteria prevented us from hearing his volleys of abuse too plainly.

The following morning Brendan's genial face showed no sign
of the previous night's resentment. We had to be on board the
Queen Elizabeth by midday and bright and early he trotted off to
be shaved by the barber opposite while Beatrice and I finished
our packing and closed up the bags. In plenty of time we arrived
on Pier 90, patiently queuing to pass through immigration.
Brendan was instantly recognised and allowed to go through
without question, but when I was asked what I had been doing
in New York, he answered for me by shouting back jovially,
'Writing under the name of Brendan Behan.' While everybody
laughed, he waited for me to reach him and then said through
closed teeth, 'and few know the truth of that statement.'

On board he became involved in a press conference, and before the whistle blew and the gangplank was hauled up, he was
drunk and belligerent, leaving New York and the startled reporters with a series of parting shots at the way of life in the city
which did not represent his true affection for the place. 'I think
the housing for the working classes here is lousy,' he said. 'Dublin puts you to shame. The buses are filthy in comparison to
our buses and the subway is a death-trap.' But he reserved his
final salvo for the newspapers: 'They go on for ever about
nothing.'

As the *Queen Elizabeth* slid gracefully out to sea, the Carib-
bean lounge in Cabin Class was the scene of heavier drinking.
Soon, abusive and aggressive, he had pinched the bottom of a
honeymooning bride, and her military policeman husband was
the first to issue an official complaint. As I was travelling First
Class, I had to leave Beatrice to cope with his obstreperous-

ness while I changed for dinner. I had been allocated a seat at the purser's table and I was about to lay into a plate of delicious smoked salmon when a harassed-looking steward whispered in my ear that I was needed urgently in the Cabin Class restaurant. Brendan's swearing had upset all the diners and, as his wife was unable to do anything with him, would I come at once and try to remove him.

I excused myself discreetly, and the steward escorted me through a series of narrow passages before I found myself a few minutes later in the kitchens which lead to the Cabin Class restaurant. Brendan was indeed shouting and, already embarrassed by approaching the restaurant in evening dress from a slightly unusual direction, I found little comfort from the startled expressions on the faces of the diners as I walked towards the Behan table. Beatrice, apparently unconcerned, was eating bananas and cream, and while she was delighted to see me she was taking no further part in the affairs of Brendan. Calling upon the head waiter to help me, we lifted Brendan on to his feet and, supporting him from either side, we half carried him out of the door while he flourished the unforgivable word as many times as he could.

Once outside we were beckoned into a nearby cabin to be confronted by the stern face of a senior officer. Anchoring Brendan's wavering figure to a chair, the head waiter swiftly departed.

'Mr. Brendan Bracken,' began the officer formidably before I stopped him.

'Brendan Behan is the name,' I interrupted.

His mistake appeared to put him off his stroke and he blustered momentarily. Then he tried again. 'Well, Mr. Bean then,' he said more softly, but soon the thoughts of Brendan's outrageous behaviour had taken precedence over his control of himself and as his words fell over each other in rage, he reverted once more to Mr. Brendan Bracken.

At the end of his diatribe I waited for his red face to shade down a little before I pointed out the unlikelihood of Brendan hearing his wrath, for his head was now sunk deep in his chest and he was not receiving at all.

'This is all the result of your press conference,' I said. 'He must not be confined in any way whatsoever. This could have very serious consequences. But if you give me your word that the bar will be closed to him throughout the trip, I, for my part, will guarantee that he causes you no further trouble.'

Beatrice shortly joined us, and with her assurances too, the officer agreed to give it a try. Waking Brendan up, we supported him back to his cabin where later a doctor visited him and gave him heavy sedation.

By the morning, his sleep had returned him to sobriety, and I told him quite bluntly of the previous evening's unpleasantness. Shocked and mortified to be the cause of my humiliation, he promised he would not attempt to find ways and means to over-come the ship's order of no spirits, and for the rest of the voyage, without the slightest resentment, he adhered faithfully to his word. By the time we docked at Southampton, he had so en-deared himself to the passengers and the ship's complement that everyone was sorry the voyage had ended.

Our ways parted at Southampton, for my father and Diana had come to meet me by car, and Brendan and Beatrice were going on to London by the boat-train. Despite all the vicissitudes, as I waved a parting farewell to them, I felt a pang of sadness, for I knew it would be unlikely that we would ever be together again in America.

XV

RETURN TO DUBLIN

Brendan remained on the wagon for the first few days in London. Already he was thinking of returning to America, and he signed the Hutchinson contract with Paul Hogarth for *Brendan Behan's New York*. The idea was for the three of us to go back in September and for the first time, I was to receive a flat fee for my part in the transaction.

I suppose it was inevitable, but Bob Lusty was worried that once again the firm would be without a publicity manager for several weeks. Although I had a very able staff who had been with me a number of years, he felt a manager was essential. The existing arrangements were to stand for the New York book, but in the interim I would have to make up my mind whether I would give up my job and work entirely for Brendan or vice versa. I could no longer do both.

This was a difficult decision. I had been with Hutchinson for thirteen years and had worked my way up from shorthand typist to a position which offered a fair degree of security. But my connection with the firm went far deeper. It had been founded in 1887 by my grandfather, then Mr. George Thompson Hutchinson, but later knighted for his services to publishing, and it had remained in the family until 1950 when the controlling interest was sold on the death of the second chairman, my uncle, Walter Hutchinson. Recently my brother, Bimby Holt, had become chairman of the parent group while Bob Lusty remained chairman of the publishing side of the business. Thus I had strong affiliation with the firm and the loyalties which accompany the ties of blood.

With the best will in the world no one could have described Brendan as a secure proposition. He was ailing and his chance of survival for more than a few years appeared remote. But it was not a decision I could make overnight, nor was it one in which I could ask for advice. I mentioned my quandary to Brendan, and he replied, very fairly, that while he did not want to be the devil's advocate, it would be a big blow to him if I ended our partnership. I made up my mind that I would wait until we had finished *Brendan Behan's New York* and then think again.

Brendan's reaction to my procrastination was not encouraging. He seemed reluctant to go back to Ireland where he would have to face the pressures of his libel case and his new reponsibilities as an expectant father, but he would not pay any attention to work either. He refused to look through the proof copy of *Hold Your Hour and Have Another* to bolster my wavering confidence that I had chosen his best articles for inclusion, neither did he show any interest in the new material for *Confessions of an Irish Rebel* which I was busy transcribing from the tapes. Instead, he spent his mornings coping with a hangover while the rest of the the day he ensured he would have one more so that, by the time he finally left London, he was in as bad a shape as he had ever been. During his ramblings he had acquired a friend who had attached himself most securely, and Beatrice, who was not anxious to transport Brendan to Dublin on her own, persuaded Alan to make the journey with her. He was an eccentric but ingenious individual and as Brendan, at the moment of departure, was no longer able to stand, Alan managed somehow to procure a bath-chair at Euston in which he wheeled Brendan up the platform and into his seat on the train. It was a chaotic send-off, but not without its humorous side. I promised Beatrice, as the train pulled out of the station, that as soon as I had re-shaped *Confessions,* I would be over to force Brendan to go through the manuscript with me.

Shortly after they had left, a two-month festival of Irish comedy opened at the Theatre Royal, Stratford, with two plays by Synge, *The Tinker's Wedding* and *The Shadow of the Glen*, and a stage adaptation of Brendan's radio play, *The Big House*. The festival was inaugurated by Alan Simpson under the name of the New Pike, and was planned as a successor to the Pike Theatre in Dublin, which many years earlier had been instrumental in putting Brendan on the map with *The Quare Fellow*. Although previously *The Big House* had been performed at the Pike in Dublin without much notice, the first British stage performance was well received.

'A play which—in his present phase of over-publicised tours and tape-recorded book-making—re-establishes Behan's brilliance as a writer,' wrote *The Times*. 'It has all the ribald verve of *The Hostage* and a higher proportion of original jokes'; while the *Sunday Telegraph* admitted that 'it makes us realise how long we have waited for a new Behan play.'

Almost simultaneously with the reviews came the official news in the press that the Behans were expecting a baby, and the newspapers were filled with photographs of Brendan looking haggard and unkempt, and captioned by even more disquieting statements that he was perpetually celebrating the event on Black Velvet, a mixture of champagne and stout. As soon as I saw the cuttings, I picked up the telephone and made a call to Beatrice's parents, and as luck would have it Beatrice answered herself. Brendan was indeed in poor form, she confirmed, and had been drinking consistently since the moment he arrived in Dublin. He rarely came home now and when he did it was usually in the early hours of the morning when he was either carried or stumbled into the front room by himself to lie on the couch until he was able to get up and go out on another batter. If I did come over, she stressed, there would be little point in my staying anywhere but with them, for the chances of connecting with him otherwise, would be remote. I was not out of my mind about the proposal, but it was a generous offer on Beatrice's part, and I agreed to accept it.

On August Bank Holiday weekend I sailed across to Dublin and stood on deck to watch the sun shining brilliantly over the hills and the countryside around the bay. I had the completed text of *Confessions* assembled vaguely in chronological order and the first bound copy of *Hold Your Hour*, and while I considered it unlikely that Brendan would look at either, I hoped that perhaps Beatrice might be able to supply some of the gaps which were blatantly obvious in the autobiography. She was at Dun Laoghaire to meet me, and told me at once that although she had informed Brendan of my coming, she doubted if he had taken in the fact.

I was sleeping in the room immediately at the top of the stairs on the first-floor landing. Brendan and Beatrice occupied the bedroom a few steps further up from my own, and we all shared the lavatory next door to my room. Whilst I knew Brendan had a horror of being shut in, I was perturbed that none of the locks possessed keys. There was a second lavatory downstairs, however, in the bathroom which led out from the kitchen, and this door could be bolted. I unpacked the bare essentials and left the rest of my belongings in my case. The house was really not big enough to accommodate the books, papers and articles essential to an author, and while Beatrice had done her best to keep the place tidy, she had not been able to overcome the space limitations, and the dining-room table at one end was a mass of letters and odds and ends.

We had just sat down to our evening meal when there was a crash on the door and a frantic rattling of the letter-box. Opening it myself, I was confronted by the swaying figure of Brendan and the hopeful looks of a taxi-driver waiting for his fare. Brendan was not the least surprised to see me and embraced me unsteadily, while his companion hovered on the tiptoe of expectation. I called to Beatrice who paid him off, while I supported Brendan to his couch in the front room.

After a few hours of sleep, he became comparatively sober and began to talk about returning to America. He was determined to make the trip and begged me to go forward with the plans for us to travel together, for he was sure that soon he would be able to steady himself up. He was harassed and unhappy and terrified of the death-grip in which he held himself, and he gave me the impression that he believed his tight grasp would be released through the use of the tape-recorder. I think it was at that moment that I decided I would be wrong to remain in my job at Hutchinson. There were other things in life more important than cosiness and security.

In the middle of the night, I was awakened by the noisy turning of my door knob and Beatrice's voice shouting, 'Leave Rae alone. She's tired after her journey.' Brendan called through the door that I should book sea passages as he did not want to fly, and when I said I would, I heard him mumble something and then there was silence.

In the morning he remained in bed until late, and when he eventually arose, he crawled downstairs to the dining-room where we were lingering over our breakfast, and sat down without speaking. In the bright light of day, I became doubly aware of how ill he looked, and as he had not been able to eat for three weeks, the skin on his face was hanging over his cheek-bones in flabby folds. Every now and again he would point at some object at the other end of the table, and if I did not hand him immediately what it was that he wanted, he became unreasonably exasperated. Even so, as soon as I had handed him the letter or article that had been important to him a few seconds earlier, he put it down without looking at it as if it were too heavy for him to carry. Suddenly a wave of claustrophobia seemed to envelop him and shouting for his shoes and socks, he asked me to put them on for him. I managed, after a struggle, to put on his socks, but his feet and ankles were so painfully swollen that to put on his shoes was an impossibility. He became frantic, pushing and shoving his feet unmercifully into the cramped space until he was successful, but he could not do up the laces and, as he shuffled to the door, I hastily tucked them down the sides of his shoes. From the window in the front room I watched his faltering footsteps reach the pavement where he paused for a breather, grabbing on to the railings as he did so. A passer-by took pity on him and helped him on his way, presumably until he could find a taxi that would drive him to a pub.

For three days the pattern repeated itself. But as I had hoped Beatrice read the manuscript of *Confessions*, and helpfully arranged for me to meet an I.R.A. colleague of Brendan's who was able to fill in some of the gaps in the story. They were both despondent over the contents of the book and confirmed what I already knew. The text as it stood could only harm Brendan's reputation as a writer. Beatrice was sure, however, that Brendan intended to get to America somehow, and suggested I take the manuscript with me where he might feel more disposed to get down to it. Sad and depressed, I left for England wondering where it would all end.

Soon Brendan was back in hospital suffering from diabetes, a liver disorder and physical exhaustion and, optimistic that compulsory rest and medication would once more patch him up, I went ahead and booked our passages. Originally I had intended to sail on the *Queen Elizabeth* as the crew knew Brendan, but there was no accommodation available and I transferred to the *Caronia*, sailing at the end of August. I cabled Berney who made reservations at the Hotel Chelsea where Paul Hogarth would be joining us early the following month. On the night before my departure I spoke to Beatrice by telephone, and although Brendan was still in hospital, she told me not to be surprised if I met up with him at Southampton, for that very day he had insisted that he was still going. He was considerably better but by no means fit, and she knew I would appreciate that when he had made up his mind to do something, there was no way of stopping him.

At Southampton I was met by a battery of cameramen and reporters at the dock and escorted on to the ship by a V.I.P. from the Cunard Steamship Company, but once they were certain Brendan was not going to accompany me they left to interview more important passengers. It was a lonely journey.

Deputising for Brendan, I showed Paul round his favourite

New York haunts and between times sat in my room trying to
improve on the manuscript of *Confessions*. Using *Borstal Boy* as
my guide, I would pace the floor in an endeavour to force myself to become a second-rate understudy. While the sketchy attempts at each sentence were fresh in my mind I would rush to the
typewriter. It was a slow and arduous task but I could see no
alternative.

The one bright moment in these gloomy weeks was the publication in England of *Hold Your Hour and Have Another*. Brendan
was very fond of quoting from the sayings of W. B. Yeats, one of
whose favourite remarks was that you should never write anything during the course of a year which you would not include in
a collection of your work at the end of it. In the light of this, the
reviews for his new book cheered me.

'Many a time I have happily held my hour and my peace and
had another, listening to him,' wrote W. R. Rogers in the *Sunday Times*. 'This book, illustrated fondly by his wife, is a collection of pieces written for the *Irish Press*—a lively, lovely rag-bag
of observation which shows charity and charm. For Behan is a
listener too, and I know no other book which so nicely captures
the down-at-winged-heel poetry of the Dublin pub-goers' talk—
the ould wans—as one would wish to capture the talk of the East
End Cockney.' Alan Brien recorded in the *Sunday Telegraph*
that 'he talks as a champion boxer breathes—the words ride on
the intake as well as the output and the merest sideswipe from
his lungs can intoxicate a weak head. But he is also a professional communicator with a craftsman's awe for what is written
down rather than scribbled upon air.' The *Observer* too was
enthusiastic and felt the book gave off 'a strong impression of
personality and the characteristically warm effluvia which
Behan's humanity generates under nearly all circumstances.'

And the American reviews of the Little, Brown edition were
later to echo these sentiments. 'Brendan Behan's new collection
should ring even to the initiated with the clink of the genuine
article—talks in the snug of a Dublin pub—unvarnished and un-
augmented, but as arresting as, say, at the early Abbey Theater

and O'Casey child,' commented the *New York Times Book Review*. 'This book should make it very clear that Behan has no serious opposition as the real thing.' Alan Pryce-Jones, writing in the *New York Herald Tribune*, conceded that while 'Mr. Behan talks massive, like a lot of large men he is extremely light on his toes. He is, on evidence, a natural writer, with a wonderful ear for idiom, a mind like a beehive, thrumming away nineteen to the dozen, and an engagingly generous spirit. It looks as though Mr. Behan's better fantasies will still carry a tickling flavour of sawdust and pipesmoke in the year 2030.'

As soon as Paul had finished his drawings, he was anxious that I should return to Dublin to get the text, for time was getting short if the book was to be published in time for the World Fair. Before I left, I gave Berney Geis the new manuscript of *Confessions* as far as I had gone with it, and he seemed pleased with the result. He implored me to try to get Brendan to finish the rest before we began recordings for *Brendan Behan's New York*. I sailed back to England on the *Queen Mary*, by now a seasoned traveller, and a table had been installed in my cabin so that I could continue working uninterrupted. The Staff were most co-operative and I would like to record my thanks to the Cunard Steamship Company for the facilities they afforded me throughout my numerous journeys. Without waiting to call in at the office, I flew directly to Dublin where again Beatrice had offered me the hospitality of her home.

Brendan had been out of hospital briefly while I was away, but he was now back in again, and although Beatrice said he was better, she doubted if he would ever be well enough in time for me to tape his views on New York. Indeed, when I visited him, while mentally he was more alert than on my previous stay, he looked worn and feeble and I was anxious not to say anything that might add to his burdens. He was up in his dressing-gown and pyjamas, and when he saw me he greeted me like a relation, pecking me courteously on the cheek without giving any indication that he was aware I had recently arrived from America. He could not stand up for long, however, and was relieved when the exchange of pleasantries was over and he could sit down again. For a while we indulged in conversation, mostly trivia, but despite his weariness, I noticed he was continually watching the corridor outside his ward as though he were expecting to see someone. All at once he got up and, with a most purposeful gait, he marched out of the room. Beatrice guessed his villainy, and opening the locker of the patient in the bed next to his, she exposed a selection of bottles which would not have been prescribed by a doctor. Shame-faced, the man confessed that these belonged to Brendan, who was bribing innocent visitors to bring in 'the message.' Furious, she shared her discovery with the matron of the hospital, and within twenty-four hours Brendan discharged himself to return to his home, his humour thoroughly soured by the removal of his loot.

For the first hour he sat in the dining-room shouting for his passport, but when he found that nobody was really upset by his threats to go to America he changed his tune and said he would wait until after the baby's birth. I reminded him that unless he pulled himself together he probably wouldn't live to see it and, surprisingly, he agreed. In a more reasonable manner he began to mention work, but his talk implied that as I had already decided to end our partnership, his words were purely academic. I hastened to correct him, and informed him of my earlier decision. He was comforted a little, but so that he should be under no misapprehension, I told him that sometime we would have to find some means by which I would be compensated for the loss of my financial security. There was plenty of time, I stressed, and we could discuss it later. At once he pointed impulsively to a plain sheet of paper that was lying on the table in front of him, and when I handed it to him he immediately signed his signature in the middle of the page.

'There you are,' he said. 'Put on that what you think fit.'

I was horrified that after all the years of Brendan's worldly success, he should be so naïve and stupid, and I answered him sharply that it was for him to carry the final authority.

Instead of being grateful for my sensible advice he flew into a tantrum, and said hadn't he enough troubles without being bothered by such incidentals. If he couldn't trust me, whom could he trust? Would I do him the favour of just this one request, he asked, and accentuated his words sarcastically. As a temporary measure and in order to appease him, I gave myself 10 per cent of his earnings to come from *Hold Your Hour and Have Another, The Scarperer, Brendan Behan's New York* and *Confessions of an Irish Rebel*, and decided that I would bring up the matter again when he was more reasonable. He never asked me what I had done, and each time I mentioned the subject afterwards I was met by the same intolerance. It was an unhappy and unprofessional way in which to conduct a business relationship, but I was not convinced that Brendan was now able to understand to what he was committing himself.

As a matter of fact, I did not think that we would ever tape-record *Brendan Behan's New York*, but hoped perhaps that he had sufficient clarity of mind to remember other details in his life during the period concerned in *Confessions*. *The Scarperer* was a much easier proposition for the serial was in manuscript and the only problem was the translation of the Irish idioms which scattered the text. If we couldn't produce the new book, at least we could finish these two other projects.

But once Brendan had satisfied himself that my existence was solely for the purpose of encouraging him to work, I was disillusioned to discover that he expected me to dance to his every whim and fancy and jump at his beck and call. He shouted for me to cook his breakfast, pick up his clothes, run unintelligible errands, and then rudely interrupted that if he had to spell out what he wanted, he would rather have nothing at all. I put up with his dictatorial behaviour for several days before I decided that I would not allow our previous affectionate regard for one another to disintegrate entirely. Early one morning, while he was alone in his bedroom, I told him forcibly that I was returning to England to cancel the New York contract while there was still time for Paul Hogarth to obtain a substitute to supply the text, and gave weight to my words by adding that, as far as I was concerned, I wished to retreat from the previous arrangements I had recently made with him.

Again I was to be astounded by Brendan's character. He had decided at that very moment, he said, smiling apologetically, to begin working again and would I find it in my heart to be patient and stay on to help him? Barely able to speak on discovering that our former easy friendship could be reclaimed so easily, I left the room at his request to set up the tape-recorder and prepare myself for the first session of *Brendan Behan's New York*.

XVI

A LEGEND—TOO SOON

We were to work in the dining-room, he said, for the chairs were more comfortable, but in reality there were too many associations with sickness and pain in the front room for him to be comfortable in it. Beatrice cleared one end of the table while Brendan dressed, so that when he eventually emerged I was ready and waiting for him to begin. He looked drawn and weary and I very much doubted whether he still had the ability to talk books, but if, in the process, it gave him an interest in living, or pleasure and security, the tapes and their contents were of no great importance.

To satisfy myself that he was not making the effort out of a sense of guilt towards me, I asked him if he really felt up to it, and he answered yes, positively, he was. I had with me photostat copies of most of Paul Hogarth's drawings for the book, and Brendan picked them up and glanced through them, one by one, showing delight at the places he recognised and questioning me on the few which he could not place. Finally, he pulled out a sketch of the Statue of Liberty, settled himself comfortably and nodded for me to turn on the machine.

His opening words described a large cocktail-party which had been given in his honour by Martini, the drink manufacturers, in Paris, and while I was unaware that I had revealed my puzzlement as to how this story had any bearing on the drawing of the Statue of Liberty he was holding in his hand, he suddenly threw

back his head and laughed freely. No, he had not gone mad, he
said, and there was a definite point to the anecdote if I could
just contain myself until he came around to it. Feeling foolish, I
let the tapes roll again, and quickly the purpose for his introduction slipped into place. Grinning triumphantly, he explained
that he had met an old lady at the party who claimed to be as
old as the Statue of Liberty, and whose parents had known
Gustave Eiffel, of Eiffel Tower fame, in the days when he de-
signed the framework of the American statue eighty years previously.

It was an extremely apt lead-in to a book on New York, and
as the morning progressed, whether or not my previous bewilderment had spurred him on, it became obvious that he was really
working and attacking the project seriously. Certainly he spoke
with the voice of a very tired man but, despite his fatigue, his
words still contained flash after flash of the spirit that had
dominated his talking in the days of his health, and had made
him the most entertaining of men. And contrary to expectations,
he was less lethargic by the end of the session than he had been
at the start of it.

After lunch Eddie Whelan, a former I.R.A. colleague, dropped
by to see him, and Brendan suggested we go at once and collect
Bill Finnegan, an equally close friend, who lived at Gratton
Crescent next door to the Black Lion public house at Inchicore.
We persuaded him to rest a few hours longer, when we hired a
taxi and piled happily into it. Delighted with the company at the
Black Lion, he warmly related his experiences of the morning
and pulled my leg good-naturedly over my needless apprehen-
sions. Again I was struck by his extraordinary ability to rise out
of himself when previously it had appeared he was only capable
of listening to the bells of hell. Insisting that he would drink
nothing but beer, he sat talking congenially, but while he did not
mention it, I was certain that his peace of mind was not caused
entirely by working again, but more from the knowledge that his
words were up to standard.

Just before the party broke up, Bill Finnegan took me to one side. 'What's happened to Brendan?' he exclaimed. 'I've not seen him so full of life since his return from America.' I smiled with silly pride as I answered. 'Oh, he's always like this after a few hours of tape-recording ...'

Each day, we worked steadily, and as he was now eating more, his mental and physical improvement encouraged all his friends to believe that Brendan would yet break away from the death rein which had previously guided him. He felt better able to cope with all his problems, and the future did not appear so black. He began to look forward to the birth of the baby and to accept his responsibilities as a father willingly, showing a new sensitivity and solicitude towards Beatrice. He was concerned that they were not on the telephone in case of an emergency, and worried that she had chosen to go into the Rotunda Hospital where earlier his grandmother had died, presumably from old age.

With quite genuine enthusiasm, he looked ahead to the day when *Brendan Behan's New York* would be finished and he could make a start on *The History of the Irish Revolution*. Somehow we had managed to appease Geis and Hutchinson, and the latter had been given British Commonwealth rights, but while I was apprehensive that the total sum of $1,000 offered me by Doubleday would do no more than cover my expenses, and not even those if Brendan took off for America, I was prepared to take a chance in the light of his present well-being. I had been given a list of books to read by Val Iremonger so that I should have some background knowledge on the subject before we actually started recording. Most of these books I had been able to buy in Dublin, but had failed to obtain a copy of perhaps the most important of all—Dorothy Macardle's standard work, *The Irish Republic*.

One morning as we neared the end of *Brendan Behan's New York*, I mentioned the omission to Brendan who confirmed that it was an essential part of my education and promised to get hold of a copy for me. He asked me how I was enjoying the book I was currently reading, *On Another Man's Wound* by Ernie O Malley, one of the leading Irish figures during the years 1916–

20, and my enthusiastic reply led to a general discussion on the subject which lasted for several hours. His reflections were magnetic and I began to consider myself a seasoned veteran on the complexities of the period. Looking back on it, however, I am left with the bitter regret that I did not record his words, for very shortly my memory of them was all that would remain of *The History of the Irish Revolution.*

Feeling securely in touch at last, Brendan reverted to *Richard's Cork Leg,* untouched for many months. While he carried the theme of the final act clearly in his head, he said he was uncertain, and in my opinion rightly so, that a play could be taperecorded as successfully as a book. At the same time, his eyes troubled him too much for writing and his hands were still very shaky, and he alluded to the possibility of dictating the third act if my short-hand was not too rusty. Failing this, he would wait a few months until his health was fully restored.

That night we went to the Bailey, in Grafton Street, on what was to be the last merry evening I ever spent with Brendan and Beatrice. We returned later contented and slept in infinite peace.

The next day, Friday, 22nd November, we recorded the finishing touches for *Brendan Behan's New York,* unaware of the minutes as they ticked relentlessly towards an assassination which was to shock the entire world. In the afternoon, Brendan decided to visit his mother at Crumlin, a housing estate on the outskirts of Dublin, and as Beatrice and I wanted to see *Days of Wine and Roses,* showing at a cinema in the centre of the city, we agreed to meet back at Anglesea Road in the evening. Before the film started, in the middle of the news, the screen suddenly blacked out, and the curtain came down. The manager of the cinema walked on to the stage and announced in a voice heavy with emotion that President Kennedy had been shot in Dallas, Texas, and had since died from his wounds. Stunned, we sat through the film, but my mind was mostly diverted to Brendan and how he would take the brutal killing. We had more or less finished one project, but had not started another; the timing could not have been more unfortunate for a man who needed very little to spark him off on a drinking bout.

We returned home as arranged, but Brendan did not show up. He had taken one drink to help him recover from the shock, and that drink had become a nightful to overflow into the dawn. When he eventually arrived he was drunk and maudlin, complaining repeatedly of the miseries of his existence. Revived by a few hours' sleep, he begged us to accompany him to the Intercontinental Hotel, not far distant from the house, but as soon as we were in the bar, he recognised an American whom he had met previously and joined him at the table where he was sitting with several others. After a minute or two he came back to us in a state of great agitation. One of the company had insulted him, he growled, for even before the introductions could be affected, she had indicated in no uncertain terms that she did not want to meet Brendan Behan and furthermore, if he persisted in his intention to sit down with them, she would complain to the manager. His American friend, who had so recently enjoyed and accepted his hospitality, felt disinclined to intervene, and Brendan was now bewildered and hurt by his attitude. Beatrice was furious on his behalf and pleaded with him to leave at once and, when he refused, she stumped out on her own.

For a while he remained in gloomy silence, staring at the glass of beer in front of him until he repaired to the gentleman's lavatory. Half an hour later, the manager approached me. Brendan had locked himself in; there had been further complaints and would I kindly remove him. Now it was my turn to be angry and, looking straight at the woman concerned, I accused her of being the cause of all the disturbance while the manager rubbed his hands in Uriah Heep fashion, begging me to help him out of his predicament. '

I felt I was being asked to do something that no woman should be expected to do. The hotel was full of male staff, and it was wrong to put the onus on me to accomplish a task of this nature. But in order to prevent, perhaps, a compulsory eviction by the police, I marched in a towering rage into the lavatory and lured

Brendan out and into a taxi for home.

Celia, Beatrice's sister, and Seamus Parker, a friend, were at the house when we arrived, and in order to salvage a few pleasant fragments from the disasters of the day, Seamus suggested we all go out in his car. While Beatrice and I delighted in the opportunity, Brendan was still surly and disagreeable and tottered off on his own. By midnight we had all converged once more on Cuiz, but when Brendan discovered that the crate of beer he ordered had been returned as there was no one in the house to take it in, he was beside himself with fury. Suddenly, in the middle of his abuses, Beatrice indicated that she was not feeling too well, and for the hundredth time, I was to be rendered speechless by the unpredictability of Brendan's character. Immediately he became tender and dutiful, alternating his attentions with hiding his concern in the pages of a book, *Guerilla Days In Ireland*, which he flipped absent-mindedly without reading a word. Every few minutes he would ask, 'How's yourself?' and when Beatrice assured him he had no need to worry, he would raise a glass of orange juice promising her, and probably himself, that this was all it was going to be from then on.

As we headed into the dawn the tensions increased and Brendan, exhausted by the ordeal of waiting, retired upstairs to bed on our promise that we would wake him up when Beatrice went to hospital. But at 5.30 a.m., when the moment came, he was sleeping so heavily that I did not dare risk being punched for my pains and we piled into Seamus's car without him. It was a beastly night, pouring with rain, and we were thankful when we reached the hospital safely and Beatrice climbed into bed. For a while, Celia and I remained with her, and at seven o'clock I was called to the telephone to hear poor Brendan mutter out his alarm at waking up to find himself alone in the house. I explained the circumstances to him and he accepted them reasonably, and arranged to meet me at Anglesea Road for lunch when, God willing, our worries would be over. Shortly afterwards, Beatrice began labour in earnest and Celia and I left, stopping at a church to pray for a safe delivery.

Blanaid Orla Mairead, my god-daughter, was born on Sunday,
24th November at 11.40 a.m. and weighed six pounds. At once
I telephoned the Black Lion at Inchicore, where I believed
Brendan to be waiting for the news with Bill Finnegan and Eddie
Whelan. The man who answered my phone call, however, assured me that Brendan already knew and had been ringing the
hospital incessantly since his arrival at opening time. While he
was not drunk he had begun to celebrate the event and I made a
mental note that I must hurry to transcribe the tapes of *New York*
before his bashing became more serious. By lunch-time I had
decided to return home immediately, and when Brendan failed
to keep our appointment, I flew to England that afternoon leaving Celia with the message that I would be back for the
christening.

During my absence, Brendan stayed with Eddie Whelan and
his wife at Rathfarnham where he remained comparatively sober.
Every day, and sometimes twice a day, he would visit Beatrice
bringing her gifts of happiness. He was thrilled with his baby
daughter and would lean over her cot gently cooing his pet name
for her of 'Miss Mouse.' But when I returned to carry out my
duties as godmother, his drinking had become out of hand and
the official ceremony at St. Andrew's Church, where both he and
Beatrice had been christened, had to take place without him.
Those of us who knew him well were not unduly alarmed, for we
understood his hatred of the television cameras which were covering the event, and noticed that, when he eventually arrived at the
end of the ceremony, he was playing at being far more drunk than
in fact he was.

While I intended to remain on in Dublin for a while for
Brendan to go through the transcription of the tapes, I realised
afterwards, at the celebratory luncheon at the Dolphin, that it
would be pointless for me to do so. Until Beatrice and the baby
were installed in their home, there was nowhere to work with
Brendan while he continued drinking to this extent. Once more,
I took off for England, and this time I was determined not to return until the tapes had been fully transcribed. But now I was to

be involved in a further complication affecting Brendan.

Hutchinson had sold American rights in *The Scarperer* to Doubleday, but by the copyright laws in America an author is only protected from piracy for the first five years following publication of his work. As the serial had appeared in the *Irish Times* in 1953, the United States edition was automatically in the public domain. Sam Vaughan, of Doubleday, hastily wrote to me to try to persuade Brendan to write additional material for the book to give them a basis for claiming copyright. But Brendan was now too ill for me to do this, and in the end, after his death, Sam Vaughan asked me to add an afterword to the Doubleday edition so that the entire book would not be in the public domain. It is very sad that at the time of publication in the *Irish Times*, no *ad interim* copyright was registered to avoid the ensuing chaos. I was able, however, with the help of Val Iremonger who had recently been appointed Ambassador to Sweden and Norway and Minister to Finland, to edit the proofs of *The Scarperer*, and I owe him a debt of gratitude for the time he devoted to assisting me while coping with packing up his family and the countless other arrangements connected with leaving.

By this time the *New York* tapes had been transcribed. The material was in a form of extended chats and required a great deal of work before it could be published. Even so, much of his laughter and witty dialogue had preserved the flavour that was characteristically his, and if it lacked the gusto and feeling which made his writing distinctive, it was a brave attempt on his part to produce a book in the twilight of his life. Brian Inglis nicely illustrates the point in his review in the *Guardian* which appeared after Brendan's death.

'It is a measure of Brendan Behan's personality and talk,' wrote Brian, 'that, reading the book, the defects do not obtrude. If anybody else wrote of Samuel Beckett as "an old and very dear friend of mine and a marvellous playwright. I don't know what his plays are about but I know I enjoy them," it would be intolerable. But Brendan adds: "I do not know what a swim in the ocean is about, but I enjoy it. I enjoy the water flowing over me." At once, the thought of that burly frame lapped by the waters off Fire Island and relishing the incongruity of his situation, disarms the critical faculty; leaving only regret that he's not around to record any more.'

At the beginning of December, Beatrice and 'Miss Mouse' were reinstated at Cuíz, and I hoped now that under my prodding, *Brendan Behan's New York* would be pulled into shape by the author himself. But when I contacted her, it was to hear that he had reverted with a vengeance to the bad old days and was more or less permanently drunk. As time was running out if the book was to be published in the year of the New York World Fair, Bob Lusty and Berney Geis prevailed upon me to try to put the contents together on my own. It was an unhappy job, particularly as the tapes reminded me of the circumstances of almost every word he spoke.

Soon Brendan was admitted to the Royal City of Dublin Hospital in a diabetic coma and suffering from a liver complaint. Rumours began to circulate round the pubs that he was dying; while those about him prayed, on Christmas Day he received the Last Sacraments. But the crisis passed like other crises, and slowly he pulled through. A few days later, on the spurious charge that he could get no sleep, he shouted for his clothes and ignoring the entreaties of the staff, as soon as he was dressed, he charged out of the hospital like a man possessed by a million arch-fiends. For the rest of the afternoon he remained drinking in a pub, but passed out finally in the sanctuary of his parents' home in Crumlin. His mother has said that she put him to bed, and not until his breathing became more regular and peaceful did she retire herself. Some time during the night Brendan, dazed from drink, must have stumbled out of the house, for he was found early the following morning unconscious in the gutter opposite, lying in a pool of blood that had flowed from a deep gash in his forehead. At the Meath Hospital the police waited by his bedside to interview him about the mysterious accident but, although he recovered consciousness after an emergency operation, he was either unwilling or unable to throw any light on the affair.

'I must have fallen,' he told Beatrice.

For several days he lay in his hospital bed scarcely able to talk above a whisper; drowsy, feeble and at times disconnected. But his remarkable powers of recovery still had not deserted him, and a week or so later he was given his discharge. At Beatrice's invitation, I flew to Dublin to stay with them, refusing to admit to myself that his health was as low as I was led to believe.

The three weeks that followed are among the most unhappy in my life. I had not seen Brendan since the christening of his daughter, and it did not seem possible that he was the same man. It was no longer a question of utilising his creative ability; not only had he aged to the point where he resembled an old man, but most of his talk was disjointed and deep in the realms of fantasy. His face carried the expression of a man who has lost all interest in living, and his eyes were mattered from an infection. It is true that he recognised me instantly, but he rambled on about an imaginary tortuous conversation he had had with my parents in which he had complained resentfully of their refusal to allow me to accompany him to America.

My first positive action was to inform Christo Gore-Grimes and Michael Rubinstein of Brendan's decline and to suggest that, after all, the libel case should be settled. I had appalling visions of him failing to turn up on the day of the trial, or worse, getting himself into a frenzy in the witness box and committing perjury. In one of his more lucid moments I told Brendan what I had done, and although I could see the decision tormented him he recognised the necessity of it as being the safest way out.

Beatrice's constant pleading with him to return to hospital for treatment merely inspired bitter rows, and he avoided his home to the best of his ability. Early each morning he would drag his body out of the house, either to see his mother or to stumble round the streets and pubs of the city to be carried home later unconscious, or occasionally, make the journey back himself in the small hours of the morning. Wisely, Beatrice never gave him the front-door key so that night after night we would be awakened around 2 a.m. by the frantic knockings on the door for Brendan to be let in, to spend the remaining hours of darkness lying on the couch in the front room. Like a domestic animal that has been shut away from human contact too long, he was without dignity in himself and in his personal habits. He very rarely came upstairs to bed, but when he did, I would hear his unsteady footsteps tread each stair before he would come into my room striving to touch some form of stability, or go to his own to keep Beatrice awake by his grumbles that she did not give him enough to eat.

Strangely, he appeared grateful for my presence around the place as if somewhere deep in the subconscious he was waiting for the miracle to happen that would straighten him out once more. Whenever I mentioned leaving, he became bothered and perplexed as if this would add the last straw to his load, but when I agreed to stay a while longer, he made pathetic efforts to pull himself together for several hours afterwards. As long as I was able to help him in this way, I was prepared to remain with him and suffer the indignities which his company sometimes involved.

Beatrice could not go with him on his tired excursions for there was no one in the house to look after the baby, and once or twice I took her place. I was fortunate in being able to keep him on his feet, but I could never persuade him to come home. One evening he insisted I take him to see his parents, and although it was very late Stephen Behan, his father, answered our knockings and graciously invited us in. Brendan's mother had already gone to bed, and while he sat upstairs talking to her, his father spoke gently but firmly of his grief and concern over Brendan's health. He would have to go into hospital, he said, or into some type of home to ease his troubled mind and we, his friends, should do our utmost to see that this happened. In the middle of the conversation Brendan called for me to join him, and for half an hour I sat with his mother watching her eyes implore me to save Brendan from himself. As we were about to leave the room, she spoke out positively. 'Take care of him,' she pleaded.

The taxi was still at the door, and at the bottom of my despair now, I asked the driver to take us home. Brendan shot up from the back seat where previously he had been reclining. 'That won't help me,' he shouted. 'Take me to Eddie and Phil Whelan. I can spend the night there.' After I had dropped him I returned to Anglesea Road on my own but I could not sleep at all.

Despite his protests that he'd be better off dead than in the mess in which he found himself, and that he was only staying alive to save funeral expenses, he still had not rid himself of the feeling in his heart that life had a purpose as long as he had a vestige of creative ability. One conversation which took place at the stage of which I am writing is worth repeating for it brings to light clearly the struggles of the man versus artist within him which ill-health, and not alcohol alone, was to bring to an end.

Beatrice had gone to bed and I was sitting with him in the dining-room well into the night, while he spoke fitfully of his miseries and his wish to be out of them all. Suddenly, without warning, he pushed back his chair, raised to his feet and his eyes filled with angry tears. 'Love is the most damnable emotion of all,' his words trembled. 'Look what I've done to Beatrice. When I married her she was a sweet and gentle person. Now she's a tiger. If I had my way I'd cut it all out and give my head a break for the other thoughts that are in it.' He sat down again more slowly and the tears trickled down his face. He brushed them away with the back of his hand and then muttered, God willing, he might be able in a few days to get back to work.

The next morning, at breakfast, he was more interested and alive than he had been since my arrival, and spoke of recording a review of Anthony Cronin's *The Life of Riley* which was shortly to be published. A knock on the front door revealed a taxi-man anxious for his fare of several days back, and Brendan seized upon the opportunity for a lift into town. As he left the room, he spoke some words to Beatrice in Irish which I did not understand. Beatrice translated them: He had asked her to ensure that I did not leave for he would be back later to begin working. At 7 p.m. he was brought home by loyal I.R.A. friends in a deep diabetic coma to be carried up to his bed. A hurried telephone call to the doctor in the middle of the night brought forward a promise that he would be round first thing in the morning, unless we felt there was anything he could reasonably do at once. As I believed that Brendan would now be taken into hospital for the reparations he so badly needed, I decided to leave the next day.

Early, I put my head around his door to say goodbye, but although he was barely conscious, I heard him say distinctly, 'Please do not go,' before he drifted away again apparently out of contact. Loathing my lack of courage to remain and watch the man that was Brendan slip further out of reach, I ignored his request, but throughout the flight home his entreaty echoed in my ears.

At the beginning of March, I heard from his American agent that he was required to write a short article on President Kennedy for a magazine, and I wrote to Beatrice to find out the likelihood of his being able to record it. Within a few days, she answered.

> Dearest Rae, I asked Brendan about the Kennedy piece and would you come over for it. He said 'tell her I'm going over,' so I haven't asked him again. He is far from well as I'm sure you will appreciate . . . I don't know what to suggest. Perhaps if you just arrived and see what happens—it might work. He might straighten out for a few days, or go to hospital for treatment which he certainly needs. I can only wait and see and keep in touch with you. Hope you are keeping fit and well. Best love to Diana and yourself from Beatrice.

Soon she had contacted me again to suggest that I come over but, on the day that I was due to fly, she telephoned that he was gravely ill and in a coma at the Meath Hospital and, as he was allowed no visitors, she thought I would be better advised to postpone my coming until his condition had improved. Appropriately, on Saint Patrick's Day he rallied sufficiently to complain about almost everything, ordering the nurses around, and once again it appeared that this crisis would pass too. But his diabetic condition and the liver complaint from which he had suffered for six years slowly overcame his determined resistance, and he drifted back into unconsciousness to die shortly afterwards.

In the ten days of his fight I had faced up to the possibility that one of these days all of us were going to have to get accustomed to the fact that Brendan no longer lived. Nevertheless, when the dreaded call came, I heard the news with a sense of great shock. I had not wanted him to become a legend all that much—all that soon.

EPILOGUE

Diana and I arrived at Dublin Airport the following morning, and drove at once to the hospital where a crowd was waiting outside for his coffin to be taken to the Church of the Sacred Heart, Donnybrook. There, in the church where he and Beatrice had been married nine years previously, his body would remain until the final stage of the journey to Glasnevin Cemetery two days later. We pushed our way through the front entrance and I saw Beatrice, heavily veiled, standing at the foot of the wide stairs which led to the wards. I put my arms around her and for a moment I felt her stiffen as if she had not recognised me, before she warmly returned my embrace, her nerves tensed to face the ordeal ahead.

'Would you like to see him before he is coffined?' she murmured, almost inaudibly. When I nodded, she led me up to his room while Diana waited in the corridor outside. Brendan's chin had been cut by the nurse who had shaved him, giving his otherwise pallid face a colour, but his eyes no longer held a haunted look, for they were shut and peaceful. I kissed him gently on the forehead, not in selfish sorrow but in the hope that the final moment had not been tormented by fears. Afterwards, I waited in the room next door with Beatrice where all the close relations and friends were collected. Suddenly she broke down. There was nothing but emptiness and misery ahead, she cried. Life for her had lost all colour.

Outside the hospital, the crowds had increased to watch his coffin, draped in the Tricolour, as it was carried to the hearse by his comrades in the I.R.A. wearing Easter lilies in their lapels. Slowly the cortège moved off while thousands followed, chanting aloud their prayers to a man they now claimed as their own. But the two-mile journey took longer than was expected, and when a coffin arrived at the Sacred Heart, Donnybrook, the many who were waiting to attend the Mass mistook it for Brendan and placed their Mass cards on the remains of a complete stranger. Half an hour later Brendan's body reached the church. Never was he more missed than on this day. With his spirit, that mocked at mortality without any disrespect for the dead, he would have appreciated the ensuing chaos.

For two days friends and strangers alike flocked to pay homage. If Brendan had not been a hero in life, the same was not true at his death. All the colour and drama associated with his name attended his funeral as thousands lined the streets and pavements from Donnybrook to Glasnevin, stopping the traffic while the I.R.A., this time aided by a posse of policemen on motorbikes, eased the cortège on its way. In death as in life he had been able to attract all sections of society, for along with President de Valera's delegate, the Tanaiste and members of both Houses of the Oireachtas, who were prepared to overlook the illegality of the I.R.A. on so solemn an occasion, came the titled, the untitled, the famous, the not-so-famous, the unknowns, the down-and-outs, and the man in the street whose day perhaps it was the most of all. While Brendan would have loved the marvellous theatre of the spectacle, he would have enjoyed particularly the sight of the old ladies with their shopping baskets standing by the graveside, the children squabbling amongst themselves for a better position, the grave-digger waving his spade in the air to make sure that his one chance of appearing on television did not go unobserved by his friends, and a colleague speaking over his grave in sonorous tones of the privilege of being interred in the Curragh camp with Brendan. At once, the verbal slip echoed in our minds with Brendan's unheard laughter. And he would have wanted it this way, for he would have preferred the humour, and the remembrance of his rich, full voice, rather than a preponderance of gloom that both were lost for ever.

Now the clown's mask has come off and the world is gazing at the discrepancies revealed, but for those of us who knew him well and shared a little of his turbulent life, the man and his mask are quite distinguishable and we remember only a fairground of circus delights without the smart of tears.

INDEX